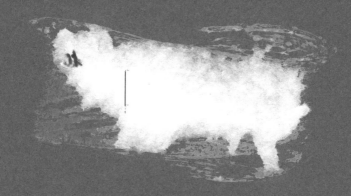

OBSESSED

The Autobiography

Richard Dunwoody

HEADLINE

First published in 2000
by HEADLINE BOOK PUBLISHING

10 9 8 7 6 5 4 3 2 1

British Library Cataloguing in Publication Data

Dunwoody, Richard
    Obsessed: the autobiography
    1.Dunwoody, Richard
    2.Jockeys - Great Britain - Biography
    3.Steeplechasing - Great Britain
    I.Title
    798.4'5'092

ISBN 0 7472 7218 2

798. 45092

DUN.

Typeset by
Letterpart Limited, Reigate, Surrey

Printed and bound by
Mackays of Chatham PLC, Chatham, Kent

HEADLINE BOOK PUBLISHING
A division of Hodder Headline
338 Euston Road
London NW1 3BH

www.headline.co.uk
www.hodderheadline.com

0747 272 182 1501

OBSESSED

Also by Richard Dunwoody

Hell for Leather (with Marcus Armytage)
Duel (with Sean Magee)
Hands and Heels (with Marcus Armytage)

For all jump jockeys,
past, present,
and those who are no longer with us

CONTENTS

ACKNOWLEDGEMENTS

A lot of people have helped me to get this far. Especially Mum and Dad who, naturally, were there at the beginning and whose love has been a constant in my life. Jockeys don't have coaches but Dad knew how horses should be ridden. Mum coached me in everything else. No son could have been blessed with more supportive parents.

For a man who spent so much of his life in that male bastion, the weighing room, I managed to find time to be amongst women. My sister Gail, Carol, Emma and now Charlie have been huge influences on my life. They may not have succeeded in always keeping me on the straight and narrow but they were able to get me back there. I owe them more than can be repaid.

Many people helped me to put this book together and I am indebited to them all. A number of my old weighing room mates remembered things that had slipped my mind and they were typically generous with their time. Luke Harvey recalled with remarkable clarity what happened at one particular stewards' enquiry and it was fun to return to that old battleground. Steve Taylor, the racing journalist, was another with a sharp memory and I appreciated his help. Michael Caulfied, executive manager of the Jockeys Association, was our reference book; our means of checking anything and everything that comes under racing's banner.

Ian Marshall, Lindsay Symons and the team at Headline Publishing were patient during the writing of the book and highly professional once the manuscript was completed. My friends Mel Fordham and Tom Maher read the book and offered valuable suggestions. Sean Magee's ordered mind was instrumental in putting together the career record that helps to define what I was doing for 17 years. Marion Paull was an encouraging and excellent copy editor.

David Walsh of the *Sunday Times* and Evelyn Bracken of the *Irish Times* were the two people involved from the day the book was conceived. Evelyn's dedication to this project went way beyond the call of duty. David, who devoted so much time and hard work, I thank especially, as I do Mary and his family for being so understanding. David and Evelyn helped me to make the book worthwhile. I hope they are satisfied with the result.

FOREWORD

B ack in 1982, when I was a young jockey on the first rung of the ladder, I rang trainers and politely begged them to put me up on their horses. Amateur, inexperienced and unknown, it was an uphill struggle. In trying to sell myself, I wouldn't tell a lie but there were times when I avoided the truth. Looking for your first ride, you didn't begin by saying you'd never ridden in a race before. Over the following 17 years, much changed and it became easier for me to get rides. But that old fundamental remained constant: you tried not to be dishonest but you couldn't be totally honest. It is how sportsmen live their lives. In this book, I have attempted to be seriously honest. Anything less and it wouldn't have been worth it. The Richard Dunwoody you know may not be the Richard Dunwoody you are about to discover.

I ache for the life I was forced to leave behind. The longing to be back in the weighing room doesn't go away, especially during the big meetings at Cheltenham and Liverpool. For the 2000 Grand National, I went to Liverpool as part of the BBC's commentary team. I'd ridden in the race for 15 consecutive years and, in civilian clothes, I found it hard. I have never liked walking in crowds and while watching jump racing, I cannot escape the feeling that I should be doing it, especially over the big fences at Liverpool. Retired, I am trying to live a normal life and, to be honest, I don't think I am very good at being normal.

Injury forced me to stop riding at the age of 35, at a time in my career when I felt I was riding well. The end came about five or six years before I was ready. I miss riding winners and the camaraderie in the weighing room. But more than that, I miss the fun we had while wasting our bodies and our time in the sauna, the mad dashes to airports, the endless journeys on motorways. They were all part of it. Afflicted by serious and potentially long-term damage to my neck, I searched the world for one expert who would tell me to carry on. All I got was reality and it wasn't well received. One of them told me that the injury would mean an arthritic neck when I was 50. So what? All I wanted to know was whether I would be OK for Plumpton on Monday.

In the end, it wasn't the real danger of paralysis in my right arm that made me stop. What did it was the realisation that I couldn't be as effective as I had been. Going out there less than 100 per cent against A.P. McCoy was what made me walk away. Against A.P. and the others, you have got to compete at level weights. Retirement was the sensible decision but I regret it. You have no idea how much.

I was Richard Dunwoody, the jockey. Now I am Mr Average Citizen. You were once at the top, respected for what you did; then you return to civilian life and, basically, you are back to mucking out. You're not the same person any more, you're worth much less. I'm not saying I don't go out and have a good time, I do. My lifestyle is good but it's as if I've been emasculated. Of course, I will try to get to the top at whatever I do; I don't like failing at anything. But if I succeed, so what?

I looked around the weighing room at Aintree, at A.P., Fitzy, Norman and Adrian, and I thought 'you lucky bastards'. If I had still been among them, I would have been my old self; brooding about a winner that I'd missed, annoyed because I'd got beaten in a photo finish, pleased that I'd given one a ride. During the three days at Liverpool, the BBC's Clare Balding asked me how much I was missing it. I said I would give my right arm to be back in the weighing room, one of the lads, taking on those big fences again. Realising what I had said, I smiled to myself. There was a good chance that if I'd stayed I would have had to give my right arm. Yet I am still not sure I made the right decision.

1

IT NEVER RAINS IN CALIFORNIA

W hat struck me was the beauty of the place. I had gone to Del Mar in California looking for a cure for a problem in my neck, right shoulder and right arm. I had been everywhere else and always the advice was the same – 'You know, Richard, your neck is not in a very good state.' 'Richard, have you ever thought about doing something else?' 'Another bad fall and you could do very serious damage.' Whatever was wrong with my neck, my head was in the sand. It was ridiculous to suggest my career might be over. Riding horses was all I had ever done and I still loved it. Doctors exaggerated the risk. So here I was in Del Mar – clear blue skies, brilliant sunshine, the Pacific Ocean and a hotel within walking distance of the racetrack. 'It never rains in California . . .'

A day earlier, 21 August 1999, I had been in Scotland and ridden three winners from four rides at Perth – not an experience to bring on thoughts of retirement. It was actually the losing ride at Perth that convinced me to go to California. Classic Manoeuvre had jumped OK for a first-timer and joined the leader at the second last. From where I sat, he was going to win but then he over-jumped and fell. It happens in racing. It wasn't a bad fall. I should have walked away unscathed. I didn't; my neck and right arm were very sore. I had been having a problem for some time. With limited use of my right arm – at times it was very weak – it had been affecting my riding. I'd taken more falls than I should have done. Sheer bloody-mindedness had kept me going but this fall bothered me. I left Perth that Saturday evening in August knowing I had to get the problem sorted. A day later I was on a plane to Los Angeles.

Paul Chek, the man I travelled across the Atlantic to see, is an exercise kineseologist and one of the best. Basically, he provides physiotherapy and designs exercise programmes to help people with particular injuries get back to fitness. He had been recommended a month earlier by his colleague Janet Alexander whom I had met in London. At the time, Janet was visiting the Harbour Club in Chelsea where I work out and she had agreed to see me. Apart from my neck and arm, on which I was having physiotherapy, my whole body felt stiff. Janet led me to an empty studio.

'Right, close your eyes Richard, turn your head from side to side, now just march up and down on the same spot.' I did as I was told. When I opened my eyes, I couldn't believe what had happened. I had moved miles from where I started, almost walking straight out of the room. I should not have budged from my starting point. It was weird, my balance was completely gone.

'Really, if you get a chance, come out to California and see Paul,' said Janet.

We had tried everything else – many X-rays and scans, I had worked with the Jockey Club's doctor, Michael Turner, I had been to see the orthopaedic surgeon Michael Foy in Swindon, and Bob Sharpe who was consultant to the Jockeys Association. I had been to see Chris Adams in the John Ratcliffe Hospital in Oxford, John Meadows in Harley Street, I had spent countless hours with excellent physiotherapists. Don Gatherer, who had worked with the England rugby team, put me on a weights' programme specifically designed to rebuild the strength in my right arm. The message never reached me. But when Janet said Paul Chek had successfully treated an ice-hockey player with a nerve injury similar to mine, I heard that.

I like travel and have never minded travelling alone. The Marriott in Del Mar was a nice hotel and the place was idyllic. Weather, water and women were all beautiful. On my first visit to Paul's office he had gone through everything with a fine-tooth comb. He has an obsessive way about him and you can tell he is extremely good at his job.

'Three months and I'll have you back riding,' he said.

'I don't think it'll take that long,' I replied.

It was out of the question. I hadn't come 5,000 miles to be told that I wouldn't be able to ride for three months. In the three days before coming to California, I had ridden six winners. For a jockey, three months is a lifetime. I couldn't miss that much. Paul said that if I continued to have falls, my neck and arm would not get better. I tried to explain jump racing to Paul and how if you were off for that amount of time, you'd be forgotten about, other people would get your horses. Janet Alexander, who was present, had some idea because she's from New Zealand, and Paul's wife Penny is English. Between us, we described how jump racing works and how important it was for me to get back quickly.

'Look, I will do more tests. You come back here tomorrow and we'll know more.'

The following morning I went for a run, determined not to lose fitness during this short break from racing. When I returned to Paul's office at lunchtime, he wanted me to meet a colleague of his, Kenny Sheppard. Kenny, a nucca chiropractor, chiefly manipulates the atlas at the top of the spine. We drove to his practice about 20 minutes away. He didn't take long to discover my whole body was out of synch. 'Well, that's not something I don't know,' I thought.

They took some X-rays, they studied the X-rays I had brought out and the information from my own scans and came to a new conclusion.

'Look, man,' Paul said, 'you'd be mad to continue riding horses, crazy.'

All the way back in the car Paul kept saying the same thing – forget about riding horses, quit right now. I had been told the same thing by other doctors but not so bluntly. I was in America and being informed in the American way. It was like I had been kicked straight between the legs. The energy left my body and back at Paul's, I found it hard to stand. They were taking my life away.

I walked away from Paul's office, very much on my own, desolate in this idyllic place. The contrast between the place and the way I felt made it all very strange. What I couldn't understand was how a few days before I had been riding as well as ever and now it was all over. Classic Manoeuvre's fall was nothing. They were wrong, I could recover, I would get back. 'You'd be mad to try,' Paul had said. I went for something to eat but it was all a blur. I barely tasted the food and then had a few drinks. I was half-shot but that couldn't banish the anguish. Back in my hotel room I telephoned some of those closest to me – my parents, my agent Robert Parsons and Michael Caulfield who is the executive manager of the Jockeys Association. I couldn't bring myself to tell them I was finished, I just said it was serious. This was Tuesday, 24 August, four months before I would bring myself to admit it publicly. That night I scribbled one word in my diary – retired.

Life moves on and the next day the sun brightened everything in Del Mar. Back at Paul's practice, he focused on trying to improve the state of my neck and arm so that I would be able to lead a normal life. Normality wasn't what I had in mind but I made a conscious decision to work at the exercises and get as much from them as I could. Paul repeated that riding horses would not be a part of the future but I didn't believe it. What if my neck and arm got strong again, if my balance returned to what it should be? Nothing was impossible. I also decided to make the most of the remainder of my time in California. I bumped into Shane Conlon who used to work for David Elsworth and we had a couple of good evenings; I even ended up with one of those better one-night stands.

Even though Paul Chek had made it clear my career was over, I couldn't accept it. Back in England, I announced that it could be three or four months before I rode again. It didn't make sense. I felt OK and well able to ride. Three weeks before I had ridden at the Galway Festival in Ireland and things had been fine. I won the Galway Hurdle on Quinze, rode two other winners there and was leading jump jockey for the week. Around the middle of August I had gone on holiday to Puerto Banus with fellow jockeys A.P. McCoy, Seamus Durack, Carl Llewellyn and the photographer and good mate Mel Fordham. It was a typical jockeys' holiday with plenty of laughs, clubbing, alcohol and more than a little womanising. We got back on 18 August and the following day I rode two winners at Newton

Abbot. Next day I was in Perth, not realising these would be the final two days of my career. Even now I find it difficult to say, to admit it is all over. In one sense I still haven't completely accepted it. In the car or over supper with my girlfriend Charlie Hutchings, I talk about what's constantly in my head.

'You know, I'm thinking of going back riding again.'

'Don't be stupid, it could never be the same,' she says.

'I could do as Charlie Swan does and just ride over hurdles. I don't see why not.'

'It's a compromise and you could end up losing the use of your right arm. Every doctor's told you it could happen.'

'I don't care about that. I just want to ride again.'

I keep myself fit by running, I keep my weight in check and every so often I test my right arm to see how much strength has returned. I can lift 12lb but that is well short of the 20lb weight I can comfortably raise with my left hand. If I never ride again, I will not forget how it ended over those days at Perth.

If my story shows how precarious is the jockey's existence, imagine what it is like for Scott Taylor. He was at Perth, too, and rode in the novice chase on the Friday. I rode the winner, Hoh Invader for Charlie Mann, but the race will be remembered for the fall that changed Scott's life. I didn't see it until afterwards. It was a terrible fall, really awkward, and once we saw it, we knew Scott was in trouble. News came through that his life was in danger. They sent for his father and we all prayed he would pull through. The weighing room is never as close as at moments like this and the mood that evening was bleak and very sad. Fellow jockey Richard Guest reported back to us and eventually he came with the news that Scott was going to live. Even though we knew his head injuries were severe and would affect him for the rest of his life, we were delighted Scott had made it. We drank late into the night.

Every jockey in that Perth weighing room realised he could have been the one in Scott's place. Some jockeys haven't pulled through. I think of Richard Davis who came up to London and stayed with me the month before being killed in a fall. Those who walk away from the weighing room shouldn't complain, and we let our hair down in Perth on that Friday night because we were the lucky ones.

There is an unrelenting rhythm to the jockey's life. The show goes on. Because of the late night drinking, the sauna at the Perth Leisure Centre was like Waterloo Station in the rush hour. Ten jockeys sat in that tiny room, all sweating pure alcohol, boasting about the previous night's exploits, and I pitied the poor members of the public who had gone for their morning sauna, unaware that the jockeys were in town. We are bound together by the highs and the lows, addicted to the exhilaration of race riding and flattered by the respect and affection widely felt for jump jockeys.

When it was time to go to Perth racecourse, Robbie Park came to collect us. Robbie was a good friend of mine in Scotland. Sadly, he died shortly before Liverpool 2000. Whenever I raced in Scotland, he picked me up at the airport, dropped me at the hotel, brought me to the races and, afterwards, dropped me back to the airport. We had a lot of good times together and I am glad he brought me to my last day's racing.

The afternoon at Perth could hardly have gone better. Blue Music for Philip Hobbs was my first ride and he won, tail swishing furiously up the run-in; Queensway, having his first run for Philip, won the handicap chase; then Classic Manoeuvre toppled at the second last when I thought we were going to win. I was annoyed with myself because the fall cost me a winner and afterwards my neck and right arm were sore. In the changing room, the young doctor on duty followed me around, asking questions like, 'What's your date of birth?' and I'm thinking, 'Look, just leave me alone.' I had to go out and ride Twin Falls and there wasn't time for my biography.

Twin Falls is 'a thinker', one of those horses that will find ways of not always doing his best. You push him most of the way because he won't freely make the effort. On the last circuit, I was driving him for all I was worth and not getting anywhere.

'I'm knackered,' I said to Robert Widger who was riding another of Philip's in the race. 'This fellow's taking the piss.'

Then the three or four horses in front of us began to slow. I was fifth turning into the straight and they left a gap between them going to the last hurdle. So I drove my horse into the gap and because he thought the others were going to squeeze him, he shot through it. 'You little bastard,' I thought. He jumped the last a little slowly but he was now in front and went away, winning by two lengths. Talk about a mickey-taker. It was a ride that pleased me; I had to be persistent and some jockeys might have given up on him. As last rides go, this was one of the better ones. It is also what made the forced retirement so hard to take. One day you are riding well, the next day someone says you should never ride again. How can you prepare for that?

All I had ever wanted to be was a jockey. At a critical time in my teenage years, that desire dominated every other feeling. I was 16, my O-level results were good and Mum believed I could and should go on to become a vet. With horses very much on my mind, I didn't want to go back to school and my teenage years were full of angst. With my intense ambition and a very stubborn nature, things were never going to be straightforward.

It hasn't been a regular life but it was the one I wanted. At first everything was focused on riding better, becoming stronger and trying to get on better horses. Over time the goals changed; the more winners I got, the more I wanted. Last season's total was never enough, next season had to be better and becoming champion became an obsession. Robert Kington and Robert Parsons, the two men who booked my rides throughout my career, know what it was like because I put them through a lot – 'Why am I not on this?' 'Shouldn't I be on that?' 'Ring him, ring him.' They will also know that however much pressure they felt, it was less than the pressure I put on myself. I remember how I felt when Peter Scudamore retired in April 1993 and made it reasonably certain I would become champion jockey for the first time. It wasn't so much joy or happiness, just an enormous release of pressure. I cried but not out of elation, just relief. The war was over. That's what Scu's retirement meant for me.

The drive to be champion wasn't much fun but I was a slave to it. The duel that I was happy to avoid with Scu came the following season with Adrian Maguire and it was the most punishing experience of our lives. Long before it was resolved, Adrian and I were becoming sick of it. Other people remember it as the greatest battle for the jump jockeys' championship, not us. From my seat inside the weighing room, it didn't matter that it was a newspaper story every day for months and that it started to interest the wider sporting public. At the end of the season, my riding 197 winners to Adrian's 194 didn't prove I was the better jockey. You couldn't say that.

On a personal level, I knew what I had put into that championship and how distraught I would have been had I been beaten. But what did it come down to? On the last day of the season I was lucky to ride three horses that won and Adrian rode only two. You had to feel sorry for him.

I wasn't comfortable with the person I had become at this period in my career and I suppose it stands to reason that I wasn't going to feel that good about what I was achieving. My marriage to Carol was breaking up and it was a bad time for us. On the day I won the championship, I had no desire to go home. Our marriage would probably not have survived in any circumstances but the pressure I put myself under to become champion made our time together a lot less happy than it should have been. I regret that. But from the middle of that 1993–94 season I was driven beyond the point of reason and for the final two months, nothing else mattered. The fear of losing overwhelmed every other feeling.

Falls and injuries are part of jump racing and throughout my career I kept records of all the horses I rode – the winners, the losers and the ones that lost me along the way. It reminded me of horses when I'd ride them in the future or if I was asked about one going to the sales. I also never ceased to be intrigued by the percentages, working out the falls-to-rides ratio for one season compared with another. At the end of the epic and punishing battle with Adrian, there had been 926 rides, 39 falls and I was unseated eight times. Throughout that ten-month season, I didn't miss one day through injury and I imagine Adrian didn't miss more than a couple of days either. I was performing at my peak and yet I didn't like what it did to me. I had to win but winning didn't fulfil me. At the end of that championship I thought, 'OK, that's out of the way, I'm never putting myself through that again.'

But it didn't work out like that. I needed another mad season and a third jockey's title to accept that this quest was killing my love for racing. Martin Pipe's winners had been the key factor in my second and third championship wins but riding for Martin brought with it hassle I no longer wanted. There was the constant need to be at my lightest and being naturally heavy-boned, I was weary of the wasting. There are only so many hours you can spend reading the *Racing Post* in the sauna. What the Pipe stable offered was the opportunity always to contend for the jump jockeys' title but by the end of the 1994–95 season, I was disillusioned with that chase. My marriage had gone, my reason was going and, to save my career, I had to regain control of my life. So I left Martin Pipe and began again, this time with a different perspective. Being champion jockey would no longer be the goal.

Understandably, it was reported I was leaving the fast lane and from now on I would be taking things easier. That was not what I wanted and in any case, it simply didn't happen. What I wanted was a change of direction, essentially a jockey's life where I would be my own boss and have a fair degree of control over where, when and for whom I rode. If I wanted to take a Monday off, I would; if I wanted to do a bit of motor racing, I would. These were things I couldn't do if committed to Britain's most successful trainer. Rather than cutting back, what I was actually doing was re-arranging priorities so that I would be able to ride at the highest level for a longer time. The change was an attempt to rekindle an enthusiasm for racing which had been drained. So I rode more in Ireland and settled on a working week that was no less exacting but seemed more fun. Basically, I was my own boss again and that was the difference.

The change worked better than anyone could have anticipated. Plenty of trainers in England and Ireland still wanted to put me up and even though the travelling was mad, it kept me sane. I discovered there were a few things that could not be changed – my competitiveness, the ambition to ride as many winners as possible and my total love for the life. It wasn't just the thrill of riding good horses that brought back the spark but the minutiae of the jockey's life. Little things stick in the mind. An anonymous admirer once sent me a dozen roses and the lads in the weighing room tortured me for days about it. The temporary boost to my ego was more than undone by the subsequent teasing. Late one night at Joe Olive's restaurant in

Naas, fellow jockey James Nash broke into a Garth Brooks song and the room was alive. You couldn't work with a finer, crazier group of men. There was a togetherness, especially on those afternoons when some jockey had a terrifying fall and we waited in the weighing room for news from the hospital. It was in those moments that the realities hit home.

I am lucky that there have always been good women in my life. My ex-wife Carol is a wonderful person and it is one of the sadnesses of my life that our marriage didn't work out. The compensation is that we remain friends and stay in touch from time to time. After the break-up of the marriage, I met Emma Heanley who gave me a life outside racing. Nothing renewed my enthusiasm for racing as much as the realisation that I didn't have to live my entire life within its claustrophobic walls. Emma opened up new avenues for me, encouraged me to explore life outside racing and when I returned, the sauna was just as hot but it no longer seemed like hell.

Injury got me in the end. I thought constant physiotherapy would get me back, but this problem couldn't be rubbed away. I went to orthopaedic surgeons and they said my neck was arthritic and there might be some nerve damage. The neurologists said, yes, the nerves in the right arm were damaged and each time I had a fall there was the chance of further deterioration. So I worked harder on my fitness, built up the strength in my arm through rest and then weight training. Partly to prove this was something I could beat, I went out and rode winners, plenty of them. No one questioned the state of my health.

The doctors would now say it was always going to be a losing battle. Any fall carried the possibility of aggravation and the bad falls left me sore and with a weak right arm. How weak? I remember a corporate speaking assignment in Galway one day and the horror of realising that I was struggling to hold the microphone – I'd had it in my hand for five minutes. There were times, too, in races when I would momentarily lose all power in my right arm. I would look down at the stick but not be able to feel it. When the right arm was at its weakest, I decided I would ignore it and make my left arm do most of the work; and because the flow of winners never stopped, I thought I could go on indefinitely. That was the plan.

Even when Paul Chek warned of the dangers of losing the use of my right arm and told me I had to stop riding, even when it was clear that only stupidity and ignorance would keep me going, I still clutched at one last straw – Paul had treated the ice-hockey player with an injury similar to mine and helped to get him back.

'The guy,' said Paul, 'had a five million dollars a year contract and with him, the risk was worth it. With you earning two hundred thousand pounds a year, it's not worth it.'

I didn't see it like that. Being a jump jockey meant far more to me than the £200,000 which, after tax and expenses, was never much more than £80–100,000 anyway. So I rested for almost four months and then met the Irish neurosurgeon Jack Phillips, desperately hoping that he would see a chance where no one else had. But the verdict was the same. 'No chance,' said Jack. The game was up and on 14 December 1999, I finally announced my retirement.

There hasn't been a day since that I have not missed riding. Cheltenham and Aintree were particularly hard. I was working for the BBC at Aintree so I was able to go there with a business-like attitude and do a job. That made it just about bearable. Cheltenham wasn't. When Istabraq was storming up the hill, winning his third consecutive Champion Hurdle, I was driving from the office down to the Fulham Road. I didn't listen to the commentary on Radio 5 Live. I didn't want to be reminded of it, didn't want to think about it.

Then on the Thursday, I was filming with the BBC's John Craven for his programme 'Country File'. We were out at the trainer Simon Dow's yard in Epsom and finished around 2.30. Up at the course, Sean Devine was entertaining his clients and employees to a Cheltenham Gold Cup day in the Queen's Stand at Epsom. Sean owns Chief's Song, a horse I had ridden many times, and after filming I went across to have a quick drink with him. I saw Bacchanal win the Stayers', wondered would I have been riding Behrajan and got away from there as quickly as I could. The build-up to the Gold Cup was starting and I didn't want to see any of it. Driving back from Epsom to the office in London, I didn't switch on the radio and waited until well after the race before checking on the result. Florida

Pearl was second. My horse. Had the horse won, it would have been tremendous for the trainer Willie Mullins and the owners, Archie and Violet O'Leary. Archie and Vi had been wonderful during my injury. I suppose I shouldn't say it but it would have hit me extremely hard if the horse had won, three months after I had officially retired. It was a relief to hear he hadn't.

Unless it is business, I now have no enthusiasm for going National Hunt racing and no desire to watch it on television. I haven't seen how Looks Like Trouble beat Florida Pearl in that Gold Cup. Why torture yourself? If I can't do it, I don't particularly want to watch others doing it. Six months after I retired I had a strange dream. I was at some small racecourse, it felt like Ballinrobe in the west of Ireland, and I was a spectator, standing by the rails as the horses and their jockeys went on the track. As they passed me, I was almost in a state of panic and knew that I just had to get out of there, as if, in civilian clothes, I was a prisoner at the racecourse. A strange dream but it made perfect sense to me.

2

LIKE FATHER LIKE . . .

_____

F ew jockeys prepare themselves for life after they leave the weighing room. Most of us are not qualified to do anything else because from the age of 12 or 13, horses are all we know. Our careers take over our lives, tempting us to look no further than the next day's racing. Given the hazards of the jump jockey's life, how can you look five years down the road? When it comes, retirement hits hard. Maybe not as hard for the few who voluntarily leave but wrenching for those forced out by injury or age. In my time, I saw John Francome, Peter Scudamore and, more recently, Mark Dwyer seemingly walk away without looking back. John and Scu had lost their enthusiasm for the jockey's life and even though Mark left because of injury, he went without regrets. For many others, it has been very different. I was 35 when the end came but I had thought I would carry on until I was 40. My dad rode a winner at the age of 50.

Michael Caulfield, an old and still close friend, says I sounded like a man in mourning over his own death when I rang to say I probably wouldn't ride again. Back in America they would probably have a support group for people like us and we would talk openly about what it is that makes leaving so tough. Since retiring I have immersed myself in business and the media, but I need time away to think about what I want to do with the rest of my life. Wherever I end up, whatever I do, the basic philosophy will be the same: I have to win.

It used to be said I would ride over my grandmother to get to the winning post first. The reality is that I wouldn't have seen her. My focus was that narrow. I saw only what I wished to see. Such single-mindedness came with a price. There was much that I missed along the way. World War Three could have broken out but as long as it didn't mean the postponement of Fontwell, it wouldn't have affected me. Suspended for some riding offence, I couldn't bear to miss winners, to watch things go on without me, and would go anywhere to get away. One year it was a few days in Vienna, another time it was skiing in Val d'Isère. The change of scenery always rejuvenated me. It was like a wake-up call, a voice inside my head laughing at my little obsession. I loved new places and new experiences, especially after Emma opened my eyes to life's other possibilities.

The wheel has turned full circle and I am now permanently on the outside. Because I know how good it was, separation continues to sting. To get by I stay well away. I have no enthusiasm for talking about what A.P. McCoy did at Newbury the other day, no desire to go racing and when I surf the television channels, I don't stop at the sight of horses and silks. You might think I cannot have really loved it. In fact, I loved it too much.

At least now there is more time for everything else. I am becoming a little more rounded and learning more about myself, who I am, where I have come from, what made me live so close to the edge during my riding career. There were times I loathed the person created by my intense ambition but I saw myself as a beneficiary as much as a victim and there were no complaints. I went with it.

Even though I lived just eight years of my life in Northern Ireland and spent the following 28 years in England, I consider myself Irish and am proud of my Irishness. I never had time for politics. When government leaders were going to Ulster for a summit meeting, I was going to Newton Abbot for an evening meeting. Maybe mine is a simplistic view but I think if you're Irish, you're Irish. That's it. I lived about 12 miles from where Formula One's Eddie Irvine was born and I think of us as fellow Irishmen. I was born a northern Protestant but I love going to southern Ireland and for a few years I kept a flat in Naas, County Kildare.

My leanings would have been obvious to anyone sitting near me at Twickenham for the first ever Six Nations Championship rugby match between England and Ireland in early February 2000. From my days of playing the game at Rendcomb College, I liked rugby but this was the first time I had seen an Ireland v. England international. I went with Charlie who got pretty excited when England scored. It was clear from early in the match that Ireland were struggling and by half-time we were losing badly. When Kevin Maggs then got Ireland's first try, I almost leapt out of the stand. We were getting something back. Since then I have been to watch London Irish play many times and later in the season we went to the European Cup final at Twickenham. I was very definitely on Munster's side. It's hard to explain one's sense of identity but on those big sporting days, it expresses itself.

In the build-up to the 1999 Grand National, I was a guest on Radio 4's 'Desert Island Discs' and had to speak about my career and choose the songs that meant most to me. Towards the end, interviewer Sue Lawley asked if I could only take one disc to my desert island, which would it be. I chose 'Clare Island', a song about a small island off the west coast of Ireland by the Saw Doctors:

> Will you meet me on Clare Island
> Summer stars are in the sky,
> Get the ferry out from Roonah
> And wave all our cares goodbye.

Ireland was where it all started. George, my dad, came from Monaghan, an Ulster county on the southern side of the border with Northern Ireland. His father, Thomas, worked in the post office in Monaghan and later managed the Magnet Cinema in the centre of town. The family, consisting of Thomas and his wife Margaret, George and his four sisters, May, Marjorie, Kay and Edith, lived on a farm called The Glen outside town. About three or four times a year, Thomas Dunwoody went racing with his friend Gus Gordon and one day, enthused by horses, he bought a pony for his son. George called his pony Black Bess and Thomas soon regretted buying the animal. Devoted to Black Bess, George neglected his books. Eventually Thomas sold the pony but by then the damage was done. The only life my father wanted now was one spent with horses.

Thomas did his best to redirect him. Through his friendship with the Pattons, a well-known Monaghan family, he got his son a job in the office of the local timber mill. The idea was for George to learn about the timber trade and become a buyer for the mill. He lasted about six months and used the money he had earned to run away. George was stubborn, a characteristic he passed on to his son. For him it was horses or nothing; they were in his blood. Many years later, I would know the feeling. This was 1936; he was 17 and desperate. He left home on his bicycle, took the lanes out of Monaghan so he wouldn't be seen and followed the signs to Belfast, 70 miles away. There he abandoned his bike, bought a ticket for the ferry to Liverpool and away he went.

George thought it would be straightforward. Off the boat in Liverpool, he didn't waste time. 'Do you know how I would get to the nearest racing stables?' he asked time and again. Maybe it was his Monaghan accent but he got nowhere. Even those who understood him couldn't help. Racing stables? They hadn't a clue. After a couple of days, George changed tack and sailed back to Ireland. He returned to Dublin and made his way to the Phoenix Park where he knew there were stables. He went to one yard, then another, but the trainers said they couldn't take him on without his father's permission, which was no help. Even though he was running low on money, he was reluctant to return home. In his own words, he 'didn't want to be collared'. He found other stables but they, too, wanted to speak to his parents. Eventually the money dried up and he grew weary of the search. He ended up at the door of his uncle in Longford who got in touch with his parents and he was put on a train and sent home to Monaghan.

Horses have that effect on you and George had, at least, shown how badly he wanted to work with them. By then old Thomas Dunwoody knew there was no point in trying to dissuade his strong-willed son. Thomas was friendly with the local GP, Dr Conlon, who knew the Curragh trainer, Cecil Brabazon. 'Bring him down,' said Cecil, and it was there that my father began his life in racing. Cecil was the father of Aubrey Brabazon, the Irish jockey who rode the Vincent O'Brien-trained Cottage Rake to win three consecutive Cheltenham Gold Cups. George worked with Cecil's jumping horses and during the summer returned home to his father's farm where he began to train a few point-to-pointers.

As time went by, George concentrated more on his own operation, riding as an amateur and training a few. Thomas died in 1952, George sold up in Monaghan two years later and, to be closer to the people he rode for, he bought a place in Ballyclare, County Antrim. He combined training with riding and even though the operation wasn't that big, it was successful. As an amateur, he rode well over 100 winners, including the decent Lord Glenfield, and would have ridden in the National on Stockman if he hadn't fractured his skull in a bad fall. He trained for such people as the Catherwoods who were later to own Little Bay, Spendid and other fine horses.

Pappa Threeways, one of the promising horses in the yard at the time, attracted the interest of a young Englishwoman, Gillian Thrale. Gillian's family was steeped in racing. Her father Dick trained at Downs House in Epsom – one of the horses he trained, Indigenous, still holds the world record for five furlongs, ridden by Lester Piggott. Leonore, her mother, was a well-respected judge of racehorses. In what was then a predominantly man's world, Leonore's eye for a racehorse earned her particular respect.

Gillian, who rode well, came to look at Pappa Threeways in 1960 but didn't buy. George may not have wanted to sell. The tradition in Ireland has always been to try to pass on everything but the best and Pappa Threeways went on to win many races for his trainer.

But George and Gillian didn't fall out and when they met at that year's Punchestown Festival, it was clear they were attracted to each other. They were married on 23 May 1962. Gillian moved to Ballyclare although her time there was short as George accepted an offer to manage Frank Shane's stud in Comber. He and his new bride moved south from Antrim to County Down. It was while they lived in Comber that I turned up. As might be imagined, the delivery was a little complicated. Mum says she almost lost me in December and the January birth was traumatic. I was turned the wrong way, Mum haemor-rhaged badly and Gavin Boyd, a very good gynaecologist at the Royal Victoria Hospital in Belfast, was responsible for getting both of us through it.

A year after I was born, Frank died, his stud farm was sold and Dad went back to training racehorses. He rented Kilbright House and the accompanying yard, between Millisle and Car-rowdore on the Ards Peninsula. Everything I remember about growing up in Ireland goes back to our time in Kilbright and horses are in most of the pictures. Those born into horse racing don't waste much time getting started. At the age of two and a half, I was led round on a small grey pony at Newtownards Horse Show and like all the toddlers in this class, I was given a rosette. As was the custom, Mum then walked me round on the lap of honour. I should have sat and accepted the applause but seeing Dad in the crowd, I slid off the pony on the wrong side and raced over to show him my rosette. Mum never saw my dismount and only looked round on hearing the crowd laugh-ing. Even then, winning was what excited me.

I am not sure when I became addicted to the buzz of riding horses but it must have been very early in my life. According to Dad, it began with Seamus, the donkey. He came as a compan-ion for one of the racehorses but ended up being our pet. As a very small child, Dad put me on Seamus and led me on a halter. Stopping one day to close a gate, he gave me the halter and said, 'Hold him now.' Seamus sensed his opportunity and away he went. He was a young donkey and could go. I took a heavy fall but it was my reaction that was forever quoted in our house. By the time Dad got to me, I was already on my feet. He expected tears but there were none. 'Daddy, Daddy, I fall off like a jockey,' I said. It was practice for something I would do well over 600 times. Dad was pleased.

If you grow up with horses and happen to like riding, there are few better childhoods. By the time I was five, I was riding Tony, a good grey 12.2 pony, following behind Dad's string and feeling very much part of the yard. School was at Dunover Primary where I was taught by two dedicated and lovely ladies, Miss Little and Mrs McIlveen. It was a small school, around 40 pupils, and I got on well there. Miss Little suffered from multiple sclerosis and has since passed away; Mrs McIlveen is still very much with us. They were serious about schoolwork and expected their young pupils to be the same. As a result, I got a very good grounding and that helped to smooth the later transition to an English primary school. Even after we moved to England, Mum kept in touch with Miss Little and Mrs McIlveen and they exchanged letters every Christmas.

In my final year at Dunover, I got into a fight when bad weather prevented us from going outside to play. When we later said our goodbyes to these fine women, Miss Little said to me, 'You have always been very, very good but just in your last year, you were getting into a bit of trouble.' That was 1971, the year Arsenal did the double and they became my team. Charlie George was my favourite player. If the devotion to long-haired Charlie suggested a mildly rebellious streak, I was also a strong-willed child. Once, when I was three or four, we were on the ferry to England on our way to visit Mum's family and I lost my teddy bear. I became totally obsessed about finding it and made an unnatural fuss. The boat was turned inside out, but no teddy. I became totally unreasonable, an obnoxious little sod who just wouldn't let go. My parents came up with a new teddy but I didn't want that. Thirty-plus years on I wonder why I have been slow to become a father and maybe one of the reasons is that I remember what I could be like as a child.

The vivid memories of Ireland are all horse-related – riding Tony, going to the races or going to a point-to-point. Dad almost always had runners at the local meetings and one afternoon we were at the North Down Harriers' point-to-point at Craigantlet, outside Belfast. My sister Gail and I were playing around the tents when I tripped over a guy rope and fell face down on to a peg. It got me just below my left eye, there was blood everywhere and I was immediately taken away to the hospital in Dundonald. At the same time, the well-known Irish amateur rider Raymond Martin had punctured a lung and cracked two ribs in a fall from a horse called Vulgan's Image. At the hospital in Dundonald I was waiting to have my gash treated when Raymond was brought in on a stretcher. He was still in his breeches and riding boots and even though he didn't look too good, it was exciting for a six year old. Gail watched Raymond being brought in, ran outside and to the first person she met, she excitedly said, 'They've brought in a dead jockey.' Raymond Martin's mother overheard and was more than a little concerned.

I had 12 stitches and still have the scar to remind me of the fall. Gail's report of Raymond's demise was exaggerated. He recovered and went on to have a fine amateur career that included victories on Call Collect in the 1989 Aintree Foxhunters and in the Cheltenham equivalent on the same horse a year later. In 1990, 20 years after sharing that casualty unit at Dundonald Hospital, I finished sixth on Bigsun in the Aintree Grand National and Raymond was seventh, just a length and a half behind on Call Collect.

Because both my parents were so keen on horses, I got every encouragement. Mum wanted me to be good at my schoolwork but otherwise, I was free to spend as much time as I liked with Tony. We went from the cantering stage and my fear of going too fast to the point where he couldn't be fast enough for me. We showjumped on the lawn, raced in the field and, as soon as we were old enough, we hunted with the local hounds. My first experience with the North Down Harriers happened by accident but it was some day. I was almost seven and the plan was for Mum to take me on a leading rein and follow the hunt on the roads. But as we were about to get going, some owners dropped in and I was told to go on and wait up by Dunover School. Mum would follow on her bike. She was delayed by the owners and as the huntsmen and harriers pulled out, I was distraught. 'Where are you, Mum? I'm going to miss everything.' My temper kept rising until I could wait there no longer. Away I went after the hunt, catching up, flying along, having no control but enjoying every moment of it. In the end, both my parents came to find me and were worried when I wasn't there. After a bit, the hunt came back towards them and they spotted us. Tony and I were not that far behind the master, having the time of our lives.

The hunt lasted for two and a half hours and when it ended I was shattered. Mum thought it would be better if one of the stablegirls took Tony home and I went in the car. At first I couldn't speak, I was so exhausted. But that passed and I told them every detail about the day. Mum says she has never heard me so talkative or as animated as I was that afternoon.

The idea of a six year old having a serious day's hunting may seem odd now but 30 years ago, kids got opportunities they don't get today. Another time, Dad took me down to Gowran Park in County Kilkenny to help with his runner, Rotomar Girl. I was seven and this was the first time Dad and I had been away together. It was a big deal for me. We stayed overnight at a guesthouse near Gowran and returned the next day. The lady of the house served us breakfast and I remember we had Shredded Wheat. Excited by the adventure of being away, I mistook the salt for sugar and sprinkled it all over my cereal. I soon realised what I had done but I didn't want to admit to such a stupid mistake. 'I'll eat it anyway,' I thought, and I did, every morsel. I didn't cry when I fell off Seamus and I wasn't going to admit the Shredded Wheat had been ruined.

The highlight of the trip to Gowran was leading up Rotomar Girl. The rules said you had to be 12 or older to lead up a horse but Dad put a cap on me to make me look older and it gave me more of a stablelad's look. It wasn't dangerous because I knew Rotomar Girl and she was the quietest mare. Jim Marsh, the stipendiary steward, wasn't taken in.

'George,' he said, 'that's a very young lad you have.'

'Ah Jim,' said Dad, 'that's my lad. He knows the mare well and he's a bit older than he looks.'

I was desperate for Rotomar Girl to finish in the first three so I would get to lead her back into the winner's enclosure. She came fifth. I could have cried, but I didn't.

So the seeds of an obsession were sown. There were hints, too, of what would become another interest in my life. Hunting one day with the North Down Harriers, I noticed a girl on her pony and began to follow her. I would have been seven, maybe eight at the time. We came to a flax pit. Anyone familiar with the rural landscape around Belfast will know about these pits, cut deep into the ground, left to fill with water and then used for the soaking of flax. I caught up with this girl as we came to the flax hole. She said, 'Come on, jump this.' From a girl, this was a challenge I couldn't turn down. I galloped Tony towards the pit. It was about 12 feet wide and very deep. He took off a little too soon and landed in the middle of it. I am not sure if I did fall off but I have a vision of holding on to the pony's tail as he climbed out. Flax-pit water is dirty and it smells. I was soaked and black from the water, only the tips of Tony's ears remained white and it must have been winter because the water was freezing. Dad turned up and brought me home. In that little escapade there was a lesson about chasing girls. Later events would show I was a slow learner.

One lesson did sink in and that concerned gambling. I have never been a gambler and even though I have once been quoted as saying jockeys should be permitted to have a bet, I don't have the remotest interest. My parents say it goes back to a bad experience early in my life. Dad had horses running in Navan and, as usual, I went along. Early in the day they met Barry Pullan, a good friend and also one of their owners. Barry liked to have a bet and was generous, giving me money whenever we met at the races. On this afternoon at Navan he gave me a pound, a lot of money in 1969. I was five and listening as Barry spoke to Dad. He had a slight stutter.

'G-g-g-good thing today,' he said, 'L'Escargot, w-w-won't be beaten.'

I weighed things up. L'Escargot was supposed to be a very good horse and he was ridden by my favourite jockey, Tommy Carberry. By the time I found Mum, my mind was made up.

'Mummy,' I said, 'I want you to put my pound on L'Escargot.'

'That's a lot of money to put on a horse, Richard.'

'It's my money. Barry gave it to me.'

'OK. It's your money.'

L'Escargot, the odds-on favourite, was beaten. I was seething. All my money gone.

'Mummy,' I said, 'I think I want to go home.'

Keen to make money, I was not prepared to lose it. Never again did I ask Mum to back another horse and it more or less finished me gambling. I was like the young boy who sneaked a cigarette and got violently sick as a result. I wouldn't do it again. Throughout my career, it was never a factor. In my list of rides there was the name of the horse, its trainer, where it ran, where it finished, the distance, a short description and analysis of how it ran. One detail I did not write down was the horse's price. For me, it had no relevance. Because I rode, people imagined I knew far more about the horse's chance than I did. At racecourses you couldn't walk from your car to the weighing room without someone discreetly asking for the day's good thing. I tried to be polite but I could have told them about L'Escargot.

In the 30-year history of the Troubles in Ulster, the late sixties and early seventies were a particularly bad time. Yet it was possible to live through those times and not be that affected by them; it depended upon where you lived and what you worked at. The difficulty for Dad was that as a racehorse trainer he regularly travelled to southern racecourses and this meant crossing the border at Newry. During the bad years, it was usual to be delayed at the army checkpoint. Being on border roads late at night was dangerous but for those involved in racing in the north, it was unavoidable. Johnny McKeag generally drove our horsebox and my parents and I would follow on in the car. Gail would be left with Geraldine Barry, a wonderful person who lived nearby.

Different memories remain of those trips but the one most often recalled was of a night in early August 1971. We had been to an evening meeting at Gowran Park and had stopped for something to eat at a place in County Kildare on the way home. Mick O'Toole, the Curragh trainer, was there. 'You're not going back up north tonight,' he said. 'Things are desperate up there.' But with Gail at home, Mum and Dad didn't want to spend a night away. It was around ten o'clock when we finished eating and it was after midnight when we reached the border. Dad drove, one of his owners, Bobby Martin, was in the front passenger's seat, Mum and I were in the back. It was the day or the day after internment was introduced and at the border, an RUC officer said it would be unsafe to drive through Newry and that we must take to the hills.

After crossing the border, we stopped at the top of the hill overlooking Newry and the town was ablaze. It is still a vivid memory. We headed towards Forkhill, then on towards Crossmaglen and through hilly roads that would eventually take us on to Banbridge and back on to the main road. Occasionally a car whizzed past us and the headlights frightened me. We were on those small roads for over two hours. Every so often, Dad would pull in to check the map. Even those brief stops were scary. It was four o'clock in the morning when we arrived home to Kilbright. Mum says it was the most frightening experience of her life.

There were other incidents. One night coming back from Leopardstown we were told at the border about trouble again in Newry. There had been a Civil Rights march and police Land Rovers were being burned in the centre of the town. Dad was driving the car pulling the trailer that carried our two runners. We tried to pick our way through Newry but at one point we were stopped and the crowd came in on us, pushing against the car. For a few moments, there was panic and fear but eventually we got through. Dad tells another story of returning late one winter's night from Navan races. He was signalled to stop by men on the road. When Dad lowered the window, a gun was pointed at his head. Even in the dark he could tell it wasn't Army or RUC. Which side of the terrorist fence, he is not sure.

'What are you doing out tonight?' asked the man.

'Coming from the races,' replied George.

'What's your name?'

'George Dunwoody.'

'George Dunwoody, the point-to-point man?'

'That's me.'

'Ah, tell us, how did yous get on today?'

But the closest encounter we had with the Troubles was an afternoon in late August 1971. We were on a shopping expedition in Belfast, Mum, Dad, Gail and me. Most of the shopping had been done and Dad took the parcels back to the car which was parked in Anne Street while Mum searched for shoes for herself. Gail and I went with Dad and we were all to meet for a cup of tea at the Abercorn restaurant. As we were going down Anne Street, there was some commotion in a pub across the road. Shots rang out. Seconds later a gunman came running out of the pub, towards us. It all happened very quickly but he knocked Gail over as he went past us and escaped down a narrow street on our side of the road. While all this was happening, Mum was heading towards the car when she realised Anne Street was cordoned off. She was told there had been a shooting. Desperately worried, she rushed off to the Abercorn, her legs so weak they could hardly carry her. When she arrived, we were already there. 'Thank goodness you're all right,' she said. Eight months later we moved to Tetbury in Gloucestershire.

Other factors influenced the move to England. My grandmother Leonore Thrale wasn't that well and was keen to have her daughter living closer. Leonore and Dick were also uneasy about their only child living in a part of the world they didn't think was safe. Dad, though, says he would never have left Ireland but for 'the few things that happened'. Mum, too, was sad to leave. Even though born and raised in England, she says if it weren't for the Troubles, she would very happily have stayed in the North.

When they told me we were moving to England, I asked if I would be able to take Tony. 'Of course,' they said, and so for me, it became a big adventure.

3

GROWING PAINS

Ambition surfaced early in my life. At first money was the motivation – be a bank manager and all that money would be mine. I don't know how long that lasted but the change came with Tony the grey pony. As soon as I learned to ride him, I knew what I wanted to be. Every signpost in my upbringing pointed to horses. For as long as I can remember, I loved being among them. The click-clack of hooves on a cement yard was background music to my childhood. Dad would exercise his string on the beach near Millisle on the Ards Peninsula. I would canter off behind them, imagining Tony was a racehorse and I was his young, up-and-coming jockey. Days at the races made me even keener. It was a different world back then and from the age of five, my parents allowed me to make my own way around Irish racecourses. I felt very much at home. I followed the top Irish jockeys of the time, analysed the form of the horses, studied how they looked in the parade ring and tried to work out how they would run.

The important decisions in my early life concerned horses. On an April Saturday in 1971, there was the choice between going to the local North Down point-to-point and watching the Aintree Grand National on television. I hated missing the point-to-point but not seeing Aintree would have been even worse. So I went to our neighbour Geraldine Barry's house and saw Johnny Cook win on Specify. At school I managed to get horses into essays, projects, paintings and anywhere else it was possible. It was the world I knew best and all I wanted.

One of the first things the aspiring jockey realises is that size matters. You look around the stableyard and there are no tall people. Mostly, everyone is slight and thin. It was always in the back of my mind – if I get too big, that's it. Even as a kid in Dunover Primary School, I knew I wasn't particularly small and it worried me. What if I kept getting bigger? Our family was very friendly with the O'Reillys who lived in Dromara and we would visit each other's houses. There were two boys in the O'Reilly house, Brendan and Michael, and although they were a few years older than me, we played together. One day I was riding Tony when Michael, their father, was around and I told him I was going to be a jockey. 'You're too big,' he said. 'You're going to be too big. You'll be a bloody policeman you will.' I was shattered and the fear that I would be too big remained with me for years.

The move to Tetbury was easy. Tony came and essentially we swapped a racing yard at Millisle in County Down for Charlton Down Stud in Gloucestershire. From being a racehorse trainer, Dad now managed a stud for an American, Bill Reynolds, and though I missed the involvement in a training yard, there was the compensation of being able to follow the offspring of the mares under Dad's care. One such mare was Black Satin, winner of the Irish 1,000 Guineas, and the others were all generally well bred. Besides, there was plenty of space on the farm for me to ride Tony. We didn't get to visit the races as much as we had in Ireland but we would go to our local tracks, Bath and Salisbury, and occasionally to Newbury. Tony and I continued to hunt and that helped me to settle. All the time I was getting better on Tony, riding faster and jumping higher. Speed excited me; the faster I went the more I liked it. I wanted to look the part, too, and how I looked on the pony mattered.

I made new friends quickly. There were lads from school and Susan Baber from the neighbouring farm. In the hay barn we made jumps and packed them with loose straw on the top, so that when our ponies kicked off the straw, it was as if we were riding over Aintree's big fences. Tetbury Junior School was OK. Because of the grounding I had received from Mrs McIlveen and Miss Little at Dunover Primary, I was actually put in a class a year above my own age group. At the end of my second full year at the school I did the entrance exam for Rendcomb College in the hope of getting one of eight scholarships. I passed it but my marks were not good enough for the scholarship. Mr Carwardine, the headmaster at Tetbury, advised me to remain another year at primary level and retake the exam. Second time round I got the scholarship and was on my way to Rendcomb College near Cirencester. The scholarship did not cover everything but because Dad's income wasn't high, it meant my parents did not have to pay a lot to have me there.

I didn't enjoy boarding school that much. On the Sundays we were allowed home, I would count the hours before the dreaded return. Rendcomb was a good school, but I just didn't like being away from the horses. On those Sundays, I would be aware that for three or four weeks I would hardly see a horse, let alone ride. Back at Rendcomb, I would make the best of it but it wasn't ideal and there were very few people with whom I could discuss racing. To make the separation easier, I kept an account of all the horses that had been bred at Charlton Down and followed their careers. Later I kept a list of the horses I rode out and tracked their progress on the racecourse. I worked at my studies and generally achieved good grades. Mum was hopeful I would become a vet. Her father, Dick Thrale, had wanted to be one and was halfway through his veterinary studies when he was called up to serve in the First World War. On his return from the war, he wanted to get on with his career as a racehorse trainer and so abandoned his veterinary degree. He always regretted it. Mum knew how keen I was to be a jockey but thought it better to be qualified in something else first. She would look at my grades and say what a shame it would be if I didn't do something with those. I didn't have much enthusiasm for the vet's life. Once I was asked to hold the tray while the vet stitched a mare after foaling at Charlton Down. As he did, I could feel my stomach turn and was afraid I would be sick. 'Don't feel I'm cut out for this,' I thought.

At the end of my first year at Rendcomb, Bill Reynolds decided to run the stud himself and my father was out of a job. We moved from Gloucestershire to Newmarket where Dad began working for the trainer Paul Kelleway. The move took me into the heart of Flat racing in England and gave me the chance to ride out regularly. Being just 12 at the time, I started riding the hack at Ben Hanbury's. The hack is generally an old and quiet horse used to lead a string of younger and keener horses. I was just happy to be riding out and to feel part of a proper racing stable. One of the older lads, Bill Brindle, took me under his wing and showed me what to do. It was how it happened in those days but now, with stable staff in such short supply, young lads, unless they have gained experience in an apprentice school, are often thrown in without anyone showing them the ropes. After that first summer in Newmarket, I began riding out for Paul Kelleway and my life divided in two – Rendcomb during school term, horses during the holidays.

As I got older and began to mix more with the stablelads and apprentices, I realised how unprepared I was for real life. Boarding school didn't train you for the rough and tumble on the outside and if ever I have children, they will not be sent away to school. I always felt at a disadvantage with the lads who were smarter and more street-wise. They wound me up and I didn't know how to take it; nor had I any clue about standing up for myself. It was no help being quiet and shy.

Rendcomb, though, had its pluses. It was good for those interested in sport and I was definitely in that group. Depending on the season, we played rugby, hockey and cricket and I tried to get into every team. I started my rugby life in the pack, first as hooker then as wing forward, but as everyone else got bigger, I remained the same size. From flanker, I moved to full-back and from there to the wing. I played midfield in hockey but I wasn't mad on the game and at cricket, I think I may have been the most defensive opening batsman to pass through Rendcomb. We would play an afternoon match, 25 or 30 overs, and I would remain at the crease for about 20 of them, all for about ten runs. I hated getting out and with the bat, R. Dunwoody would have made G. Boycott seem cavalier. The lads cursed me for it and batsmen lower down the order had express instructions to run me out.

I never considered myself particularly bright but hard work got me good O-levels – seven As, one B and one C in nine subjects. A few of the lads regarded me as a swot but it was the only way I could get on. Generally, I felt I didn't figure things out and retain them as well as others and so I got into the habit of writing things down. That helped. I still find it useful. I was competitive in the classroom but there was another side to my character; a part of me likes to release the valve occasionally and let off steam. During my riding career it happened every so often; we would stay up late, drink a bit and often end up with female company. On the day after our O-levels ended, the options at Rendcomb weren't great but we made do. Allowed a day off, Timothy Pratt, Richard Evans and I biked it out of the college and stopped off at Tim's house for a few beers for lunch. Afterwards we went to an off-licence and bought martini, vodka and cider. Armed with our alcohol we cycled to a field overlooking the school, sat there and drank the lot. The plan was to cycle back to the college in plenty of time for the six o'clock roll call. The best laid plans of mice and boys . . .

First we got merry, then a little stupid and in the end, we hardly knew where we were. Half-conscious, wholly drunk, we sailed past our six o'clock deadline. Eventually Tim and I began to come round and realised that we should be getting back to Rendcomb. We shook Richard but we might as well have tried to wake the dead. What was the three musketeers' motto? One for all, all for one? We decided to abandon our friend. Stumbling back on my bike, I saw deer in a nearby field, running and jumping hedges, and in my drunken haze I wasn't sure if they were real or not. Reality hit as soon as we got back to Rendcomb. Missing us at roll call, they knew something was wrong and one look at us told them precisely what. We were paralytic. We explained about trying to rouse Richard, but when they went back to where we had been drinking, Richard was gone. Search parties were organised and everyone was frantic. What if he got sick and choked? They headed off in various directions and as they did Richard came cruising back in a car. A local farmer had picked him out of a ditch and driven him back to school.

The headmaster wanted to see us the following day and suspended us for three days from the beginning of the next term. It wasn't a ban we were entitled to appeal against. My parents weren't impressed. Mum always felt that because I was a scholarship student at Rendcomb, I had to be particularly responsible. The school had given me an opportunity, she said, and I had let everyone down. Not long afterwards the O-level results arrived and I was half forgiven.

That summer I rode out every day at Paul Kelleway's. It was one of the smaller yards in Newmarket so I was allowed to do more than I would have done at a bigger establishment. Paul took an interest in me from an early stage and really brought me on, and of course Dad was working at the yard and kept an eye on me. I got to ride Donegal Prince in his work, even schooling, and he went on to win some big races afterwards, including the Schweppes at Newbury. For a racing-mad 16 year old, it was a summer from heaven. One day I would go to the races to lead up a horse, the next morning I would ride work with Greville Starkey or even, on one special occasion, Lester Piggott. At that time I wanted to be a Flat jockey but my physique was never going to allow that.

The more experience I had of riding out and the more time I spent among racing people, the more I wanted to be a jockey. Mum still talked about my becoming a vet and my O-level results were encouraging. My form master agreed it was a realistic aim and it was decided I would take three science subjects at A-level. I went along with this even though I knew that if I was going to be a jockey, I couldn't spend another two years at school, followed by a further five at university. In my mind, becoming a vet was not on. I was desperate to be a jockey. At Rendcomb I read John Hislop's two instructional books on riding and, alone at night, I practised the exercises designed to strengthen the muscles most useful to a jockey. One exercise involved getting into the riding position and holding it for five or eight or ten minutes. I did it every night, always trying to hold the position longer than the night before.

In September 1980, I moved into the sixth form but I no longer wanted to study biology, physics and chemistry. They were tough at this level. I suppose hard work would have got me through but my heart wasn't in it. At the time I was worried about my weight. Michael O'Reilly's prophecy still haunted me and Dad said I had the same heavy-boned limbs as him and would always be on the heavy side. I could feel myself getting bigger and would look anxiously at my hands. 'They're pretty big but I can't get heavy, I just can't get heavy,' I thought. I bought books on food and analysed the number of calories in each individual foodstuff. I had to come up with a new regime for myself so I counted them, allowed myself a set number and stuck rigidly to the targets. Because sixth-form students at Rendcomb had their own rooms, it was easy to get away with not eating much. If you didn't eat at the table, everyone presumed you must be eating in your room.

From that September, concern with my weight became an obsession. The less I ate, the less I wanted to eat. Biscuits, chocolate, all sweet things were out and because my shape changed gradually, I didn't notice it. It did affect my life though. Rugby in particular was getting harder. I was lighter than I had been two years before. During the Christmas holidays I rode out for Paul again and he was one of the few people to suspect something might be wrong. He reckoned I wasn't eating properly. Around that time Mum also felt I wasn't myself and she worried even more when she found books on dieting and calories in my room.

At first I enjoyed the discipline of not eating much. It proved to me how serious I was about becoming a jockey and how I could control my weight. As happens, the dieting eventually took control of me. My weight dropped from nine stones to eight and continued falling. It was a gradual process because I didn't stop eating completely and I didn't make myself sick. But the need to keep my weight down had taken over my entire life. There wasn't a weighing scales in school but I didn't need one – if I used more calories than I consumed, I had to get lighter. All the time my energy level decreased and as it did, my appetite disappeared. One morning towards the end of February 1981, it all came to an inevitable climax. In the previous five years at Rendcomb, I had never once rung home in the morning.

'Mum, I want to eat but I can't,' I whispered.

'What, Richard?'

'I want to eat but I can't. I feel really weak, awful.'

'Richard, you must go immediately to see Matron.'

A short time later, I collapsed. My blood pressure was dangerously low. They put me into sick bay at school. Matron telephoned my mother to say the doctor was coming to examine me and he sent me on to Cirencester Hospital. They did all kinds of tests that revealed nothing. Mum came down to see me and was shocked at how emaciated I had become. They said it could be an ulcer or that I had picked up some virus. At the time there wasn't much understanding about the illness and it was unheard of for boys to be anorexic. Most of the doctors wanted to rule out the possibility. Boys don't get it. One doctor did suggest I was suffering from 'an eating disorder'.

My mother knew what the problem was. She had been suspicious during the Christmas holidays when I nibbled food and became increasingly fussy at the table. Seeing the dieting book in my room convinced her that I was obsessed about my weight. A few days after my collapse, one of the teachers at Rendcomb telephoned her and said that he had a sister who had been anorexic and that I had the same symptoms. In a way, she was relieved because it explained what was wrong with me. I spent three days in the hospital at Cirencester and then went home to Newmarket. Full recovery took a long time and I found it impossible to eat food that was heavy or stodgy. Even a slice of bread was hard work.

It was a tough time for all of us at home. I had no strength and suffered from violent mood swings. I was so weak I couldn't get out of the bath, so Dad had to help me. My relationship with Gail had not been very good and during this time it was at its worst. Gail had resented the fact that I was sent to boarding school while I thought it unfair that she was allowed to attend day school and live at home. I would have willingly swapped positions. It was a pity because a few years earlier, we got on really well and played together all the time. For the first few days after I got home from hospital, Gail could not have been kinder. She was only 13 at the time and was terribly frightened when she saw how thin and frail I was. Girls expect their big brothers to be strong and Gail couldn't believe what had happened to me. She tiptoed around the house and was very sympathetic for a while but then the tension resurfaced. Gail now says she was trying to wind me up but, to be honest, I was the bigger problem. In my darker moods I tended to take things out on her and she didn't have to do much to get on the wrong side of me. One of the things I could stomach was drinking chocolate and I liked a mug of it in the evening.

One night the chocolate was gone and I flew into a rage. I freaked when I realised Gail had drunk it. I get wound up at the best of times but with this condition, I exploded. That night Gail got it. I shouted and kept shouting. Mum came and sent Gail to her room for annoying me and it took me some time to cool down. Anybody witnessing that evening would have reckoned I needed to be locked up.

The anger told a lot of how I felt about myself. I didn't like what anorexia had done to me and hated feeling so helpless. Gail wasn't the problem but that didn't stop me. Basically, I had starved myself to be a jockey but in doing that, I lost the strength necessary to ride horses. The frustrations caused by the illness were taken out on those closest to me.

How did it get to that point? Once I began to study the precise calorie levels in different foods, the fascination with controlling my diet deepened. I enjoyed the feeling of saying no to the things I wanted. Hunger was a small price to pay for that and as for the gaunt face and thin body, I didn't even notice them. Keeping my weight down wasn't the only motivation for the starvation diet. I decided if I spent two years doing A-levels, I would then be too old to be a jockey. Subconsciously, not eating was a way of letting my parents know how badly I wanted to leave school and get on with a riding career. They had to understand how determined I was. Just as my grandfather had been made to understand when Dad ran away that time.

In our family it was something we never spoke about. The illness happened and was consigned to the past. My parents didn't bring it up and when I eventually went back to Rendcomb to complete that school year, no one there ever mentioned it. It suited me not to talk about it. But it was a traumatic event in my life and now, with the benefit of hindsight, it wasn't a good idea to sweep it under the carpet. During my career as a rider, I was often asked by parents to speak to their young son who hoped to be a jockey. In a few instances, I saw my 17-year-old reflection, the evidence of serious under-eating and the fear of getting too big or too heavy. To those boys I always said the same thing: 'You cannot ride well unless you are physically strong. You've got to keep up your strength.'

Feeling miserable, I made one important decision.

'I'm not going back to school,' I said to my parents. 'I've had enough. I want to go and ride out. I want to be a jockey, so I'm not going back to school.'

'But Richard, not many lads who ride out end up becoming jockeys and without an education, you'll have nothing,' my mother said.

'I don't care. I'm not going back.'

Nothing was going to change my mind. Mum felt I was making a mistake but realised it would be useless to insist. I had already made myself ill through dieting, so what would I do if forced to return to school? Instead she came up with a compromise. I was to go back for the last term of the school year and once that was out of the way, it would be horses. That was reasonable and as it was going to take a little bit of time before I was strong enough to ride, I agreed. Still, I felt no elation. My parents suggested I visit Uncle Humphrey Graham and Aunty Polly in Portsmouth. They thought the change of scenery would do me good and not having me to look after was certainly going to make their lives a little less stressful.

I loved Humphrey and Polly but at this time I was very down and disillusioned; 17 years of age and not much over seven stones in weight, I felt and looked miserable. I'd chucked in my A-levels, given up the idea of going to college and all for the chance to ride horses. Where was my life going? 'You'll end up with nothing,' my mother had said. There was no easy solution. I didn't want to spend another two years at school; that much was clear. I had to regain my strength before I could even think about riding; that would take longer. Maybe I was going to be too big anyway. At the time, I couldn't see life getting better and suicidal thoughts even entered my head. Throw myself under a bus or off a bridge and it would end everyone's problems.

Over the following weeks, however, I began to eat tiny amounts of easily digestible foods, not enough to rebuild my strength but sufficient to stop the debilitation. I returned to school for the final term and took Classics in Translation as a tenth O-level, getting an A. I also did the mocks for my A-levels but never considered staying on for another year. When my classmates were going home on their summer break, I was leaving school. By now I was strong enough to ride and everything seemed better when I started riding out at Paul Kelleway's again that summer. I was to work at Paul's as a 'pupil-assistant', an unpaid lad who mucked out like everyone else but who was there to learn, and I was desperate to get on in this world. I was going to be a proper jockey.

As I rode out, my strength improved and so too did my moods. As a rider, I could survive in the yard or on the gallops but I struggled socially. When it came to girls, I was a disaster. I may have taken Gay Kelleway to a hunt ball when I was 14 or 15 but I had very little contact with the female sex. Whatever efforts I made ended in failure. All I had to do was speak to a woman and I would turn crimson red. When I went to stay with the Bosleys, there was a girl there with whom I temporarily hit it off. We went out together and ended up back where the lads stayed. There were bunk beds and things looked promising. Coming from boarding school, I wore pyjamas that had Chinese horsemen running all over them but the night didn't progress as I hoped. Actually, there was no progress. Afterwards the girl told everyone in the yard about my 'Chinese horse pyjamas' and the lads just ribbed me to pieces. I never wore them again. The embarrassments helped me to mature and in the year after school, I grew up more than I had in the previous six.

Though hopeless in the lads' canteen and chronically shy at the disco, I had no doubts about my future. I wanted to be as good a jockey as I could be and I understood from the beginning that whether I made it or not was entirely down to me. Riding out at Kelleway's got me into the game but to move up, I had to move on. Paul was a Flat-race trainer and even though the idea of being a Flat jockey appealed to me, I accepted that I was too big. Jumping it had to be.

At the beginning of September, I joined John Bosley's yard in Brize Norton. My parents had been friendly with John and Sylvia for many years, and I was now good mates with their son Martin. As pony-riding youngsters, Martin and I stayed with each other and got on well. Years later he would be best man when Carol and I got married. John trained National Hunt horses, a lovely man who was very easy to work for. Moving in with the Bosleys was a perfect stepping stone between the comfort of living at home and having to look after myself. In fact, those three months with them completed my recovery. Even though reasonably strong, I still was not able to eat properly when I went there. Without anything ever being said, the Bosleys eased me back to full health. They didn't know about the problems I'd had, although Sylvia did think I was unusually thin. She had ways of beefing me up and, being a visitor, I tried to eat what was put in front of me. With Sylvia's cooking, it wasn't hard. During those months she was like a second mother to me and I always appreciated it.

By now I was in a hurry to take my career onwards and that meant working in a big stable where I would get to exercise and work top class National Hunt horses. That December, six months after abandoning Rendcomb College, I joined Captain Tim Forster's yard in Letcombe Bassett and I was on my way.

The experience of being anorexic left its mark. I would always struggle with my weight. Big-boned and quite tall for a jockey, it was a constant battle and too many hours were spent in the sauna and in a steaming bath. But through the years of deprivation and wasting, I nearly always ate a proper evening meal. Watching what you eat is important for a jockey but my illness had taught me to pay attention to what I wasn't eating.

4

CALL YOURSELVES JOCKEYS?

I t was the winter of 1982 and it was a desperately cold one. I was on £15 a week as a pupil-assistant to Captain Tim Forster at Letcombe Bassett and the three lads I shared a house with in Letcombe Regis weren't much better off. Turning on the heating in our cottage was a luxury we avoided. I was close to penniless and though my three companions, Peter Grady, Neil Morrice and Robert Robinson, were a step or two higher on racing's ladder, they weren't keen to spend money on an optional extra such as heating. 'Richard, it's your turn to get wood for the fire,' Peter would say on those evenings when the temperature dropped. I was the youngest and newest tenant at 1, Old Manor Cottages, so it was always my turn. We would then spend hours wrapped in layers of pullovers, trying to set light to the sodden logs. And there were other ways of fighting off pneumonia. We played squash at the sports club in nearby Wantage and regularly used the public sauna. In the evenings, we played darts or pool and always hoped it was someone else's turn to buy a round. In the mornings, icicles hung from the inside window latches and I perfected the art of dressing under the duvet.

Mum would sometimes come from Newmarket with a box of food and for a few days my popularity soared, but the days of plenty were few. Feeling hungry one evening, I went to the fridge and demolished the remains of a chicken Peter had roasted for our lunch earlier in the day. Having had my fill, I went to bed. Around 1 a.m. the lads returned from the pub. Ravenous in the way the inebriated can be, they went to the fridge. Chicken sandwiches would do nicely but the bird had already flown. They dragged me from my bed and explained, none too politely, that I had no right to the chicken. I got the message.

So impoverished were we in those days that the £30 clothes voucher offered to all participants in the Stable Lads' Boxing Championship was enough to lure us into the fight game. We went to the village hall in Compton on the other side of East Ilsley to train for our fight debut. I must have gone four or five times and enjoyed the sparring. To make it to the finals, each contestant had to get through a preliminary competition. With the sparring under my belt, I thought I was grand. No way would I make a fool of myself. The preliminaries were held during a one-day session at a barracks in Chelsea and each fight consisted of three two-minute rounds. I drew Ricky Pusey, a jockey who worked for trainer Fulke Walwyn. He went on to win the 1985 Stayers' Hurdle at the Cheltenham Festival on Rose Ravine. In the boxing championship, Ricky was one of the shorter straws.

Technically, he knew what he was about and I figured that I had to make it a real scrap. From the bell I went after him. Ricky moved this way and that, throwing jabs and hooks that I stopped with my face. The difference between the gloves used in sparring and real gloves was enormous. Real ones hurt. Angry, I chased harder. Ricky kept picking me off and even though I was in there for less than two minutes, I took a lot of punishment.

'You bastard. I'll have you,' I swore as I charged blindly towards him.

Ricky moved easily out of reach. I couldn't get near him. Blood streamed from my nose; it felt smashed. One eye throbbed and Ricky kept drilling his left fist into my face.

'You bastard,' I said again, full of rage but with no way of making him pay.

The referee told us to break and with my face a total mess, he said, 'You. I'm giving you a warning. Bad language.' Thanks. Back into the fray, I ran straight into more trouble but was too stubborn to go down. Frustrated, I kept going after him. Just before the end of the first round, the referee halted the massacre. By the time I'd showered and dressed, my nose was swollen and I had a black eye but I felt a strange satisfaction. Although hell had been beaten out of me, it had been perversely enjoyable. I liked being in there and I had got rid of a lot of pent-up frustration. The clothes voucher also came in very handy.

Six months before he died in 1999, I went to see Captain Tim Forster. I had been schooling close by at Henry Daly's, who had recently taken over the Captain's yard, and had decided to call in on the Captain on my way to Ludlow races. Even though Tim wasn't well, his resilience was remarkable, his zest for life undiminished by illness. It was November time, the season was in full swing and he talked of his former charges and how much he was looking forward to the big races ahead and to his point-to-pointers running in the spring. I came away feeling uplifted and sad. Sickness had been the Captain's long-term companion but he accepted it. As much as anybody could, he epitomised the spirit of National Hunt racing. He used to say the only thing more boring than a two-mile handicap hurdle was a three-mile handicap hurdle. That was the kind of form he was in on that November day. Proper racehorses jumped fences. Nothing excited him like a steeplechaser. Point-to-point racing was the soul of the game, his idea of the perfect day out. At the end of a life devoted to steeplechasers, he loved them more than ever.

The Captain could train, too, as his three Grand National winners proved. His reputation for grooming young jockeys came about towards the end of his career with the arrival of Luke Harvey, Anthony Tory, Carl Llewellyn and Chris Maude. When I joined in December 1981, there were few young jockeys about the place. Hywel Davies was stable jockey but he had been groomed at Roddy Armytage's. Within the game, the Captain actually had a name for being a little reluctant to give opportunities to unproven amateurs or young conditional jockeys.

He agreed to take me on after an approach from Major Dick Ker and his wife Bidger, friends of my parents who knew the Captain. I started as a pupil-assistant so I could ride as an amateur and use the point-to-point circuit as my training ground. This was important because my experience up until then had been mostly at Flat stables in Newmarket. The Captain took me on without seeing me and we met for the first time on the Monday morning I started. He was a daunting figure and I never really got that close to him. It used to amuse me in later years to hear the Captain say he taught me everything I knew because even though we rarely discussed how I rode, in a way it was true. He was always in the background, pulling the strings. He gave me some opportunities in the first two and a half years but not many. He looked on me as he looked on his more backward young horses – this one needs time. He realised how physically weak I was. As I got stronger and rode winners, he used Hywel and me like pawns, moving us about in a way that kept us very competitive. Mostly, though, the Captain was very loyal to his stable jockey and at the time that was Hywel.

It was a great place to start and I had enormous respect for the Captain. I'm glad that shortly before I retired and before he passed on, we were able to reminisce about our time together. There was never that much said between us, but I'd always hoped that he took some satisfaction from the winners I rode.

Chance led me to 1, Old Manor Cottages. The boys had a place available and if I preferred it to the stablelads' hostel, it was mine. Sharing a house seemed the wiser option and I went for it. It couldn't have worked out better and, almost 20 years later, I'm still in touch with two of the original three, Peter Grady and Neil Morrice, while on several occasions I bumped into Robert Robinson when he was riding in hunter chases on the northern circuit. Peter now runs a successful livery yard near Newmarket and Neil continues to work in racing journalism. Throughout my career, Peter would ring before the big meetings at Cheltenham and Liverpool to wish me well. He says that on the Sunday evening I first showed up at the house, they were all struck by my appearance: short hair, neatish dress, polished shoes and obvious determination to make something of myself. Blame my mother.

It's true, though, that riding out with the Flat strings at Newmarket taught me to look tidy on a horse. At the Captain's, some of the younger lads might have mistaken me for the real thing. I would have seemed confident and was a young man in a hurry. At the time, my grasp was greater than my reach and, deep down, I knew it. Steve Norton, one of the Captain's lads, was an example of how far I had to go. Steve didn't have a licence but he was a horseman and he could settle a keen animal far better than I could.

About eight months after I started, the Irish rider Mick Furlong joined the Captain's and moved into our house. Mick was a lovely horseman. He had ridden the 1977 Cheltenham Gold Cup favourite Bannow Rambler but was brought down by Lanzarote. We talked a lot about riding and Mick made so much sense. On a difficult horse, he would sit quietly, letting the animal have its way before gently calming it. I would look on, amazed. This man was unbelievable.

We had our moments at the Captain's. With the crew we had, it couldn't have been otherwise. John Humphreys, who has since passed on, Peter Feltham, Neil 'Ginger' Price, Robert Elson, Steve Norton and David 'Taff' Rossiter were among the senior lads; Michael Caulfield and I were two of the younger brigade. Luke Harvey arrived the year after me, a young innocent from the West Country. I looked after three horses, as did every other lad in the yard. I got in at 6.30, mucked out, rode out and certainly earned my £15 a week.

You would occasionally get to lead your horse up at the races and that was great fun. As soon as he got to the racecourse, Ginger would tie up the horses and find the nearest pub. Towcester was one of our favourite tracks because the pub was such a short walk from the course and it had an excellent pool table. A few drinks didn't have much effect on the older lads but they sure affected me. Most of the time I was leading up, I was half-gone. The first time I led up John Francome should have been a big occasion because for many years he had been my hero. But that afternoon, Francome was on the Michael Henriques-owned Our Laurie and I was on scotch. Our Laurie led me round and although I smiled a lot, I wasn't able to say much to Franc.

Schooling sessions at the Captain's were also memorable. He soon allowed me to join a small group, jumping the young horses over hurdles, and this would invariably lead to disaster. The Captain would never use a lead horse and many a morning one of the babies, as we called them, would head for the wing, another for the wire fence and one would be stranded across the hurdle. There was always someone on the floor and the Captain would look to the skies. 'My God,' he'd say, 'and you want to call yourselves effing jockeys.' Later, when I had progressed up the ladder, I was allowed to school over the bigger obstacles, the fences, but there were still countless catastrophes. Very Light, a good old handicap chaser, cartwheeled one day with me, straight in front of the Captain. Casbah, another great servant, was proven blind after breaking Mick Furlong's collarbone in another fall. But perhaps most amusing of all, Professor Plum took charge of me having jumped the fences, skipped cleanly over the gate at the top, deposited me head first onto the Ridgeway and made his way home for his breakfast.

I was generally quiet but, occasionally, not quiet enough. Another morning the Captain's string was heading back from the gallops. I'd ridden work to suit myself, not Ginger. I hadn't stayed with him in the gallop and he didn't like it. I muttered something under my breath, some smart-alec comment I should have kept to myself. Ginger just came up to me and pulled me clean off the horse. I landed on the ground and the horse bolted. It was a long, embarrassing walk back to the yard.

During the first few months with the Captain, I weighed about 8st 7lb and was not that strong. Without much experience of jumpers, I rode too short. No one shouted the odds on me becoming a champion and by the time I got round to registering my point-to-point rider's certificate, it was too late for the 1981–82 season. I was disappointed because there might have been a couple of rides that spring. The mistake went pretty much unnoticed by everyone else.

Some people might say that I looked the part from the first day but looks are deceptive; there was a little style but no real substance. Hywel Davies looked at me more closely than anyone else. Was I a threat to his position as stable jockey? Not over the first two or three seasons. Hywel says the pluses were that I looked reasonably stylish and was obviously determined but against that, I was too shy and lacked self-confidence. He thought my reluctance to open up with people worked against me and admits he never had the same feeling about me as he had about Adrian Maguire and A.P. McCoy in their first seasons. First time you saw Adrian and A.P. you knew they were going places. The same could have been said about Richard Johnson and, even though he is very young, Tom Scudamore now looks like a rider for the future. I was a different case. Graham McCourt lived just down the road in Wantage and we got to know each other well. Graham thought I was physically weak and lacked finesse. The success that eventually came, he says, was down to single-minded ambition and stubbornness.

After my first six months with the Captain, I returned to Newmarket for the summer and rode out for Bruce Hobbs. This helped to keep me fit, and among the Flat-racing riders I was conscious of style but I was still not strong enough for even the smaller Flat horses. Every day a grey horse called Mardi Gras would blaze up the gallops with me, much to the amusement of the other lads. But by the time I returned to the Captain in early August, I was armed with my amateur's licence and a determination to get my career started.

From my days at Rendcomb I had been an avid reader of the *Sporting Life* and now I scoured the entries for upcoming amateur races, both on the Flat and over jumps. Finding a horse without a jockey, I would ring up the trainer and say I was available. My pitch was that I was young but experienced, attached to Captain Forster's yard and still had my seven-pound riding allowance. Most declined my offer but I kept finding new people to ring. Eventually one of the calls hit the jackpot.

Dr Arthur Jones, a small trainer with about 15 horses near Swansea in South Wales, agreed to put me up on his eight-year-old Mallard Song in a two-mile Flat race at Chepstow on the August Bank Holiday Monday. Although he had won two hurdle races when trained by Josh Gifford, Mallard Song had not achieved much since joining Arthur and started at 33 to 1. Two of the leading amateur riders of the day, Oliver Sherwood and Jim Wilson, had rides in the 13-runner race. Willie Muir, who now trains, was on the favourite, Champagne Charlie, and even though riding an unrated outsider, I was as nervous as if riding the Derby favourite. 'Don't forget to breathe,' said one of the other jockeys to me in the weighing room. It didn't help that I couldn't get a pair of riding boots to fit. This was a Flat meeting and the available boots were too small – not good. I *had* to look the part.

Gulping for breath, I kept Mallard Song close to the pace and even though beaten for speed by the winner, Radfield ridden by Adrian Sharpe, he stayed on well, despite my unrythmical urgings, and finished a good second. I was thrilled. Dr Jones was equally pleased and said he was delighted with my riding. He calculated the percentage of the second-place prize money that a professional jockey would receive and gave it to me as a gift. Thinking of cold winter evenings at Old Manor Cottages, I was in no position to be the principled amateur and took the money. Arthur Jones is still at Clydach in South Wales and still has the letter I sent him. He has only just realised that Mallard Song was my first ride.

Coming home from Chepstow that evening, my mind buzzed with excitement. Riding a two-mile Flat race was far more demanding than I'd expected. Dr Jones was happy but I was too exhausted to give his horse a genuinely strong ride and could barely take the saddle off or even stand up afterwards. You could ride on the gallops all you liked and go for as many runs as I did but there was no substitute for the real thing. Still, I was on a high. I had ridden a long shot, finished a decent second, hadn't done anything stupid and with my head in the clouds, I took the wrong exit off the M4 on the way home and ended up having to take the ring road round Swindon before continuing on to Letcombe Regis. Mallard Song had, however, used up all my concentration and when the car in front of me stopped at traffic lights, I ran straight into the back of it. Not much damage was done to the other vehicle but the front of my poor Morris Marina was a mess. I'd never liked the Marina's yellow colour and even though it was worth repairing, it wasn't worth getting upset. The car finally met its end six months later, the evening before my first point-to-point ride, when I over-turned it on the Ashbury–Wantage road. Too excited again.

Mallard Song's run didn't lead to an avalanche of opportunities. Back at the Captain's, they would have said it was a Flat race, nothing to do with the real thing and couldn't anyone get round when there were no obstacles in the way? Real progress was measured riding work on the Captain's keener horses. If you could handle Professor Plum and others such as Swords-man, General Sandy or Drumgora during their work, you were getting somewhere. It took a long time and many laps of the gallops at breakneck speed, totally out of control, before I was ever happy on the difficult horses.

There was a way forward at the Captain's, but I had to be patient. As the stable's amateur, it was said I might be offered rides on Colin Nash's small team of point-to-pointers. Colin, who has since died from motor neurone disease, combined horses with farming and was Master of the Old Berks Foxhounds. He and Captain Forster had long been good friends and there was an understanding that if the Captain's amateur was any good, he would get the rides on Colin's horses. Everyone benefited – Colin got a jockey, the jockey got opportunities and the Captain ended up with a more experienced jockey. My first ten rides under National Hunt rules were for Colin Nash and he also gave me my first winner over fences, Game Trust. Colin got me going in point-to-points and the same Game Trust was my first winner between the flags. What set Colin apart was decency; he was just a nice man. I was twice unseated and fell twice in my first eight rides for Colin but he still stuck with me. Who would have blamed him if he had decided to change jockey? All Colin said was that I was so enthusiastic, I threw myself over the fence before the horse.

It was a generous explanation but, in fact, I just hadn't got things sorted out in my head at that stage. Concentrating on looking the part, I wasn't getting back far enough in the saddle, nor had I learned to slip my reins properly. I had so much to master. For the first and only time in my life, I started regularly calling cabs at fences – I shot one hand up in the air almost anticipating a fall. It can be a sign of losing your nerve and I was disgusted with myself. Mick Furlong recommended I drop my irons a couple of holes. A few clear rounds sorted me out and it improved. Over the years, I was pleased that for all the bruises and physical damage, the falls never deeply affected my nerve. If anything, the older I got the more invincible I felt. I always said I was too stupid to be really afraid.

The first winner came at the hunter chase meeting at Cheltenham in early May. It was the final race of the evening, darkness was falling, many people had already made their way to the car park but it was perfect. Game Trust was a lovely honest mare who made it all very easy for me, and even though she got in too close to the last and had me sitting far back, almost on her tail, she galloped strongly up the hill to win. It may not have happened in a hurry but I was finally getting somewhere. I had ridden Mallard Song the previous August, five months passed before I got my second ride and now, three months later, my first winner. Winners, though, can be like buses – you wait for ages for one and then they come in convoy.

Over the remaining four weeks of the season, there were three more winners and the last was significant because it was my first ride for Captain Forster and my first race against professional jockeys. I'd had 18 rides under rules and finished enough races to be allowed to ride against the professionals but the Captain still thought it too soon. He walked into the yard, his stick in one hand, his other hand making a gesture that suggested total despair.

'Good God,' he said to me. 'I can't find another jockey. I've got to give you the ride on Swordsman at Fontwell. You'll just have to ride it. Whatever you do, don't fall off.' With plenty of racing on that Bank Holiday Monday, Hywel was elsewhere and Anthony Webber, whom the Captain tried to get, was committed to Kim Bailey's Spinning Saint in the same race. I wanted this chance but was a little afraid. Swordsman wasn't easy, not the horse I would have picked for my first ride against the pros. The lads in the yard sensed my trepidation.

'What are you going to do on this fellow, Richard?'

'Swordsman? You won't be able to ride one side of him.'

I half agreed. Then another voice inside my head said, 'Hold on, this is a ten to one shot. You wouldn't get the ride if he was well fancied.'

Knowing Swordsman would attack his fences, I dropped him in behind at the back and tried to settle him. He was brilliant, absolutely brilliant. He took control running down the hill, winged the fences and gave his 19-year-old jockey a truly exhilarating and very memorable ride. We took the lead at the second last and went on to win comfortably. This could hardly get much better. Even the Captain seemed half pleased. Although he never let on, maybe he did have a quiet belief in my ability and afterwards he said well done. I went back to Newmarket for the summer break feeling better about my career. Four winners from 23 rides in my first full season as an amateur didn't make me the next Francome, but I wasn't totally discouraged.

5

FALLING INTO PLACE

On Saturday afternoon, 24 February 1984, the jockeys in the weighing room at Kempton pulled their helmets on and watched the end of a three-mile handicap chase being televised from Doncaster. Ridley Lamb was in front on Fortina's Express with Hywel Davies closing on Solid Rock. Both horses were travelling and they rose together at the final obstacle. Solid Rock took the fence by its roots and crashed, giving Hywel a sickening fall. Fortina's Express went on to win but that no longer interested the lads at Kempton. They waited for the television cameras to return to the scene at the last fence. Hywel lay motionless on the ground, his horse equally still. 'Hywel's been buried,' said one of the lads. 'Poor bastard,' said another. Called for the next race, the Kempton jockeys stayed where they were, anxious for news of their fellow jockey. They feared the worst.

John Francome, who was riding at Kempton, reckoned the lads weren't in the right frame of mind for the race they were about to ride. Franc got a pair of riding boots, packed them with newspaper so they would stand on their own and placed them upside down on the weighing-room floor, not far from where the boys watched TV. When they turned round, they saw the upside-down boots and Franc crouched alongside them. 'OK, Hywel,' he said, leaning down, 'you can come out now. The lads have gone.' In that second the mood changed and the boys went out to ride their race. The medical people who attended Hywel later told him that on the way to the hospital he stopped breathing a number of times but each time was revived. He eventually regained consciousness, took a month off and rode the winner of the Grand National the following year. Ridley Lamb, a charming Northerner who won that Doncaster race and the Gold Cup in '87, was subsequently killed in a car crash.

That Saturday afternoon I was in the middle of a seven-day concussion ban after a crashing fall from Alan Blackmore's Silent Tango at Huntingdon. Mine had also been a bad fall. I lost consciousness for about 15 minutes and Silent Tango was killed. Jockeys judge the seriousness of a fall by how much or how little they remember of it. The medical people got me back to the weighing room and I lay there on the bed, totally out of it. I didn't recall a thing. Eventually Hywel came in.

'What are you doing there?' he said. 'You're all right. Come on.' He walked me to my car, drove me home and then four days later, it was his turn to have the lights switched off. His fall at Doncaster was, however, my big break.

Having had four winners in my first full season riding, it was too soon to turn professional, but I hoped the victory on Swordsman would lead to more rides from the Captain. Early in the new season the opportunity came on the handicap hurdler Cabin Boy who was fancied and favourite for an amateur race at Newton Abbott. Too keen to win, I was too hard on the horse when his chance had gone and partly caused his fall at the second last. I had travelled to the races with the Captain and it was a long journey home. He wasn't pleased. It would be two months before I rode another of his horses. My second season had gone into a tailspin before it started. By the end of January, I had just 51 rides and three winners. Things improved in February but it was still going to be an ordinary season until Hywel met with his bad luck.

Seven days after Hywel's fall, the Captain had three runners at Hereford and he needed me to ride all three. With Hywel out, there was nothing unusual in that and of the three only the novice hurdler Hurry Up Henry seemed to have a winning chance. What was surprising was I'd picked up rides in the other four races at the meeting. It was uncommon for a seven-

Times change. In the days before chinstraps, Dad is shown here in his cork helmet, held on by the draw-strings of his cap.

Aged 12, with Mum and Gail at Charlton Down stud.

Even at nine months, a decent set of wheels brought a smile to my face!

Aged two and a half with my first 'winner' at Newtownards show.

Riding Fast Friend on the gallops at Newmarket, aged 15. She was a keen filly and I was never happy to give her too much rein. *(Anthony Kelleway)*

With my first big race success, Prideaux Boy, having won the Mecca Hurdle at Sandown in 1985. *(R.H.Wright)*

Giving Syd Woodman the rundown on yet another winner at Fontwell in 1984. The tooth wasn't lost in a fall but at school in the playground in 1973.
(Gerry Cranham)

In the living room at the cottage I shared with Chris Nash in 1984. Phone, *Horses in Training* and the *Sporting Life* were then the essentials to success. *(Gerry Cranham)*

'Bloody jockeys!' Captain Tim Forster inspects his novice chasers as Hywel Davies, leading, and I trot past before schooling over the fences again. *(Gerry Cranham)*

The worst moment of my career. West Tip slithers to the ground in the 1985 Grand National. Hywel has negotiated the fence safely on the winner, Last Suspect (left), as Scu makes for home on Corbiere (right). *(George Selwyn)*

Very Promising takes the last a length ahead of Scu and Half Free to secure my first notable winner for the Duke in the 1986 Mackeson Gold Cup. *(Gerry Cranham)*

(Left to right) John Durkan, Simon McNeil and Norman Williamson at our home in Sparsholt, Christmas 1990. John was to die of leukaemia in 1998 – a huge loss to his family and the racing community.

Showing off again, Sharky. Simon Sherwood has the reins pulled from his hands as Cavvies Clown blunders at the second last in the 1988 Gold Cup. They soon recovered, but Charter Party, with me on board, had already taken their measure. (*Ed Byrne*)

With Carol at Kempton Park in 1992. At the time, Carol was becoming more used to being on the other side of the lens, assisting Mel Fordham with his racecourse photography.

Desert Orchid powering home in the 1990 King George VI Chase to give him his fourth victory in the race and me my second. *(George Selwyn)*

One small step for Man, one giant leap in my mind. Remittance Man, a spectacular chaser, shows his scope at an open ditch before going on to win at Wincanton in October 1992. *(John Beasley)*

Remittance Man clearing the water jump at Newbury on his way to winning the Hopeful Chase 1990. *(Alan Johnson)*

pound claiming amateur to have a full book of rides on a seven-race card.

'You'll never get through it,' said Captain Forster. 'I don't know what's going to happen but you're not going to be able for it.' Given a choice, the Captain had a natural preference for pessimism but even allowing for that, it was clear he just didn't think I was strong enough for such a demanding day.

That afternoon, Hereford was heaven – seven rides, four winners, a second and two thirds. The winners were for different trainers and apart from Kim Bailey's Spinning Saint, they were long shots. After winning on Pucka Fella in the handicap chase, I rode Toy Track for the Captain in the novice chase and he ran the race of his life to beat Martin Pipe's short-priced favourite and Triumph winner, Baron Blakeney. Going out to ride Three Chances for Bob Champion in the hunters' chase, Kim Bailey joked that it would be better if I didn't win because it would cost me three of my seven pounds allowance. I was riding Kim's Mister Bee in the last and he suspected the three pounds might make a difference. Three Chances won easily, Mister Bee did have three pounds more and was beaten by a neck in a hard-fought finish. On the one hand I was elated, on the other cursing for missing a fifth.

Before Hereford, I was perceived as an OK young amateur but that changed overnight. Suddenly people were asking when I was going to turn professional and what my plans were for the future. The following morning, I turned up for work as normal at the Captain's.

'Well done yesterday,' he said when we met. 'That was great.' We talked for a little bit about the immediate future and the Captain suggested I shouldn't turn professional just yet. He wanted to see if I could overtake Dermot Browne and Simon Sherwood and win the Amateur Championship. Next season would be time enough to turn pro. My parents agreed with the Captain and I thought if I could keep improving, it didn't matter whether I was amateur or professional.

Tiger Woods said something after winning the 2000 British Open Championship at St Andrews that struck me as being true. Recounting his progress over the three years since winning the Masters in 1997, Tiger pinpointed the difference between winning and improving. 'Winning,' he said, 'is not always the best way of measuring progress. I became a much better golfer in 1998 than I had been in 1997 but I didn't win much. The rewards came later.'

By the end of the 1983–84 season, I had spent two and a half years at Captain Forster's for a total of 28 winners. Even though I gradually improved my riding over the following 16 years, the progress achieved during that time was on a different scale from anything that would come later.

I started from a low level and because I accepted that I wasn't very good, I worked at getting better. I only had to look at how Hywel schooled horses to realise how much I had to learn. We talked about it a lot. Hywel encouraged me to get them in close and teach them to fiddle a fence because it was not on to go in on a long stride all the time. He also made me understand that if a horse was having his first run of the season, it didn't make sense to be too hard on him because he probably wasn't fully fit. It was always in my nature to be very self-critical and at this time I thought I was a pretty ordinary rider, nothing special. Once Luke Harvey and I went up Gramps Hill near Letcombe Bassett to see a small point-to-point trainer who had told us he needed an amateur jockey. We both volunteered but only one of us could ride his horse.

'Ride down there,' he said, 'I'll watch you both and then make my decision.' We auditioned and came back for the verdict. 'You'll be just fine,' he said, pointing at Luke. Unluckily for Luke, the horse proved to be virtually unrideable on the course and nearly finished his career before it had even started.

To my mind, I over-used the stick, I now rode quite long, I couldn't use the stick in my left hand and I wasn't strong. I could get wound up and aggressive – Graham McCourt used to call me Mr Angry in those days – and mentally I was average. There is a short entry in my diary for a Sunday late in November 1983 – sit closer, grab hold of them, less stick. I looked across the weighing room at Peter Scudamore and it was there, the attitude and the focus that I needed. During the summer of 1984, I went to the British Racing School's chief instructor, Johnny Gilbert, and asked for help on my style in a finish. Johnny thought the problem was rhythm and he got me to practise on a bale of straw. There was so much to improve.

One of the difficulties for young jockeys is that there are no designated coaches. You've got to get help where you can find it and work it out for yourself. Dad was good for me. He would watch closely and tell me what he thought. One Saturday at Chepstow I rode Swallow Prince for a small West Country trainer who told me I had to be really hard on the horse to get the best out of him. This was 1984, a time when the best jockeys used their stick pretty severely and I wanted to show I could do the same. I crucified the horse. That evening I went home to Newmarket and Dad, who had seen the race on television, raised it with me.

'You used your stick too much on that horse today,' he said.

'The trainer told me to do it.'

'Never use your stick like that again.'

Dad didn't say much but if something was on his mind, he'd say it then be quiet. You knew he wasn't happy. I watched my Chepstow performance on video and I had been very, very hard on the horse. I suppose I wanted to show I could be as strong as Scu or Graham or Hywel. It was indefensible. I didn't need to ride like that. I reviewed it again; it looked worse second and third time around. Although conscious of my over-use of the stick, four or five seasons would pass before I learned to use it nearly properly. Young jockeys on the way up think only of their next winner and in a driving finish their will to win over-rides their common sense. For a long time it did with me.

Not having a lot of success during my first two years at the Captain's had its compensations. The modest winners' tally kept my feet on the ground and even though there were some favourable comments in the racing press, it was restrained. I also got the opportunity to ride for some of the smaller trainers who are the heart and soul of National Hunt racing – Colin Nash, Alan Blackmore, Jill Evans, Arthur Barrow, Penny Barnes and Lindsay Bower. As I moved up the ladder, Syd Woodman, a lovely man who died later in the eighties, put me on a lot of his horses and Michael Oliver had faith in me.

Maybe my career would have taken off anyway but the four-timer at Hereford was an enormous boost. Ten days before the Cheltenham Festival, the timing could hardly have been better. Michael Oliver gave me my first ride at the Festival and Bashful Lad ran well and blunder-free to finish fifth in the Kim Muir Trophy Handicap Chase. But the thrill of the meeting was Oyster Pond in the Grand Annual Challenge Cup. He was a keen front-runner who jumped quick but was known to head-butt a fence occasionally. Although beaten quite comfortably into second place by the Jonjo O'Neill-ridden Mossy Moore, Oyster Pond ran a fantastic race. It was the fastest I had ever gone on a steeplechaser and probably the most exciting ride of my young career.

What struck me about the Festival was how hard it was to win there. Although John Francome was the leading jockey of that era, Scu, Graham and Hywel were up there in the top echelon but in 1984, all three were still waiting for their first Festival winner. 'I hate this place, hate it,' Hywel used to say. I can still see Scu, head down and silent in the weighing room after Cima finished second to Dawn Run in the Champion Hurdle. Not many expected Cima to beat the Irish mare but Scu took defeat badly. At least we had one thing in common.

Twenty-four winners for the season weren't enough to over-take Simon Sherwood and Dermot Browne in the amateur championship but I'd made some kind of mark. *Pacemaker* magazine judged me Amateur of the Year and there seemed to be agreement that I had promise as a rider. Even though my wages had risen from £15 to £20 a week as a pupil-assistant to the Captain, the time had come to turn professional. My family had subsidised me for long enough.

Michael Oliver wanted me to commit myself to riding all of his horses in the 1984–85 season but I had done well with the Captain. He had been very good to me and I was reluctant to leave him. I would start my professional career as his second jockey. I would also get plenty of rides from a number of small and medium-sized trainers with whom I had established good relationships.

The time had come, though, to move from Old Manor Cottages. It was a young man's house, always great fun and at times a bit wild. With my attitude becoming more serious, I needed somewhere quieter. Colin Nash's son, Chris, invited me to share a cottage on the farm where his dad trained. It was ideal. My first pro season went well with 46 winners from 383 rides in Britain and my first winner in Ireland. But more important than the numbers were the big race successes. In racing all winners are welcome but some are more welcome than others. You can ride three winners at Plumpton on Monday but it doesn't compare with winning the big, televised race at Newbury on Saturday. On the first Saturday in December, I won the Mecca Bookmakers' Handicap Hurdle at Sandown on Graham Roach's Prideaux Boy and five weeks later, again at Sandown with snow on the ground, the Anthony Mildmay, Peter Cazalet Chase on the Michael Oliver-trained West Tip.

Michael had also booked me to ride his new acquisition, Von Trappe. 'This is a really good horse, a flying machine,' said Michael on the day I first rode him. Great horses often come with quirks; nature rarely gives them everything. Von Trappe had the engine of a champion but his straight back meant he would never be a natural jumper. That season, Michael tried to prepare him for the Sun Alliance Chase but he took a heavy fall at Cheltenham on the day of my 21st birthday party in January and Michael opted to revert to hurdles, targeting the Coral Hurdle at the Festival. It was a decision with which his jockey wholeheartedly agreed. Michael also had West Tip in fine form. After winning at Sandown, he won his next two races and had the Ritz Club Handicap Chase as his Festival target.

The Festival was hugely important back in the mid eighties but not quite the giant it has become. On the Wednesday morning of the 1985 meeting, the Cheltenham sauna had its usual quota of jockeys and as it was the big event of our year there was a true festival spirit in the air. It wasn't unusual in those days for someone to bring a few bottles of champagne into the sauna and share them around. Someone did on that Wednesday morning. Graham McCourt was there, Hywel, Paul Croucher, Graham Bradley, Dermot Browne and most of us would have had a glass or two. I certainly did and I could feel the effects.

It wore off, though, when Von Trappe gashed himself coming off the sand chute in front of the stands on the way to the start. Once there, I thought 'this horse isn't going to be able to run' but he was fine when I trotted him in front of the starter. How he then stayed on his feet after Crouch and his mount Rufus T Firefly fell in front of us early in the race remains a miracle. Once we had avoided that, the rest was easy. There have been many Cheltenhams since that first one but the feeling Von Trappe gave me coming down the hill is one I will not forget. He was running away. 'I can't believe this, I just can't believe this. We should win here', I thought. At the last there was still plenty under the bonnet and he stormed up the hill. It was seven lengths at the line, I had my first Festival winner and I sampled my first Cheltenham reception. Having tasted, I was hungry for more.

The second came 24 hours later when West Tip out-battled 19 rivals to win the Ritz Club Chase. If Von Trappe had been a cruise, this was more a regular day at the office. Naturally inclined to run at his own speed, West Tip wasn't keen to go with the fast early pace but I didn't want us giving a start to the others. Rarely can you come from off the pace at the Festival. Soon after the tapes went up, I pushed hard and by halfway I resorted to the stick. After giving West Tip a smack on the far side, my stick broke in two and got caught up with Dermot Browne who was upsides. What remained wasn't much use and I threw it away, using hands and heels through the last mile. The old horse went as quick if not quicker for no stick and jumped like a stag to beat Acarine and Robert Stronge by four lengths.

It was an impressive performance, confirming West Tip as a serious challenger for the Aintree Grand National 16 days later. His jockey was now a name with two winners at the Festival and on board the favourite for Liverpool. I was a new face and the media latched on to the fact that I would be the youngest jockey riding in the National. Previously I had been mentioned in despatches, now I was the next John Francome, and could I do 'Wogan'? I had a reasonable relationship with the press; I helped as much as I could and they treated me fairly. When I said it was insulting to John Francome that a rider in his first professional year should be described as his successor, I meant it. John had been an outstanding jockey; I was a kid with plenty to learn.

After my appearance on 'Wogan', I somehow became the housewives' favourite for the big race. It was my first big success with the opposite sex. 'You seemed pretty relaxed on "Wogan",' said fellow jockey Mark Richards a few days later. I was relaxed all right; the several drinks I'd had in the BBC's Green Room before going on had diluted my chronic nervousness.

Despite the fuss, it wasn't difficult to keep my feet on the ground. I remembered a line in a report following my third win under National Hunt Rules. I'd won on Colin Nash's Gambling Ghost in the hunters' chase at Newton Abbot and one writer complimented me for my meticulous preparation for the ride – I had walked the track, which is something jockeys routinely do at a course they haven't ridden. Sometimes you were criticised unfairly but, more commonly, you received more praise than you deserved. I only had to remember how far I had come.

Exactly a year before, Brendan Powell had driven me to Aintree on the Friday because we were both travelling on to Hereford on Grand National day. That night, we went to a large, almost deserted, disco in Southport along with Mark Low and Adrian Sharpe, and shamelessly posed as jockeys riding in the National. Adrian was the only one who actually had a ride. I said I was Richard Rowe and to honour our bravery, the manage- ment of the disco wished to present us with a bottle of sparkling wine. Hoping it would impress the only two single girls present, we gratefully made our way to the stage. Later the DJ smiled and the girls were gone, whisked from under our noses.

Two days before the 1985 National, I rode Run To Me in what used to be the Topham Trophy. It was my first experience of the big fences. As a boy I dreamt of riding over them; I built the little fences with straw on top and when my pony sailed over them, I was at Aintree. For once, reality was better than the dream. Run To Me jumped from fence to fence and was travel- ling as well as any until Robert Earnshaw and Richardstown brought us down at the fourth last. I couldn't wait for West Tip and the National.

Going into big races, I preferred to have just a general plan which could be changed if the race didn't ride as expected. With West Tip, the idea was to hunt him round in the middle of the field for the first circuit and then gradually pick off the others on the second. His stamina was his greatest strength. I was sure he would last the four-and-a-half-mile marathon. I also wanted to stay well away from Sam Morshead and Solihull Sport. Although Sam has always been one of my favourite people, I felt his horse was sure to fall. At the first fence, Solihull Sport came from nowhere and jumped right across me. He came down. We just escaped.

West Tip jumped and raced beautifully through the first circuit. It wasn't taking a feather out of him and without being asked, he eased his way towards the leaders on the second circuit. When the Irish-trained Dudie fell, I found myself upsides Corbiere and in front. It had been effortless and as we headed down towards Becher's for the second time, I wanted him to take it nice and carefully.

Becher's is different from other fences at Aintree and not just because of the steep landing area. The fence is on a bend and as you approach, especially in those days, it seems like you are jumping into the crowd on the right-hand bank. There's also a lot of screaming and shouting, making it difficult for a horse to keep his concentration. I held on to West Tip's head as we neared the fence and let him go in to pop it. But his mind wasn't completely on the job. He went slightly left to give himself a little more room but he got in a bit closer than he should have done and didn't get high enough. His ears were pricked as he crumpled. Had he stood up, it would have taken some horse to beat him.

I travelled back to the weighing room in the ambulance but the only damage was psychological. There were tears in my eyes. This was the race I had always wanted to ride in. During my first professional year I got the chance, I was on a horse that I believed was going to win. This was my big opportunity, then it was gone. I didn't understand how such a good jumper could have fallen. By the time the ambulance dropped me off near the weighing room, I was coming round. I was young, I'd had two winners at the Cheltenham Festival and I was pleased that Hywel had won the race on Last Suspect for the Captain. Journalists asked how well I had been going. 'Running away,' I said, 'but we'll come back next year and win.' Some of the older guys would have laughed at my innocence. Great jockeys such as Scu and Francome had never won a National and here was a kid who believed all he had to do was turn up in 12 months' time.

Back home, I went for the video. What had happened? It was clear the horse was flying and had jumped the five fences before Becher's without the hint of a mistake. The difference at Becher's was the crowd, the noise and the drop. The horse in front runs the risk of being distracted. In the previous ten years at the National, Golden Rapper, Andy Pandy, Alverton and Delmoss had all fallen when leading or close to the lead at Becher's second time round. I hadn't wanted to be in front that early but the horse had been travelling so well – too well, maybe. I looked and looked again at the video but couldn't see that I had presented him badly at the fence. Next time, though, we would not lead into Becher's. Next time, we would get it right.

6

YOU'VE GOT THIRTY MINUTES

I left Britain a boy and returned a man – at least that's how Hywel Davies likes to put it but then Hywel has always been a fair talker and after his near-fatal fall at Doncaster in 1984, he got even worse. According to him, I came of age on a jockeys' trip to America, Australia and New Zealand in the summer of 1985. The offer to be part of the British team came at Aintree two months earlier and I was chuffed, even though I would be travelling reserve. To be selected on the same team as Peter Scudamore, Steve Smith Eccles, Hywel and Graham Bradley at the end of my first professional season was way beyond my expectations. It was an opportunity to experience new places in the company of men I looked up to and there was a good chance I would get to compete. The series of challenge races would be fun and there would also be a social side to the trip. The lads weren't altar boys and I was looking forward to enjoying myself. It was my first trip outside Britain or Ireland and I had to get a passport. I was 21, a young jockey just about comfortable inside the racing world but an innocent outside it. In one respect Hywel was right. Compared to my team-mates, I was the boy.

From the age of 17, I had worked in racing. I'd hardly lived beyond horses. Girls were always on the agenda but for the most part, they remained an aspiration. We would go to the pub, look around and end up playing pool all evening. Some lads had it, others didn't. I was clueless. During the summer of 1983 I went over to Ireland to ride out for Michael Cunningham in County Meath. There was a lot of craic over there and I stayed in a guesthouse in Athboy with one of Michael's lads, Figgerty, another who taught me all he knew. One evening, we met some girls at a pub in Trim and later in the night I ended up chasing mine around Trim Castle – not exactly a classy performance.

Around the time of my 21st birthday, I had started seeing a girl more regularly. One evening at the cottage that Chris Nash and I shared, we had an argument, she threw a glass of water at me, I ducked, the water splashed over the television set, found its way into the electrical panel at the back and caused a blowout. We got the television repaired but the relationship was irreparable. I believed I knew what I wanted but unfortunately there weren't many takers. Racing came first and relationships demanded a commitment I wasn't prepared to give. But the yearning for female company never waned.

On the nights when I did go out, I enjoyed a drink. In the weighing room it was significant that John Francome was tee-total; Jonjo O'Neill might take an occasional glass of wine, as did Peter Scudamore. Aspiring young jockeys could hardly miss the point. But then I would look at Hywel and Graham McCourt, with whom I had more contact. They were good, dedicated jockeys and they both enjoyed a few drinks. I was on their side. As sportsmen who had to watch our weight continually, we would never be able to drink much anyway and drinking in midweek was generally a non-starter. But I would occasionally feel the need to let go. It was a hard grind and if, on the one night you went out, a few drinks helped you relax, why not? I was looking forward to finding out how Scu, Ecc, Hywel and Brad let their hair down.

The trip began in the US, where we rode at Fair Hill in Maryland. It was hot there. Mrs Valentine, who has owned so many nice jumping horses in Britain and Ireland, invited us to a party and we were off to a fine start. The day after we arrived, there was the draw for the horses in the riders' challenge, then an afternoon's golf and the following day we were riding against America's jump jockeys. Brad loved his golf, the other lads were keen enough but I was the odd one out. I wasn't any good then and even though I tried over the years, I hardly got much better. Golf didn't suit me. I have always wanted some order in my life and whether it was riding, cricket, rugby or table tennis, I had to be proficient and as good as the people I played against. To get to that level in golf, you have to have talent and patience. Talent, I hadn't much of; patience, none. Think of the ideal golfer, even-tempered and calm . . . you can see why it wasn't me.

For me, the racing at Fair Hill was excellent. Scu, on a supposed no-hoper and not really having enjoyed the rock-hard ground and the extreme heat, offered me his ride in the second last race. Trained by Janet Elliott, Pine Hollow was a 20 to 1 shot and Scu felt it was safe to pass him on. It wasn't, we won and Scu wasn't the happiest. Two years later Jonathan Sheppard, the leading trainer over jumps in the US at the time, invited me back to America to ride Flatterer in the Breeders' Cup and I did wonder how important that win on Pine Hollow may have been. I ended up riding a fair bit for Jonathan over the years.

From the US we flew via Los Angeles to Melbourne in Australia where we rode at Moonee Valley and Flemington. Back then, jump jockeys in Australia were mostly stablelads who rode occasionally over fences and were treated accordingly. We were put up in a lads' quarters that hadn't been used for six months. It was cold and damp. Brad and I and one very large spider shared a room and in the cold war between the humans and the arachnid, the spider won by a distance. Having come from a country where jump jockeys are more appreciated, we voiced our complaints and were moved to Melbourne's prestigious Southern Cross Hotel.

Ecc rode two winners at Moonee Valley and I had a winner at Flemington. Riding a horse called So Just for the Australian trainer Jack McGreal, I tracked Hywel on Arctic Thunder all the way and the race developed into a duel. He knew I was there but didn't know if I could go past him. By now there was an edge to the rivalry between us; he was Captain Forster's stable jockey, I was his hungry understudy. Earlier in the season, he had beaten me in a tight finish at Windsor and next morning he had pinned the photo on to the noticeboard in the Captain's tack-room. During my first couple of seasons, Hywel had given me lots of good advice but as I began to get a few winners, the relationship moved on to a different level. Hywel had to protect his position. I understood that. And now, at Flemington, a left-handed track, I was tucked in behind him, wanting to beat him. Knowing how weak I was with the stick in my left hand, I tried to get up on his inside, so I could use the stick in my right. Hywel's horse hung slightly out to the right at the last hurdle; I got a run up his inner and beat him three-quarters of a length. Was I pleased? You bet. After pulling up, Hywel saw a gleam in my eye, he says, that he hadn't noticed before. He recognised it, though.

It would be nice to think it was the ride at Flemington that convinced my peers I was a man but, sadly, no. That came later and away from the racecourse. We were actually back at the Southern Cross and had met up with Ian Watkinson, a former jump jockey from Newmarket who had moved to Australia. Ian knew a few women and had persuaded them to come and meet us. For some reason we were all in my room when two of them arrived. They came straight upstairs and were invited in.

Ecc picked out the nicest one – 'Ah, you'll come and have a drink with me?' Then Scu, Ian, Brad and Hywel came to a sudden decision. 'We were just leaving,' all four said at the same time and before I could jump off the bed, they were heading towards the door. The lady left in the room wasn't a contender for Miss World and she was a fair bit older than me, and a fair bit larger. Afterwards the lads claimed she was probably no more than 45 or 46, just looked a lot more. Hywel says as he left the room, he heard the beginning of the conversation.

'You're a young thing,' she said.

'I'm only 21,' said I, feebly.

'Well, you won't be "only 21" when you leave this room.'

I didn't want to cause any offence but I did want to leave. The lads had other ideas. I tried the door but they were on the other side, holding tight.

'Come on lads, stop messing,' I said. 'Let me out.' They laughed and held it tighter. I gave up and turned my attention back to the room. A stopwatch had appeared on the bedside table.

'You've got thirty minutes,' she said.

It was my initiation, they said afterwards, and Hywel, who

never tired of telling the story, says when I eventually did come out, I was a man.

In New Zealand, we arrived in Tauranga on Thursday and it rained non-stop for two days. The weather kept us indoors and as we were not now scheduled to ride until Monday afternoon, cabin fever set in. Ecc introduced me to a couple of women who worked in the hotel. They seemed quite friendly. We had a drink and they invited us back to one of their homes. Another five or six people came along and it seemed like it would be good fun. It was looking like a party. Back at the house, the women put on 'The Bolero', the song from the Dudley Moore movie *Ten* where Bo Derek runs along the beach to its accompaniment.

Now as the song played on, our hostesses started to undress. Ecc and I, although taken aback, certainly didn't complain. As they got down to their underwear, the 18-year-old daughter of the woman I was with walked into the room. It was excruciatingly embarrassing but paled into insignificance when her young son burst in later. The others had left and I'd joined his mother in a state of undress in the middle of the sitting-room floor. Two days rain in Tauranga does funny things to a man.

The racing didn't go as well as it had in the US and Australia. In New Zealand I got moderate horses. After Tauranga, we moved north to Auckland and raced on Wednesday at Ellerslie where I rode See You Later. The best you could say about it was that it was an experience.

'Watch that fellow. He's not the nicest of jumpers,' said the New Zealand lads. See You Later stepped at every hurdle, narrowly avoiding disaster, and was a horrible ride. He wasn't going to win no matter how he was ridden and there was no point in risking life and limb. Why travel to the other end of the world to get broken up on a moderate racehorse that couldn't jump anyway? It wasn't the bravest ride I've given a horse.

See You Later's trainer, Mr Graham, was a policeman and I suppose you could say this was the beginning of the up-and-down relationship I had with the law.

'You could have been a bit more forceful on him,' said the policeman/trainer.

'He wasn't jumping that well,' I said.

'He might have jumped better if you had helped him at his hurdles.'

'I think you need to go and learn how to school horses before you run this thing again.'

He went crazy. It was the first time in my career I took on a trainer after riding his horse. I can't recall ever doing it again to the same extent. It's not something jockeys do. Maybe it was the fact that I wouldn't be looking for more rides in New Zealand, but I was annoyed. It seemed to me no one had ever bothered to teach See You Later to jump.

We left Auckland the following day, stopped in Los Angeles on the way home and, once there, Brad and I decided to have a holiday. We stayed in a hotel at Hollywood Park and got in touch with the Irish jockey Jimmy Duggan who was riding work there for the summer. It didn't take long to track down Jimmy and we also met Steve Youlden, another good lad who used to ride in England. Through friends of theirs, we rented an apartment on Redondo Beach. This was the life. On the spur of the moment, Brad and I had decided we would spend the bit of money we had made on the trip and so here we were, staying in this cool apartment on a beach in LA – the sea, the sun and, Jesus Christ, so many women.

We had some time. On our third consecutive evening at the local nightclub, Jimmy started to chat up this cute American girl. I stayed in the background at first but as the night wore on and fuelled by more Dutch courage, I was a little more talkative. By the end of the evening, I was getting along really well with the girl Jimmy had discovered. Her name was Timi Del Conte and for the next ten days or so, we explored Los Angeles. She took me to my first drive-in movie in her mum's Chevrolet. It was the James Bond film *View To A Kill* where quite a few scenes were shot at Chantilly, the French training centre. For the first time in my life watching horses was not my priority. It was a great holiday that also consolidated a very close and enduring friendship with Brad, a true star.

The team had left England in early June; Brad and I returned on 11 July, much heavier than when we left. It had been a hell of an experience. For a boy still wet behind the ears, it was also an education – or, as Hywel would say, an initiation.

7

AS GOOD AS IT GETS

Young and relatively innocent, I was at that point in my career when I could sleep on the night before an important race. Still, an alarm call was rarely needed. It was 6.30 a.m. when I got out of bed on the morning of 5 April 1986 – Grand National Day. A light covering of snow lay on the fields around the Post House Hotel at Haydock, near Liverpool. 'Should make the ground a little bit softer for my horse,' I thought. Usually I tried to be business-like in my approach to the big races. You had a horse to ride, a job to do; it didn't help to get caught up in the emotion or the excitement of the day. The National was different. No matter how hard I tried, I couldn't cut myself off from the occasion. From a horse-obsessed childhood, there were too many memories of the race. Back then it was my favourite and if ever I was going to be a jump jockey, these were the fences I wanted to tackle. It was 6.50 when I left the hotel car park and, already, I could feel it, the buzz.

That morning on the gallops at Aintree, West Tip felt good too. The dawn rendezvous was part of the National Day routine, it got you and your horse into the mood. It helped focus the mind, stretch his legs. A quiet canter and a couple of interviews with bleary-eyed media. Back at the Post House around 8.45 a.m., I sat down to breakfast and began my own build-up. Even though my career was progressing gradually, I felt I had come a long way in a short time. A year before I had stayed at the Scarisbrick, a nice hotel in the centre of South-port, but I changed to the Post House because it was out of town and close to the sauna at Haydock racecourse. Racing people stayed at the Post House and it was where I wanted to be. Liverpool had gone well; two winners in two days and Glenrue's almost-all-the-way victory over the big fences in the Topham Trophy was particularly satisfying. It was my first win-ner for Terry Casey, a gentle and softly spoken Donegal man who had ridden winners for my father back in the days when Dad trained in County Down.

Over breakfast I scanned the National field for trouble. Most of the problems in the race could not be anticipated but I liked to search anyway. Essex, the Czech-trained challenger, was an entire horse – that is he had not been gelded – and having seen him before, I knew he could run very freely. His trainer, Vaclav Chaloupka, was on board and both horse and jockey were having their first experience of Aintree. Couldn't be behind them jumping a fence. Dudie's was another set of colours I noted. He made mistakes. Had to stay clear of him. Then I mentally rehearsed how I wanted to ride the race: line up in the middle, travel down the middle to Becher's first time, ease towards the outer just before Becher's and then track back towards the inner, jump the Canal Turn at a slight angle to save ground, try to get a little daylight before jumping The Chair, get a lead down to Becher's second time round, hold on to him, leave it as late as possible.

Breakfast over, bags packed, I got to Aintree early and walked the track. West Tip was my only ride of the day and as I walked, I envisaged where I would be at every point in the race. Eamon Murphy, the Irish jockey, took a bad fall in the first race and was unable to ride in the National. So for the second successive year, I would be the youngest rider in the race. Last year I felt the youngest but not this time. Even though partnering what I considered to be the best horse, I wasn't particularly nervous. My innocence in reaction to West Tip's fall a year before had survived. 'We'll be back. We'll win it next year,' I had said at the time. Now, we were back and I felt calm. Was there a horse I would prefer to West Tip? No. Could we win? Very definitely.

★ ★ ★

In my fourth season as a rider, I was beginning to feel a legitimate member of the weighing room. In 1984–85, I'd had 46 winners including my first two Festival successes and the other jockeys were gradually beginning to see me as one of them. Being picked for the British team to ride overseas brought with it some recognition and, just as important, at the start of the 1985–86 season David Nicholson had asked me to be second jockey to Peter Scudamore. Although going through a lean time, the Duke was one of the sport's big players and I didn't hesitate. Second jockey to the Duke and the Captain, first call on most of Michael Oliver's horses and with a number of smaller trainers keen to use me, I was set up for another good season.

And 1985–86 was a good season with 55 winners from 504 rides, nine winners more than the previous one; not that I was congratulating myself. When I looked at my riding performance I tended to see only the weaknesses. The mistakes interested me more than things I'd done well.

In my rides' ledger I paid particular attention to the number of fallers and especially to the number of times I was unseated. At the end of the 1985–86 season, 31 of the horses I had ridden had fallen and a further ten had unseated me. That meant a fall for every 12 rides, close to the average for National Hunt racing but too many. I knew where the fallers came from – an almost demonic desire to win. It didn't matter that the horse was tired or not jumping well; quite regularly, chance or no chance, I threw him at the fence. Later in my career, the average would be one fall in 18 rides and that was where it should have been.

I was young and far from mature. When in Australia riding against the Aussie jump jockeys, I bought myself a new stick and had my name engraved on a little brass plate on it. It was thin and whippy and didn't have the felt covering that everyone uses now. I bought it in the same way a young gunslinger might pick up the newest six-shooter. This would make them go faster. Two weeks into the new season, I used it on Dina Smith's hurdler, Homeward, at Worcester and even though the horse won, that didn't justify my use of the stick. The horse was cut and bleeding. In the winner's enclosure afterwards the sheet was pulled over him very quickly and we hoped the vet wouldn't notice. He did but the stewards let me away with a warning. I should have been banned.

Being part of David Nicholson's team did not produce much in the way of winners. It was a tough time for the Duke, the VAT man was on his case and the horses were suffering from a virus. But from my first days at Condicote, it was obvious how much I was going to learn. The Duke and Scu were different characters but they shared extremely competitive natures and from an early stage, I sensed the move would work for me. Whereas the Captain was an ex-army man who saw success as a welcome bonus on occasion, the Duke simply *had* to succeed. No one with whom I worked took schooling more seriously or schooled horses better. With the Duke, everything had to be right.

You came to his office dressed for work and mentally ready. I never did meet Frenchie, his dad, but over the years with the Duke I got a good idea of what he must have been like. Frenchie Nicholson was regarded as the sport's greatest trainer of Flat jockeys, a hard taskmaster with the knack of getting the best out of his young apprentices. The Duke had similar talents; there were times when you wouldn't like something he said but you respected him. You tried to impress him. In the days before a race, the Duke would talk about how his horse might be ridden, he would want to know your ideas and get you thinking about the race long before he legged you up. He had views on most things and wasn't slow to air them but he would listen too. For me, loyalty was his greatest quality. When you became his stable jockey, you were his man. You got unswerving support.

At this point in my career, Scu's influence on me was even more important. Because I was riding out for the Duke once or twice a week and schooling on Sundays, Scu and I spent a lot of time together. I had looked up to him before I got to know him and admired him even more when we worked together. Scu was straight and bright. You knew where you stood and while he was ambitious for himself, he was always fair with others. He went out of his way to help me. I used to go racing with him, too. His sons Tom and Michael were toddlers then and I watched them grow up. What most impressed me about their dad was his single-mindedness; he had once shared the championship with John Francome but when John retired, Scu believed it was his destiny to become the number one jockey. So when the Duke hit his two bad seasons from 1984 to 1986, Scu was continually anxious. Towards the end of the 1985–86 season, Fred Winter asked him to be his stable jockey and Scu accepted. He temporarily fell out with the Duke as a result of not letting him know before other people. But Scu's departure to Fred Winter created a huge opportunity for me.

Of all the jockeys I've competed against, no one's riding better reflected his character than Scu's. It was the will to win. Scu would galvanise a horse in a way that not many others could. It was always easier for the horse to go with Scu than fight him. One afternoon at Wolverhampton I was riding against him in a finish and I was amazed by his strength. He used his legs like nobody else could and when he hit a horse, it responded. A.P. McCoy has been rightly praised for his strength but Scu was stronger. I appreciate we are talking about two of the very strongest jockeys but if I were a horse, I know which one I would rather be ridden by, and that is not to take anything away from A.P.

At that time, there was a machismo aspect to the way we rode horses. Hywel Davies was tough, Graham McCourt was tough, but Scu was on another level. Whatever he did with them, he could really grab hold of them. He could wind them up like no one else could. I looked at Scu and thought of how far I had to go. Then I would look in the mirror, remind myself that I had been 19 when I started to shave and that I was always going to be a slow maturer.

It bothered me, too, that I struggled to use the stick in my left hand. Horses, in my experience, tended to hang left more than right and were best straightened by the jockey using the stick in his left hand. But rather than pull my stick through and use it in my left, I'd put it down and try to disguise my weakness. 'Why didn't you hit him a smack?' one of the lads would say afterwards and I would pass it off, annoyed with myself. That season I really worked on using the stick in my left hand.

Things were improving in other respects. The Captain started putting me up on some of his better horses, Michael Oliver's two stars West Tip and Von Trappe returned from their summer breaks in good form and those smaller trainers, who had done much to get me started, continued to give me plenty of rides. But racing is such an up-and-down game; the big fall comes in the middle of your best season, the big winner turns up when things are going badly. After having an average first four months to the 1985–86 season, I had a miserable run through the last three weeks of December. Von Trappe won at Cheltenham on 6 December and over the following three weeks, I rode 42 consecutive losers which took us up to the second day of Kempton's Christmas meeting.

Nothing seemed much different when Philip Mitchell's Garfunkel finished an average third in the first race and Colin Nash's Hot Handed was battled out of it by Arbitrage in the second race – Scu's strength had once again put me in my place – 44 losers and counting. Then, out of the blue, a bolt. My last four rides of the day all won – Roadster for Colin Nash, Von Trappe in the Feltham Chase and the Philip Mitchell pair, Tugboat and Sylvan Joker. After Hereford almost two years before, this was my second four-timer and again the timing could hardly have been better. The Kempton winners were my last four rides of 1985 and at the turn of the year, I was feeling a little better about life.

Did it last? Like hell, it did. Von Trappe fell when running away at the water in the Embassy Final at Ascot and that was the story of his career. Had he been able to bend his back and get his hocks underneath him, there is no knowing how far he could have gone; another one in the battalion of 'if only' horses.

The snow fell on 6 February, covering Britain's racecourses, and over four weeks passed before the temperatures rose and the courses reopened. When suspended or injured, jockeys hate to miss even one ride but when racing was called off because of bad weather, we were like schoolboys freed from the classroom. Through those days we played squash at Wantage Sports Centre, played snooker, went sledging down in Kingston Lisle and, occasionally, we would all go for lunch in Faringdon or the Chinese restaurant in Wantage and some of us would get very drunk. Graham, Jimmy Duggan, Luke Harvey,

Martin Bosley, Mark Richards and Hywel would come along. They were good days.

The thaw eventually came and racing resumed just three days before the Cheltenham Festival. Many of the horses weren't as fit or as sharp as they would normally have been. Two memories remain from that year's Festival – Dawn Run's win in the Gold Cup and my losing on Roadster in the Mildmay of Flete Challenge Cup. Having had a bad fall at Ascot, I wasn't overly excited about riding Von Trappe in Dawn Run's Gold Cup. It was my first ride in the race and while I couldn't consider myself a proper jockey until I rode in the Gold Cup, I would have preferred a safer jumper. How could Von Trappe survive three miles and a quarter at top speed without making a calamitous mistake? Four fences from home, he fell. It was a shame because even though he'd blown up at the top of the hill, he was beginning to run on again. He was only eight to ten lengths off the leaders and he had such a turn of foot at the end of a race. It would have been interesting to see how close he could have got.

After Von Trappe's fall, I picked myself up and watched the leaders stream down the hill towards the third last. They cleared that and galloped on towards the sweeping bend into the straight. Lots of people watched from the inside rail, obscuring my view. I walked down the hill towards the ambulance, listening for the crowd's reaction and as the horses turned into the straight, the commentator mentioned Dawn Run's name and there was an almighty roar. The whole of the Cotswolds shook. It was a strange experience for me, up near the top of the course, as if on another planet looking down. The noise died and everything went quiet. Something had happened. She'd been beaten.

'Too bad,' I thought and moved closer to the ambulance.

Then there was another eruption, this time louder than the first.

'What happened?'

'She got back up, she's won.' The ambulance man was listening on the radio and nearly jumped out of his seat.

In the weighing room afterwards, all hell broke loose. It was amazing that hard-headed jocks were moved by the mare. What a way for Jonjo O'Neill to cap his career. We were based at different ends of the country, so I hadn't ridden against him that often but he was someone for whom I always had the greatest respect. At the end of the previous season I had finished on the same winners' total as Jonjo, 46, and even though he was winding down at that time, it egged me on to be on the same mark as him.

Roadster was the one winner I should have had at that Festival. We were just ahead of John White and The Tsarevich jumping the last but were outpaced in the last 50 yards and beaten half a length. My immediate reaction was to think I hadn't done much wrong; the old horse hadn't quickened and had been touched off. That was only partly true. I hadn't been strong in the finish and, given how well the horse had jumped, I could have been more aggressive at the last fence. What really bothered me, though, was that I'd missed the chance to ride a Festival winner for Colin Nash, a man who had done so much for me at the beginning of my career.

Colin would have been the last to suggest I could have done better and knowing him, he probably didn't even think it, but deep down, I knew. That evening I bumped into Dodger McCartney as I left the course. Simon was his real name but we called him Dodger. He was a punter and we all thought the world of him. According to the Jockey Club's instructions, we are supposed to be careful about who we fraternise with and must avoid undesirables out to prise winners from us. Not that Dodger could ever be classed as one of those. Some of the rules relating to jockeys date back to an era when they were the serfs of the sport, and should have been updated long ago. There have been many times when we have been treated like second-class citizens. Regulations have been changed without consulting the Jockeys Association, and certainly not in our best interests. The inference is that jockeys are more susceptible to disreputable characters. There is no evidence to support that.

As for Dodger or anyone else coming to me for information, it didn't often happen. Occasionally I would say I thought this should win or that should win but the well-informed punter would not have had me at the top of their list of good judges. Dodger certainly knew better than to look for my opinion. I just wouldn't have had a strong view most of the time. On the other hand if he told me he reckoned I would win such and such a race, I felt better about my chances. Dodger knew the form inside out. At the races he would lean against the railing at the point where the horses exited on to the course. Sometimes as you passed he might say, 'Go on Woody, kick him home,' and you would think, 'Good, Dodger's backed us, he thinks we're going to do it.'

As a small boy back in Ireland, a big losing bet – well, it was big to me at the time – on L'Escargot had satisfied my thirst for gambling. Betting never interested me but if jockeys are forbidden to bet, why shouldn't it be against the rules for the trainers too? Jockeys are monitored extremely closely on course by many cameras. Behind the scenes at home, a trainer could influence the result far more easily.

I tended not to look closely at races until the eleventh hour, taking the *Racing Post* into the sauna around midday and going through my rides and my rivals. Sometimes after mounting my horse and going down to the start, I would get the feeling that they were spot on and we were going to win. That would be as close to a conviction as I would get and I wasn't always right.

But Dodger studied the form religiously. When I met him leaving Cheltenham that evening, he said, 'Woody, I think you should have won on Roadster.' I thought, 'Ah Dodger, you backed him, did you?' His comment stayed with me and I was sore about it. It dug deep because he was probably right, and it was Cheltenham.

West Tip also ran in the Ritz Club Handicap Chase at the Festival and being short of fitness after the February freeze, did well to finish seventh, beaten 11 lengths by Charter Party. It wasn't the kind of run that turned too many heads but he was still on course for the National. The situation became a little confused when the Captain's Port Askaig chased home Maori Venture in a good chase at Lingfield the following Saturday and there was speculation that I might have to switch to Port Askaig for the National. The Captain thought I should ride his as I was attached to his yard and Port Askaig's form seemed almost as good as West Tip's. I didn't want to change horses but the Captain could be extremely persuasive.

'Fifty-fifty,' I would say to people when they asked.

Thankfully, West Tip made the choice straightforward. Two weeks before the National, he ran the trial I needed at Newbury, staying on in his inimitable high-action style to beat Beau Ranger in a handicap chase. The Captain didn't argue. 'Clear it with Lord Chelsea,' he said. I rang Port Askaig's owner and asked permission to ride West Tip. Lord Chelsea was fair about it and Graham McCourt picked up the ride on Port Askaig.

It was around this time that I began seeing Carol Abraham who lived in Wantage. We had known each other for about three years. Carol and her friend Sarah Simmons used to drop into Old Manor Cottages at Letcombe Regis. There were a couple of dates but it fizzled out. I wanted the relationship to progress but Carol was just 15 and even shyer than I was. Now and again we would bump into each other. Carol had always loved horses and at this time rode out for trainer Henrietta Knight. Once I won on the Knight-trained Matt Murphy in a point-to-point at Tweseldown and Carol led me up. Without us realising it, the seeds of a future relationship were sown. Then, early in 1986 when I was 22 and Carol was 19, we started going out with each other again.

About six months later I was in a sauna with Graham McCourt at the Wantage Sports Centre. Graham and I tended to talk about things we wouldn't discuss with too many others.

'I think, Graham, this is the one. I'm hooked.'

'Don't be mad . . . at your age,' was Graham's immediate response.

Five months later Carol and I were engaged.

Down at the start, walking round in circles, the usual banter among the jockeys dies away. Even the toughest fear what they are about to face – 30 fences, four and a half miles. I am nervous but it is the fear, the danger that turns me on. This is what I have always wanted. This is what makes me feel worthwhile.

The tape shoots up and the anticipation is over. Forty horses and their riders gallop towards the first fence and I'm in the middle of the line across the track, looking for daylight but not wanting to go too fast. There are always fallers at the first and I don't want to jump behind something that might fall. West Tip moves well and his class allows him to get that little bit of space going to it. He jumps it perfectly. Graham and Port Askaig fall about eight yards to my right, but I don't see them.

From the first to Becher's five fences later, I concentrate on getting the horse in his rhythm and stay alive to what is going on around me. We have a number of horses in front of us but plenty of space and I ease towards the outer as we near Becher's. We jump it from the outside in and he lands safely. West Tip is a natural for this race. He's aware of what is happening around him; he notices when a horse makes a mistake and if it looks like falling he will almost shift in mid-air to get out of the way. Sometimes he sees things before I do and fills me full of confidence. He is an intelligent horse who doesn't want to fall. We're now hunting round, in seventh or eighth place but never far off the pace. Last year's fall is on my mind and my race is ridden to ensure we get a lead down to Becher's second time.

At the first, second time round, a loose horse careers sideways not far from us. He crashes into the Charlie Mann-ridden Doubleuagain. They are brought down and the thought flashes before me, 'the luck of the National'. It could have been us. Going to Becher's second time around, Classified, Young Driver, Monanore, The Tsarevich and Northern Bay are all in front of me. I again move towards the outside. 'Stay in, stay in,' shouts Sommelier's rider Tom Taaffe but I still shift a little further out and we both jump it safely, barely pecking on landing.

The relief calms me. Now it's simply a matter of holding on to West Tip, staying two or three lengths behind Monanore, Classified and Young Driver. Crossing the Melling Road on the long run to the second last, I try to see who is still going well. Young Driver is the one to beat.

We join him at the last fence and then, mindful that it is a 495 yard run-in, I don't ask the last question until we reach the elbow about 150 yards from the post. A year before, Phil Tuck felt he was winning on Mr Snugfit but Last Suspect devoured the ground after jumping the last, so I dare not look behind. What if there is another Last Suspect? West Tip thinks the race is won, his ears are pricked, he is now half-racing, half-taking in the excitement. I try to get serious, hit him two smacks but he's not taking a blind bit of notice. We win by two lengths and I slap his neck in disbelief. On the walk back to the winner's enclosure, West Tip jig-jogs. He's still on his toes. He's enjoying the adulation.

I look around the crowd, everyone's going mad. I've done it, I tell myself. You've come back here and made up for last year. There is just a smile on my face but inside, I am euphoric. This is as good as it gets.

One of the downsides of achieving success at an early age is that you can't fully appreciate it. It comes too quickly and because you haven't lost enough, you don't understand what winning means. As the youngest jockey in the race and winner of the Grand National, I thought, 'This isn't as difficult as people say.' As I weighed in, the Duke waited by the scales and stretched out his hand to congratulate me. With Scu on his way to Fred Winter, I was set to become the Duke's stable jockey for 1986–87 and this win delighted my new guv'nor.

After leaving my saddle in the weighing room, I was taken back outside for the usual round of interviews. The day began to swirl – a BBC interview with Des Lynam and a press conference. Then there was the parade up and down the course with me standing and waving to the crowd in what resembled a Popemobile. It was desperately embarrassing. What was I doing waving like some celebrity to the public? I had ridden the winner of a horse race.

Along the way I managed to make a few quick phone calls, first to my parents and then to Carol who watched the race with her family in Wantage. I had asked Carol to set the video at my house in Stanford-in-the-Vale and I looked forward to sitting down and having a long look at the race. For now, though, I was keen to ensure we had a venue for a party that evening and remembered the good night we'd had at the Cotswold Gateway in Burford when Hywel won 12 months earlier. The Cotswold Gateway would do me. Everyone turned up – my parents, Carol, Graham, Hywel, the Nashs, Brendan Powell, Martin Bosley and plenty of others. Next morning it was up to Michael Oliver's stables to see West Tip and on Monday night we had another party at Timmy's Chinese restaurant,

Liaison, in Oxford. There was no National Hunt racing until Wednesday and we used the short break to celebrate the victory in the way it should be celebrated.

The season continued and ended with a few little twists that perfectly summed up the fickleness of the sport. Everyone's heroine at Cheltenham, Dawn Run went to the French Champion Hurdle at Auteuil, fell at the fifth from home and broke her neck. She died almost instantly. On Jonathan Sheppard's talented hurdler, Flatterer, I was right behind the mare when she and her French jockey Michel Chirol came down. It didn't seem one of the hardest falls and the ground was well watered. I didn't think for a second there would be a problem.

/At the other end of the spectrum there was Von Trappe at Kempton. Having fallen in the Embassy Final at Ascot and the Gold Cup at Cheltenham and being unseated in another Cheltenham race a month later, I was sceptical about Von Trappe's chances of taking me from the beginning to the end of any race. But in a competitive handicap chase at Kempton in May, he took on and beat the useful Everett, Glenrue and other decent chasers. He ran away with it, making lengths at the last three fences and, almost incidentally, lowered the course record by two seconds. There may have been surer rides than Von Trappe to the ambulance room, but none were quicker.

When I got round to watching the video of the National, I replayed the sequence from the last fence to the post. I didn't look very good in the finish. When I sat down to ride West Tip I bounced the saddle like an unfit amateur. It was also obvious that having started my career riding too short, I was now riding too long. Because we had won the race, there were people queueing up to tell me how good I had been, but the opinion that stayed in my mind was that of Martin Blackshaw, who was then training in France. Martin had been a very good rider and finished second to Red Rum on Churchtown Boy in the 1977 National. Martin, who has since been killed in a car accident, said it had been a reasonable ride but I would get a lot better when I pulled my irons up a couple of holes and got stronger. I agreed.

8

VERY PROMISING

C arol and I had been going out for just ten months when there was talk about getting engaged. It was me who made the running. Carol would laugh and wonder was I joking. I was 23, Carol was just 20 but we were wrapped up in each other and very comfortable together. I had sold my house, a two-bedroomed terraced, in Stanford-in-the-Vale and moved to a bigger one in Bampton, detached with four small bedrooms. In the evening, Carol would come over and cook supper while I watched a recording of that day's racing or went through the following day's cards. She would stay for a while and then go home to her parents' house in Wantage. Carol was smashing, I thought the world of her and did believe we loved each other. Through my eyes it was fairly straightforward; we should get engaged early in 1987 and a year later we would be married.

From reading the reports of my win on West Tip in the 1986 Grand National, it would have been natural to conclude that I was a mature young man. If being able to negotiate Aintree's big fences means you're mature, then I suppose I was. If saying the right things in the post-race press conference proves you've got things worked out, then I had. This is how I'd figured it out: I had lived the lad's life for a couple of years, gone through the drinking nights that on occasions ended with some girl in the back of a car, but those days were over. That was me in my amateur days at the Captain's. Now I was first jockey to David Nicholson and had moved into the big league. Changes were necessary. I needed to settle down and focus more on my career. Even though I had just moved into the house in Bampton, I was already thinking of buying a larger one, suitable for the two of us, with some land, a few boxes and a couple of horses. I wanted a more settled life, a more regular lifestyle. Earlier nights, better diet and someone to be there for me. I'd done my messing round, now it was over. Carol worked in racing, at first riding out for Henrietta Knight and then as secretary to the Wantage trainer, David Gandolfo. She understood the jockey's life. Being married, I reckoned, would be good for my career.

Four days after Christmas in 1986, David Nicholson sent Very Promising to Ireland for the Black and White Whisky Champion Chase at Leopardstown and the horse became the Duke's first winner in Ireland, beating Bobsline and Frank Berry. The race was worth almost £33,000 and in terms of prize money, it was the second biggest win of my career up to then. Leaving Dublin that evening, I stopped at Shannon Gems jewellery shop in Dublin Airport's duty free. There was one engagement ring I liked. Seven weeks later, we were back at Leopardstown with Very Promising who was this time beaten into second place over three miles by ForgiveN'Forget in the Vincent O'Brien Gold Cup Chase. It was Valentine's Day and on the way home, I stopped again at the jewellery shop. This time I bought the ring.

I had travelled with the Duke and Dinah Nicholson to Ireland and that Saturday night we met up with Carol at the Dragon Chinese restaurant in Burford. It was a good evening despite the afternoon's result, but it was not until we got home later that I produced the ring and asked Carol to marry me. She was a bit taken aback that I had actually gone and bought the ring before we had properly discussed it but she still said yes. Then she started to tease, why had I done it? I wasn't sure what to say.

'It seemed like the right thing to do,' I stumbled.

Like a coffee break in mid-morning, breakfast at the Duke's became a ritual. I went to Condicote on Sundays and Thursdays and after first lot, the Duke and I would retire to the house where Dinah prepared breakfast. Not everyone liked Dinah's coffee; it was very strong but it suited me. There was also toast, preferably brown toast, two slices for me, coffee and one slice for the Duke. On Thursdays he would have his *Sporting Life*, I'd have the *Raceform Update*, and on Sundays we would discuss the week's racing – how this horse should be ridden, whom we had to worry about in this race and that. When I had eaten my two slices, the Duke would religiously reach across and whip away my plate. For a heavy-boned jockey, two slices of toast were enough. I often imagined that Frenchie, his dad, probably did the same for his young jockeys.

I liked the Duke and I liked the feel of the job. It felt good to sit in the seat that had been so recently filled by Peter Scudamore and the Duke had a way of making you feel part of the team. It was obvious that he and Scu had enjoyed a very good relationship. When the Duke had financial problems a couple of years before and his bank bounced the cheque to cover the lads' wages, Scu stepped in and paid the staff. Shortly afterwards a number of the Duke's owners helped him through a very tough financial crisis. Like so many racing people, the Duke's talent was for horses not balancing books. When a virus got into his yard in the mid-eighties, the operation could not sustain lean years. The Duke trained just 17 winners in the 1984–85 campaign and 22 the following season. Michael Oliver, West Tip's trainer, tried to persuade me to say no to the Duke.

'What do you want to go to him for? Come to me, we have nearly as many winners as he has,' Michael said. But I looked back to the seasons before the Duke's two disappointing years, to the times when he trained between 50 and 70 winners a season. That was much more his level than 17 or 22.

The Duke had a certain style that made him intimidating. What he believed, he believed passionately and he had principles. His stable jockey was his man. When Scu was in the position, the Duke considered him the best. Now I had taken over, and I was given that status. I had his loyalty. About six weeks after the announcement of my appointment, Solar Cloud was due to run at Auteuil in France. This was mid June 1986, the time of year that fell between the old and new seasons. Scu, technically, might still have been stable jockey and he said he would like to ride the horse that he had ridden to victory in that year's Triumph Hurdle. But the Duke said no, his new man would ride it. Then Scu indicated that he would like to continue his partnership with the Duke's best horse, Very Promising. Scu got on well with the horse and equally as well with the owner, Paul Green. It was understandable that Paul might have wanted to stick with Scu but the Duke again put his foot down. What happens, he asked, when Very Promising clashes with the Fred Winter-trained Half Free, whom Scu would be contracted to ride.

With the Duke's job came a definite hardening of my attitude. When asked to become his stable jockey I asked for time to consider things and even though I desperately wanted the job, I also wanted a decent retainer. For the first year or so we agreed on a figure for each horse in the yard which would be paid by the owners to me but this didn't work out. It was impossible to expect owners to pay extra for my services if they felt I didn't get on well with their horses or, in some cases, if I didn't ride their horse in any of its races. So it was decided I would get more than the jockey's normal 9 per cent of the penalty value or prize money. The amount varied but it worked out much better and, financially, I was well rewarded riding for the Duke and later Nicky Henderson.

Deals such as the one I negotiated with the Duke come with certain responsibilities. I had to be more committed and better prepared. I installed a sauna in the garage of my new house in Bampton and that summer, 1986, I decided against taking a holiday. Carol went to Greece while I kept riding and watching my weight. Steve Smith Eccles, who was then the most senior jockey in the weighing room, the one with the number one peg, warned me that by the middle of November, I would realise my mistake. The Ecc was right. The season was long and, by November, I was mentally drained.

Ecc's personality made him a natural leader in the weighing room. On the last day of the season it was Ecc who said, 'OK lads, you've got this far, look after yourselves today,' and every time he said it, I thought, 'Christ Ecc, you're right. We might just make the summer holidays here.' At the close of a day's racing, someone might say, 'Hard luck, Ecc,' if he'd ridden a couple of losers. His reply was always the same. 'If I walk out of here in one piece at the end of the day, it's been a good one.'

The last day of the season invariably produced a lighter mood, an almost end-of-term giddiness. On the last afternoon of the 1987–88 season I rode Terry Casey's Bold In Combat in the three miles and two furlongs hurdle at Stratford. Buoyed by the prospect of the holidays, Ecc was feeling even fresher than usual. As the field passed the stands, he was upsides Tarnya Davis (now Sherwood) and began to pat her behind. That led to an attempted kiss by Ecc that Tarnya managed to lean away from. Undeterred, Ecc then placed his hand between her legs. I was directly behind them and even though it was the most audacious sexual harassment you could imagine, it appealed to my wicked sense of humour and I could barely stay in the saddle for laughter. Tarnya, it should be said, was well able to look after herself and Ecc's messing certainly didn't bother her. Appropriately, Bold In Combat won the race.

On another famous occasion the trainer, Jeff King, came into the weighing room at Uttoxeter to complain to Ecc about a ride he had just given his horse. Ecc listened for a bit and then just smacked him. It was a good while before Jeff put Ecc up again but he did and that incident was eventually put aside. Jeff had been one of the toughest and best riders never to win a jockeys' championship but he was very hard to please when you rode for him. Even if you were riding someone else's horse, Jeff might tell you he thought you had given it a bad ride. After winning the Coral Hurdle on Von Trappe at the 1985 Festival, Jeff said I had been too hard on the horse from the last hurdle. There was no argument from me. I had been too severe.

Neither did I argue too strenuously when the Duke first told me that I had got it wrong on one of his horses. It was the two-day meeting at Ascot in the middle of November and the fall of the two-mile chaser Long Engagement was what annoyed him. The horse jumped carefully over the first four fences and fell at the fifth. I didn't think I had done that much wrong.

'You weren't positive,' he said afterwards. 'One way or another, you've got to be positive. Be positive, don't change your mind.' It was one of the Duke's big things, you had to be decisive presenting a horse at a fence. So next day I was riding French Union in a big two-mile chase. French Union was a brilliant jumper but I fired him at a fence from nowhere and decked him. I had been positive, though, and the Duke never said a word.

Five years later, the name of the horse had changed but the story was the same. The Duke believed I didn't get on with Duntree and there was some evidence to support his view. After the horse had won on his seasonal appearance at Cheltenham under Hywel Davies (I chose to ride the better fancied Windy Ways for Nicky Henderson in the same race), the Duke put me back on the horse for his next race at Kempton. He fell. The Duke complained but for Duntree's next run at Sandown, I was still his pilot. This time I was unseated. Now the Duke hated his jockeys to fall off, as he would say. If the horses remained upright you should remain on their backs. It was your job. Still, his loyalty was unshakeable. I rode Duntree in his next run, this time at Warwick. He buried me again after I threw him at the last ditch. My parents were there that day and were more than a little concerned that I had parted company with Duntree for the third consecutive time. They met the Duke soon after the race.

'This horse hasn't got a jumping problem,' he told them, 'there's nothing wrong with his jumping.' Their expressions must have indicated they found that hard to believe. 'This horse does NOT have a jumping problem,' said the Duke, prodding my mother on the arm with his forefinger. Nevertheless, he put me back on him next time and on this occasion we didn't fall. Maybe the horse didn't have a jumping . . . The season ended with Hywel getting another chance on Duntree. This time he was unseated.

Through the first four months as stable jockey to the Duke, I had 194 rides, 18 falls, one unseated and one slipped up. Twenty out of 194 was more than one fall in every ten rides and far too many. I was trying too hard, asking tired horses for enormous leaps. Yet the Duke and I did get off to a good start. With just a handful of runners in September and early October, the Duke sent five horses to Stratford on 18 October. Four won. Three weeks later I had my first big race ride for him on Very Promising in the Mackeson Gold Cup at Cheltenham. I was very conscious that Scu on Half Free was one of my big rivals even though we were third favourite and he was fourth favourite in a wide open handicap chase. Very Promising was on springs and not a difficult ride and that day he was at his best, jumping like a buck and travelling fluently through the race.

When I nudged him to the front three fences from home, only Half Free was able to chase. Into the straight, my challenger closed the gap and was just a length behind jumping the last but Very Promising put his head down and battled bravely to win by two lengths. I gave the horse a reasonable ride, kicked on at the right time and when Scu came at us, we still had something left. But I was too hard on him from the last fence and the finish is not one I ever want to see again. I was still trying to prove myself against Scu and the other top jockeys. I wanted to show I could be as forceful as they were in a finish. I was not going to hold back but neither was I thinking things through. If the race was won with 100 yards to go, it was pointless hitting the horse beyond that point. Why stretch the horse to make him win by a greater margin? Head down, all I saw was the winning post.

But the winners were flowing and the Duke had a number of nice horses. As well as Very Promising, there was French Union, Long Engagement, Voice of Progress, Cottage Run and Burnt Oak. All had won before the end of November. As the winners' tally improved and I got to ride better horses, I became more competitive, setting the bar ever higher. I wanted more winners this season than last season, more this month than last, more today than yesterday and the satisfaction of having a winner was no longer enough to ease the disappointment of missing one. The Duke has said he never knew anybody who took losing as badly as I did. Given that Scu had been his jockey before me, I must have been a sad case.

The disappointment Michael Oliver felt when I chose to take the Duke's job turned into something stronger when I opted to ride Charter Party over West Tip in the Cheltenham Gold Cup. At the beginning of the season, the Duke agreed that I could ride West Tip for Michael in all of his races. Neither of us anticipated West Tip running in the Gold Cup but in what was an average season for staying chasers, Michael was right to enter the horse. The Duke, however, had Charter Party primed for the race and was adamant I would ride his horse.

'You've got to ride mine, even though we have that agreement,' he insisted. I couldn't see West Tip winning the Gold Cup but I thought if things went right for Charter Party, he might have a chance. I decided it would be Charter Party.

Michael, though, had said whoever rode West Tip in the Gold Cup would ride him in the Grand National and in the days before the Festival, the racing papers ran stories saying I would be jocked off for Liverpool. That was worrying enough in itself but it was complicated by the fact that Ultan Guilfoyle, a BBC television producer who became a very close friend, was making a documentary about my life and focusing on the build-up to the National with West Tip.

Having won on the horse at Aintree 11 months earlier, I felt Michael might have been a little more sympathetic to my situation. The Duke paid my retainer and I was not retained to ride West Tip. Michael asked Richard Linley if he would ride his horse in the Gold Cup and it was presumed he would keep the ride for Liverpool. Then Richard dislocated his shoulder again while winning on Gala's Image in the Arkle Challenge Cup on the first day of the Festival. Peter Hobbs deputised in the Gold Cup and Michael put me back up for the Grand National.

Nerve-racking? Not nearly as much as the Gold Cup itself. Half an hour or so before the scheduled start of the race, it started snowing and on the way down to the start, the snow began to gather and ball inside the horses' feet. The jockeys knew straightaway the race could not begin; with balls of snow in their hooves, the horses would slip badly and besides, when they kicked those balls of compacted snow backwards, they'd come flying at us like bricks. Charter Party was not the most reliable jumper in ideal conditions and I'd already fallen from him earlier in the season. Down at the start they told us to return to the paddock and even though we were wet and freezing, the stewards wouldn't let us back into the changing room because we had been officially weighed out. We stood around the weighing scales, waiting to see what would happen.

Helicopters were brought in to blow snow off the fences and away from the take-off and landing areas. After about an hour we were told to remount, the course was again raceable. I was well able to contain my enthusiasm for riding Charter Party in these conditions and when he made a mistake at the third fence, I thought, 'Oh, this is just great.' We got over the next, the water fence, and then it was the first ditch. 'OK, pull yourself together, you're going to jump this,' and I drove him in on a very long stride. He said no. That was it, we were on the floor and out of the Gold Cup. It was a big error of mine at the time. I would lengthen the horse's stride and say, 'You get there, you jump,' and often the horse would do exactly what Charter Party did – he'd decline to jump, put in an extra stride and then not be able to get high enough to clear the fence. Rather than work with the horse to help him get to the other side, I would try to bully him into doing it my way.

Picking myself off the ground, a thought struck fear in my heart. West Tip might win. I ran away from the obstacle, across the inside of the course and down to the last fence. 'Please, don't let West Tip win, don't let him win.' They came to the last in a line – The Thinker, Cybrandian and Door Latch. West Tip was two or three lengths behind but close enough to get to them. It was torture. I could see West Tip staying on strongly up the hill and overtaking the three leaders. The horse that I turned down would win the Gold Cup. Thankfully it didn't happen; he finished fourth, beaten four lengths. Michael Oliver's decision to run him in the race had been totally vindicated. And as for mine? I was upset at having passed up the chance to finish fourth in the Gold Cup. It could have been worse but even if someone had sat me down and said, 'Look Richard, you made a logical decision to ride Charter Party. On form he was a more likely winner than West Tip. Don't be so hard on yourself,' it wouldn't have made any impact. To me this had been a mistake and I wasn't allowed mistakes. By now I was on a treadmill. I had to get it right and if I didn't, I beat myself up about it.

That Cheltenham had its moments. French Union gave me my third Festival winner when taking the Grand Annual Chase on the opening day and then Very Promising ran an outstanding race before finishing a neck second to Pearlyman in the Queen Mother Champion Chase on the second day. We knew Very Promising stayed a good bit further than the race's two miles and after jumping the third last, I went for home. Scu was on Pearlyman and would have anticipated the acceleration, Colin Brown and Desert Orchid were right there too. Going to the second last, Scu and Pearlyman came swinging up alongside us, travelling incredibly well. They went half a length up, giving me something to aim at as we approached the last.

'OK, let's go now, let's wing this.' I gathered up Very Promising, hit him in the air and we just flew the fence. We landed running and got back in front of Scu but he then wound up Pearlyman sufficiently to regain the lead inside the last 100 yards.

It had been a fantastic race and for once, I wasn't in despair about losing. I felt I'd given the horse a decent ride but Pearlyman was one hell of a two-miler. I suppose what pleased me most was that I had taken on Scu in one of the big races at Cheltenham and even though my horse was beaten, I didn't feel I'd been outridden. If I could have stood back at that point and thought about it, I would have realised that the journey I had begun wasn't actually about winners but about something greater. More than numbers or titles at the end of a season, I sought the respect of my fellow jockeys, of Scu and Ecc and Graham and all the lads. I walked back to the weighing room after the Champion Chase feeling just a fraction taller than before. 'Hard luck,' they said. 'Ah, it's OK,' I replied and meant it.

The hassle over West Tip and whether I would keep the ride finally convinced me I needed someone to help book my rides and keep trainers informed of my plans. Jockeys were only just beginning to employ agents and while there was a certain resistance to them from trainers and other jockeys who refused to employ one, they made sense to me. With my commitments to the Duke, there weren't enough hours in the day to keep in touch with all of the other trainers for whom I rode. A good agent could do that effectively. Robert Kington was well known and respected within racing. He had ridden for Fred Winter and his sister Marilyn was, in fact, married to Scu. With the introduction of agents, the landscape did change.

'Your agent rung up looking for my ride,' one of the older jockeys would complain. I didn't have a lot of sympathy, although I mightn't have said so. My feeling was that I was entitled to ask, to let the connections know I was available. Ultimately, the decision was the trainer's or the owner's, never mine. Over the years there were times when there was resentment in the weighing room over my pursuit of rides that were considered to belong to others. If I felt the ride might be available, I had a duty to go after it. Times were changing.

As soon as Robert came on board, my workload lightened and I had more time to concentrate on how I rode. Robert wasn't just an agent, he had ridden himself and would offer his opinion about how I had performed in a particular race. He didn't mind being honest when he thought I had ridden badly and I respected him for that.

West Tip ran another fine race in the National to be fourth. Carrying ten pounds more than when winning the year before and racing on ground quite a bit faster, he wasn't the force he had been in 1986. I pushed him along to keep his position on the first circuit and although he stayed on well over the last mile, he never really looked like getting to the leaders. Beaten 13 lengths by Maori Venture, he wasn't good enough on the day, but we didn't leave Aintree without a winner. Against the Grain beat Dixton House and Playschool to win a competitive novices' chase.

Later in the month I went for one day to the Punchestown Festival. It was my first time there and I made the visit well worthwhile by winning the BMW Champion Novice Hurdle on the Duke's High Plains. My other ride at Punchestown that afternoon was Another Shot for Peter McCreery. 'This fellow jumps so low, you'll feel your feet brushing through the birch,' the lads in the Irish weighing room told me. I'd pulled my irons up a fair bit since West Tip in 1986 and I thought they had to be exaggerating, but they weren't. My feet felt birch at every fence. Somehow we got round and finished third.

Having ridden 55 winners the previous season, I rode 70 in my first season as number one jockey to the Duke and finished third in the jockeys' championship behind Scu and Mark Dwyer. The Duke, too, had enjoyed a good year and lifted his 1985–86 tally of 22 to 42. The new team at Condicote had started well.

9

A SPECIAL PARTY

For the big day, sportsmen and women prepare differently. Some stay perfectly calm, treat it as just another match, another race, another challenge. If what you have done in the past has been good enough to take you this far, why change? Others, the truly confident, look upon the big occasion as an opportunity to show what they can do. I was at the start of the Derby at Epsom in 1986 and will never forget how calm and in control Greville Starkey was as he walked round on the favourite, Dancing Brave. 'God,' I thought, 'how can he be so cool?' He could have been riding in a maiden at Pontefract. That confidence ultimately led to their defeat but the memory of Greville remained with me for a long time. Through the first half of my career, I could never be like that. Riding a horse that I thought should win a big race, I tended to see it as the definitive test of my ability, even of my character. Whatever I had done in the past meant nothing, my worth as a jockey depended upon what happened in the next big race.

It is the day before the start of the 1988 Cheltenham Festival, Monday 14 March. I am riding the favourite for the following day's Champion Hurdle, the Mercy Rimell-trained Celtic Chief, so I've decided to have a quiet day at home in Bampton and concentrate on preparing properly. I believe this is the most important race of my life. Celtic Chief beat his principal rival Celtic Shot by eight lengths at Sandown five weeks earlier and is everyone's favourite to win tomorrow's big prize. Favourite for the Champion Hurdle – I only need to start thinking about it to get tight and tense. My day is organised to leave no time for thinking.

So this Monday morning begins with an hour in the sauna and after that I visit Val Ridgeway who has been one of my physiotherapists since I first started riding at Captain Forster's. Val is an exceptional remedial therapist, the guardian angel who has watched over a number of jockeys. A fall from Another Coral at Sandown on the previous Friday has left me sore but this visit will have me in good shape for Cheltenham. After Val there is a meeting at the Jockeys Association, then an appointment with my accountant and, finally, a hair cut. It is late afternoon when I get home and start studying videos of previous Cheltenham races. I look again at the Pearlyman/Very Promising race in the 1987 Champion Chase and I play the tape of Charter Party's win in the Ritz Club Handicap Chase of two years before. Scu got the horse jumping well round Cheltenham that afternoon and I want to learn from how he did it.

Carol, my fiancée now, has come round and we have a light supper but already I know it's going to be hard to sleep tonight. People think I am confident, they say I seem sure of my ability. It's not true. Things can go wrong in a Champion Hurdle, it happens so quickly and there is very little time to make up for a mistake. And I know that Mercy Rimell is not that happy about my riding her horse. She has always been a big fan of Scu's but because he is committed to riding Celtic Shot for Fred Winter, he is unavailable. At least Celtic Chief's owners, David and Leila Sewell, are keen to have me riding the horse.

It is eight o'clock in the evening, too early to go to bed but I am thinking of nothing but tomorrow. 'Go for a run. Not that long, enough to get your mind off the race.' For 35 minutes I jog around the streets of Bampton village, a demented jockey running from something he can't escape.

In bed, I toss and turn. The run has awakened every sinew in my body and as I lie there, my mind moves into overdrive. 'You can't make a mistake tomorrow, this is the big day, this is the winner that can change your life.' I try to stop myself. 'Get a book, read.' But the words don't register, horses stampede through my head. I get up, go downstairs, get another glass of water, check the time. Two o'clock in the morning and I still haven't closed an eye.

Maybe it's the bed. I go to the spare room and try to sleep there; 4 a.m. and still no sleep. I turn on the light again, start reading. No good. What's happening here? Just go to sleep. A little after five, I drop off but it is a light, fitful sleep. On and off, I doze for two hours.

Outside the Cheltenham weighing-room door as I arrive at 10.30, Snowy Lewis greets me with a smile.

'Hello Richard, everything well?'

'Just fine, Snowy, just fine.'

Through the 1986–87 season I had felt tired and when it ended, I couldn't wait to take a break. However well intentioned, the decision not to take a holiday during the summer of 1986 had not been clever. Horses have five or six races each season, I'd had five hundred. They get turned out on grass for three months and I refuse to take a couple of weeks off. I wasn't going to make that mistake again. A group of us were off for ten days in Trinidad and Tobago. The party included Peter Scudamore, Steve Smith Eccles, Graham Bradley, Simon Sherwood, Mark Caswell and Willie Humphreys. Most of the wives and girlfriends came too. For Carol and me, it was a first holiday away together and we had a fabulous time.

I was now comfortable in the company of Scu and Ecc, and Brad I knew well from our time together in America two years earlier. Away from their working environment, jockeys laugh a lot and tend to be up for things that saner people would avoid; not that we ever totally cut ourselves off from horses. When we were in Tobago we flew to Port of Spain in Trinidad for a day at the races. Most of the women, including Carol, didn't share our curiosity about Trinidadian racing and stayed on the beach in Tobago. They did well to miss the drama of the short return flight.

Our twin-prop aircraft encountered a violent tropical storm as it began its descent into Tobago and the pilot decided it was too dangerous to land. Instead he hovered over the airport, waiting for the storm to pass. It was a long, long wait and the plane was being tossed this way and that. One of the girls from our holiday group who was on the flight began to scream, her fear accentuating the potential danger. Scu was ashen-faced and very quiet. I'm not a great traveller but a few drinks at the races earlier in the day had made me strangely philosophical, almost nonchalant. 'If we're going down, we're going down,' I thought. Ecc, of course, became a little louder as the storm got worse. Taking a look at the frightened faces around him, he chirped up, 'If this little beauty goes down, there's goin' to be a lot of spare rides next season.'

We eventually landed. It was one of three bad flying experiences I've had. Coming into Heathrow a few years later on a flight from Dublin, we were about to touch the ground when the plane accelerated and took off again. No one blamed the pilot; there was another aircraft on the runway. On another occasion when I flew into Cork in 1999 en route to Killarney races, it was very windy and just as we were about to land, the pilot decided it was too dangerous and made off for Dublin. That moment when the landing suddenly and unexpectedly becomes a take-off is frightening.

Another vivid experience of flying came in a dream. I was on a flight; it must have been transatlantic because flying over the vastness of the ocean unnerved me. Suddenly the plane went spiralling out of control, started plummeting down and nose-dived into swamplands somewhere in the US. It seemed so real. I was terrified and woke in a cold sweat. The next morning there was a report on the radio about a plane that had dropped from the sky and crashed into the alligator-filled swamps in Florida, the Everglades. I am no soothsayer but it had been so realistic it was disturbing.

In my waking hours, I was getting used to crash landings and even though I had more than my share of falls through the first four seasons, I had been very lucky with injuries. That wasn't going to continue and even though I reduced the percentage of falls in the 1987–88 season, it was also the season when they began to leave their mark. With the benefit of hindsight, I think the unlucky run of injuries this year related to a bad fall from the three-year-old hurdler, Bob's Ballad, in early December at Fontwell. I can only imagine how it was because I remember nothing of it. The horse was very keen and had run away with me on the way to the start; then, after taking charge of me from the third, he was weakening when he fell at the downhill hurdle, the fourth last. I was badly concussed and ordered not to ride for seven days.

Towards the end of December, we took Very Promising to Ireland to try to win the Black and White Whisky Champion Chase for the second consecutive year. Very Promising's owner Paul Green had L'Ane Rouge in an earlier novice chase and he asked me to ride it. Trained in Ireland by Homer Scott, L'Ane Rouge looked like winning as he rose at the last fence but he collapsed in a heap on landing. I was fired into the ground. It was a bad fall and afterwards my neck was very sore. I agreed with Dr Halley, the racecourse doctor, to give up my ride in the next race and return for Very Promising later in the afternoon. I was just about OK and Very Promising finished third to Weather the Storm and Bobsline.

Two days later I rode Chase The Line for the Duke at Cheltenham. The horse over-jumped at the first hurdle, went down on his belly and as he came up, his head crashed into mine. It was like being hit by a sledgehammer and it aggravated the damage caused by the L'Ane Rouge fall. I could do nothing except pull the horse to a stop. My neck throbbed, I had no strength in my arms and not much feeling in one of them. It was clear the injury was serious.

'You've got to get this right,' said the Jockey Club doctor Michael Allen. 'You don't mess around with something like this.'

I went to see Dr Christopher Earle, a Harley Street specialist, and had a Mylogram. This is a procedure whereby fluid is injected into your spine so they can tell more from the X-rays. It was an incredibly uncomfortable experience; your spine is like a steel rod and your head feels like it's going to fall off. The test showed up nothing major and Michael Allen told me to take four weeks off.

Bad falls are part of the sport. You know the danger but once you allow the fear of it to take control of your riding, you're finished. One of the jockeys' defence mechanisms is machismo. We talk about 'decking horses' as if we and not the animals are responsible for the falls. Most trainers tend to take the horse's side; the Captain used to say, 'All my horses jump well until bloody jockeys get on them.' When the falls are serious and we walk away, we take some sort of perverse pleasure. I had this conversation with Jamie Osborne a number of times and it is my view that jockeys have to look at it that way. You get buried in a 35 m.p.h. fall and as you get up, unscathed, you turn the experience around – if I can walk away from that, I can walk away from anything. You smile to yourself, feeling for the moment invincible.

I suppose there are safer ways of getting kicks but, unfortunately, the kicks aren't as good without the danger. You know the risks are high when you ride an average novice chaser on rock-hard ground around Taunton. Of course, you hope your agent will protect you from obviously dangerous rides but as a jockey, you have to agree to almost everything else. I have long believed that before going out to the paddock on occasions like this, you leave your brain in the weighing room. If you go out and start thinking about even simple things like the stiffness of the fences or the hardness of the ground, you are not going to be able to do your job. It is paramount to put your brain into neutral.

I had finished high up in the jockeys' championship for the two previous years and as a result I was getting offers to ride in unusual places. Without thinking too deeply, I accepted. It was a good but possibly not the safest way of travelling the world. In 1987–88, I rode in seven different countries besides England and Ireland and one day went to Hanover in Germany to ride a horse called Our Cloud for Norwegian trainer Arnie Carlsson. Our Cloud was a good jumper but approaching a large privet hedge situated on a bend, he sadly broke his shoulder, tried unsuccessfully to rise at the fence and catapulted me into the ground. We were towards the front of a big field, but even though the horses were bunched tightly towards the inside, each one miraculously missed me at the back of the fence. I was very, very lucky. It was always going to be a major factor riding abroad. On-course medical facilities, or lack of them in some countries, would send a shiver down my spine and I really had no wish to visit the hospitals of Europe no matter how good they may have been.

But there was occasionally good money to be made and the first attractive opportunity to come my way was from Jonathan

Sheppard who offered me the ride on Flatterer in the French Champion Hurdle in 1986. Jonathan had spoken to Marigold Coke, the Captain's secretary, with whom he was friendly. As always she had put in a good word for me. After Dawn Run had fallen fatally early on the final circuit, Flatterer ran a brilliant race, in extreme heat, to chase home Le Rheusois. A year and a half later I was invited across to America to partner him again in the Breeders' Cup at Fair Hill in Maryland. Getting there wasn't straightforward and I needed the Duke's co-operation. It was something we both became very good at; if he wanted something he could persuade me to go with it and when I needed something I felt I could win him over. Not only was the Breeders' Cup worth $125,000 to the winner but it was a big international race and I had a very high opinion of Jonathan as a trainer. The difficulty was the timing; I was due to ride Very Promising in Devon in an important race against Pearlyman on Friday afternoon and had to be in Maryland to ride Flatterer on the Saturday. At first the Duke said no, it couldn't be done, but relented when I convinced him I could ride Very Promising and still get to the US on time. I didn't ride in the later races in Devon after winning on Very Promising, and got to Heathrow in time for the 7 p.m. Concorde flight to New York. It was the first and only time I flew Concorde but for one who doesn't care for long flights across the Atlantic, it was perfect. I got to New York, hopped on a light aircraft bound for Unionville, Pennsylvania, stayed the night with Jonathan and his wife Cathy and then travelled on to Maryland the next morning.

The story didn't end well, though. Flatterer, a horse I considered to be among the best I've ridden, went lame after jumping the eighth fence. It took all my strength to pull him up. On feeling him go, I took him to the inside of the course on to the flat track but he would not give in despite the injury. At the following bend, approaching it at a much tighter angle than the rest of the field, he knocked several horses sideways. It was only when we turned uphill in the straight that he eventually relented. He would never race again. I felt sorry for Jonathan and his owners, Bill Pape and George Harris. They were shattered. 'Seeing Flatterer injured,' Bill said at the time, 'was like being backed over by a cement truck.'

Gacko, the French horse, went on to win and even this memory is tinged with sadness. Roger Duchene, the experienced French rider who rode Gacko that day, later died in a fall at the smaller water jump at Auteuil.

The list of jockeys I have known who were prematurely killed or seriously injured is depressingly long. One in particular stays with me. In the summer of 1988 Carol and I went to Greece with a group of racing people including Paul Croucher. It was June, a month before Carol and I were to be married; because of my riding commitments, it was easier to have a holiday before the wedding. We went with a good crew – Marcus and Gee Armytage, Jamie Osborne, Ray White, Carl Llewellyn, Martin and Sarah Bosley and Tarnya Davis who was going out with Crouch at the time. We had an unbelievable fortnight, one of the best-ever holidays and Crouch is there, in all the happy memories.

Crouch rode for Nicky Henderson and Kim Bailey and was a very good rider. But it was his attitude to life that I respected. You could say he was mad, then again we all probably were, but he was also a really good guy. Maybe it was because I was serious and intense that I admired him so much. I could lose my reason because I'd missed a winner. Crouch rode winners and losers and understood that both were impostors. A trainer could have a go at him over a particular ride but Crouch would sometimes find it hard to keep a straight face. It was water off a duck's back. We went racing together a fair bit and he was the best company. He could always see the bright side.

He was in his element with us on that holiday and one afternoon will stay with me for as long as I live. It was a glorious day, blue skies and brilliant sunshine. A few of us went up the coast in a small boat skippered and crewed by a couple of locals. They took us to the Blue Caves, which could only be entered from the sea. Inside it was dark, beautiful and mostly enclosed. Over on one side there were traces of light coming from an underwater opening to the sea. The Greeks did not speak any English but one of them used his hands to say it was possible to swim down and find a way out into the open sea. He suggested we do it. I shook my head. 'No way.' Everyone else in the boat felt the same, except Crouch.

'Yeah, I'll do it, I'll do it,' he said.

He slipped out of the boat and went down to see how far he would have to go to get to the hole. He came up.

'It's a bit down,' he said. The Greek lads encouraged him. He went down again to check, but still wasn't sure. They were daring him now.

'OK, I'll do it.'

Down he went. We left the caves and by the time we chugged back outside, we expected Crouch to be waiting for us. There was no sign of him. We waited. Still no sign of him. Now every second seemed like a minute and just as our worry was turning to panic, Crouch appeared out of the water. His head and body sprang up, almost like a cork from a champagne bottle. It had been a long swim under water and the tunnel to the sea was narrow and longer than Crouch expected. Instead of swimming through it, he'd had to crab along on his chest and arms to get out. He was covered in scrapes and scratches when he got through. It was a great relief to get him back into the boat.

Two months later Crouch was driving home after riding down in the West Country. As he neared Lambourn, he called a few friends and suggested meeting at The Ibex pub in Chaddleworth. He was, as usual, in good form. After a drink, Crouch left the pub and 200 yards down the road, his car skewed off the tarmac, smashed into a tree and he was killed. The previous month he had been at my stag night and a week later at our wedding and then he was gone. He was buried in Devon, on a hillside overlooking a beautiful valley. It was an intensely sad funeral. Carol and I stood there, both of us had thought the world of him, but it was only Carol who cried. 'What are you doing?' I said to her. 'What are you crying for?'

Later I tried to rationalise my response to Carol. Why had I been so dispassionate? 'Tragedies happen, this is life, no point in getting upset about it,' I told myself. Now, all these years later, I see it more clearly. I was becoming so single-minded about racing that other emotions were being shut down. Being hurt or upset just got in the way, and it was better not to acknowledge their existence. Carol's natural grief gave me a glimpse of what was happening to me and, not liking it, I turned on her.

★ ★ ★

When I started out as a jockey I simply wanted to ride winners but after four or five years, that hunger moved on to a new level. As the winners came, the ambition to ride more intensified. In the end, the ambition controlled me. This was how it had been when I tried to cut down on my eating at Rendcomb College many years before. Eventually, the diet completely controlled me. In the end I wanted to eat but I couldn't. Now I was experiencing the same phenomenon. Leading up to the 1988 Champion Hurdle, it seemed to me like the biggest race I would ever ride. Celtic Chief had to win, everything had to go right, I couldn't make a mistake. I wanted to control this so badly, it ended up controlling me. Desperate for a good night's sleep before this race, I couldn't sleep at all.

Anyway, the idea of controlling everything is pie in the sky. Racing has a way of re-acquainting you with reality. In the race before the Champion Hurdle, I rode Jim Thorpe for Gordon Richards. A 20 to 1 chance here, but he turned out to be one of the best novices of his year. Going to the last we were third, three lengths behind the leader Danish Flight and tracking Abbey Glen but we still had an outside chance of taking it. Jim Thorpe clouted the last and I was thrown sideways and forward out of the saddle. It was a heavy fall but the horse stayed on his feet; I had been unseated. I was physically very sore and cross with myself for exiting in such a way. Celtic Chief's owner, David Sewell, said I didn't look that healthy but once the Champion Hurdle preliminaries began, the soreness disappeared.

With 21 runners in the Champion Hurdle, it wasn't the day to miss the break. Lined up in the middle of the field, that's what happened. Celtic Chief stood for half a second before jumping off and we started the race further back than I would have liked. We got back to mid division soon enough but he wasn't travelling well and struggled to keep his position away from the stands. In the end all he did was plug on and he was never going to do better than his eventual eight-length third place behind Celtic Shot and Peter Scudamore. The start hadn't helped but neither had it been the difference between winning and losing. David and Leila Sewell thought similarly; they felt the horse had been beaten fairly and squarely.

I wasn't sure what Mercy Rimell thought at the time but I was to find out two weeks later in the *Racing Post*. My good friend Neil Morrice wrote the report. 'Dunwoody To Blame Storms Mercy' was the headline. Mercy didn't exactly live up to her Christian name. 'Celtic Chief,' she said, 'was asked to come from an impossible position, no horse could have won from where he came.'

'That bloody Morrice,' said Dad, 'I'm not talking to him again.'

As first days at the Cheltenham Festival go, that was diabolical. The second wasn't much better. I rode Nick The Brief for Terry Casey in the Sun Alliance Novice Hurdle and the horse ran a fine race to finish fourth, beaten just over three lengths. I knew he stayed well and kicked for home from the third last. Afterwards, John Upson, the owner, said he thought I may have gone too early and made too much use of the horse. It is understandable that connections find ways of excusing their horses' defeats but this was now turning into a very difficult week for me. I didn't feel I had done much wrong on Nick The Brief but when you're low, it doesn't take much to push you lower.

Then I rode poor old Very Promising in the Champion Chase and this time we were well beaten by Pearlyman. Desert Orchid beat us for second. Not as good as he had been 12 months earlier, Very Promising battled bravely to the end. On the run-in, I crucified him and should have been banned for excessive use of the stick. The horse was giving his best, he was never going to beat Pearlyman and he suffered because I was frustrated. Agathist in the Coral Hurdle was my last ride on Wednesday. He was favourite in the ring but beaten about 30 lengths in the race.

What was it Hywel used to say about Cheltenham – 'I hate this place, I can't stand this.' That evening, I knew how he felt.

But the thing about racing at this level is that you never have to wait too long for the next opportunity. In some respects you're like the loser standing at the one-armed bandit – you can keep putting coins into the slot. Two days down at the Festival, there was still one to go and I had two very important rides on the final day, Kribensis and Charter Party; Kribensis because we thought he had an outstanding chance in the Triumph Hurdle and Charter Party because it was the Gold Cup. I had been thrilled that Michael Stoute asked me to ride Kribensis after the Duke had put in a good word for me.

Realising he didn't have a Triumph Hurdle horse, the Duke recommended me to Michael when Steve Smith Eccles looked like being claimed by Nicky Henderson. Even though he could be opinionated and uncompromising, the Duke always gave you support and would go out of his way on occasions to find you a winner.

Kribensis gave me the perfect start to Gold Cup day. I sat just behind the leaders and bided my time, knowing the horse had so much class. We got a good run into the straight, took it up at the last and stayed on well to win by three lengths from Nigel Coleman on Wahiba. Remarkably, Nigel and I were first and second in the Triumph Hurdle a year later but the order was different. Nigel riding Ikdam beat me on Highland Bud. He is another jump jockey whose career ended before it should; a very bad head injury forced him to stop.

Throughout his career, Charter Party was an in and out jumper. The Duke used to say it wasn't the horse's fault; he hadn't been properly taught when first schooled. Later in life he contracted navicular disease which meant he was often lame and not the easiest to train. Getting Charter Party to the start of the 1988 Gold Cup in peak condition was an exceptional performance by the Duke and it remains a great testimony to his ability. People just didn't appreciate the size of the achievement. As soon as I mounted Charter Party, I realised we had a big chance.

'This fellow,' said Dan Jones, Charter Party's lad, 'hasn't taken a lame step all day. He's been grand.'

For Charter Party, that was very untypical. The Duke would be at the start on Gold Cup day just in case there were problems. The horse had always been highly thought of in the yard. Few horses could work with Very Promising over any distance the way Charter Party could and on those days when he got his jumping together, he was high-class. On this day, he was at his best and gave me an unbelievable ride. We raced about fourth or fifth, close behind the two leaders, Golden Friend and Cavvies Clown. At the top of the hill, I moved into second behind Cavvies. ForgiveN'Forget moved up to third on the outside. He, too, was going well but after jumping the fourth last, he fractured a leg.

Cavvies made a bad mistake at the second last, hitting the fence so hard that he pulled the reins out of Simon Sherwood's hands. I felt I had them beaten anyway and that Simon had thrown the horse at the fence because he sensed the race was slipping away. On our own now, Charter Party popped the last and went on to beat Cavvies by six lengths. After the last, I hit Charter Party all the way up the run-in. I was much too hard on him. Eleven years later, when I announced my retirement, this finish was shown again and again and I hated seeing it. I hit him a couple with the right, then I pulled the stick through to my left hand and then pulled it back and tried to hit him again with the right. If it had been nowadays, I would have gone down for a month and deserved it. All I needed to do was give him a couple of taps just to keep his mind on the job. But you pay for your mistakes. If I never again see gallant Charter Party come up the hill to win the Cheltenham Gold Cup, I certainly won't mind.

I was now past the foothills, climbing towards some distant summit and determined not to be sidetracked. There was a post-Cheltenham party at John and Sylvia Bosley's in Bampton that Thursday evening. My parents were there and it was a pleasant evening, albeit a quiet one after a hectic week. I had become very wound up and now, three or four hours after the last race, I couldn't unwind. A year or two earlier, I might have got drunk but now I was thinking of the next day: Fakenham. One ride for Philip Mitchell, Garfunkel, should win. Fakenham is not the most glamorous track and, in deep Norfolk, it is one of the tougher drives. On the night I won the most important event at jump racing's Olympics, I had an eye towards Fakenham. Fellow jockey Ian Lawrence drove me. It took us about three-and-a-half hours to get there, four-and-a-half hours to get home. Garfunkel did the business. Another winner.

10

HORSE POWER

S omeone once said it takes 20 years to become an overnight sensation. For the first six years of my riding career, I
had been a ruthless examiner of my performance and
even though considered to be one of the top jockeys, I wasn't
nearly as good as I wanted to be. I had the ability to make
horses run for me but they ran for a lot of jockeys. When I
looked, it was the weaknesses in my riding that stood out.
During those years, my falls-to-rides ratio was far too high, I
wasn't strong or stylish enough in finishes and often I didn't use
my stick correctly. Then in 1988 and 1989, it began to change. For
no particular reason other than six seasons of trying, I started to
get it right and something that had seemed elusive was now
attainable. I discovered the satisfaction of getting off a horse and
being able to say, 'Yeah, I've given that a decent ride.'

I look back on my notes and the progress is there in black
and white. At the end of the 1987–88 season the winners'
column totted up to 79, my highest ever total, but it wasn't the
winners that pleased me most. Over the ten months of the
season I had ridden 582 horses in Britain, taken 29 falls and
been unseated four times. I worked out the percentages; falls-to-
rides was under 6 per cent, close to one fall in every 18 rides.
Through my first three seasons riding as a professional, the
ratio was nearer one fall in every 12 mounts. Even allowing for
the fact that I was now riding better horses, the improvement
was significant.

At the 1989 Cheltenham Festival, I won the Arkle Challenge Trophy Cup on Waterloo Boy and the way we'd done it felt good. Walking away from the owner Mike Deeley and with the Duke at my shoulder as I returned to the scales, I knew that at last I was getting somewhere. In his final preparatory run for the Festival, Waterloo Boy had come up against Sabin du Loir and Peter Scudamore at Ascot. On ground faster than he liked, Waterloo Boy had struggled to live with the front-running Sabin du Loir. A mistake at the second last destroyed whatever chance we had and I immediately accepted that we were beaten, easing Waterloo Boy and saving him for the re-match that would take place at Cheltenham. We were beaten 20 lengths at Ascot but I couldn't see why we wouldn't be a lot closer at the Festival where the stiffer two miles would help us and where I would ride the horse more positively.

At Cheltenham, Sabin du Loir started 5 to 4, Waterloo Boy 20 to 1, but to me it felt a much more even contest. Waterloo Boy was a lovely horse, always tried his hardest and the best chance we had against Sabin du Loir was to take him on early and not allow him to dictate the pace. Waterloo Boy responded brilliantly. We were able to stay in touch with Sabin du Loir and, pressurised by our closeness, he made a few mistakes. At the last, we were marginally in front and increased that advantage by getting away from the fence quickly. Sabin du Loir was momentarily caught for speed and the bigger danger was the northern horse, Southern Minstrel, who loomed up beside us. He was ridden by one of the strongest jockeys in the weighing room, Chris Grant, and if I could have picked a rider other than Scu whom I didn't want taking me on in a tight finish, it would have been Granty.

But by now, I was ready. I had worked hard at using the stick in my left hand and actually found I could be more effective with it in a finish. I was also physically stronger and a bit more polished. Hard-pressed to the line, we beat Southern Minstrel by half a length; Sabin du Loir was a length further back in third. Up to that point in my career, I felt this was the best ride I had given a horse.

Later that year, I rode Crossroad Lad for Tim Thomson Jones at Cheltenham and got into a battle with Scu on the Martin

Pipe-trained Blake's Progress. It was nip and tuck all the way from the last but we nicked it on the line. Beating Scu in that kind of finish helped my confidence no end. So driven was he and so focused, he was extremely hard to beat in a close finish. At last I felt I was approaching his level. A month later, I was riding the ex-Irish-trained City Index at Nottingham and after jumping the last, I had only In-Keeping and Scu to beat. I was going easily; he was under pressure. Halfway up the run-in I looked across at him and smiled.

'Go on, Scu, give her another smack,' I joked as we sailed past, knowing that it would not make the slightest bit of difference. Not only was I growing more confident, I was also showing a little less respect to my peers.

As my riding improved, doors opened. Although I rode primarily for the Duke, the size of his team allowed me to ride for plenty of outside stables. Towards the end of the 1988–89 season, Nicky Henderson asked if I would ride his better horses. Although it was going to be hard to balance the demands of the Duke and Nicky, it was too good an opportunity to turn down. Nicky agreed to pay me in similar terms to the Duke and I was determined to make it work. Things got even better. After Simon Sherwood retired, I took over the ride on Desert Orchid, and Jonathan Sheppard offered me the ride on Highland Bud who had been sold from the Duke's and was to become the best steeplechaser in the US.

Even now it is hard to recall the scope, power and ability of some of these horses without feeling regret at no longer being at the helm. During my six years with the Duke, there was always a core of class steeplechasers. Very Promising was already a decent two- to two-and-a-half miler when I arrived and he improved. As Very Promising reached the end of his career, Waterloo Boy came along, picked up the torch and the stable had another cracking chaser at the minimum trip. In the way that Very Promising had blazed the trail for Waterloo Boy, so it was that the best of the three, Viking Flagship, came along as Waterloo Boy was finishing and as I was moving on to Martin Pipe. I twice won on him at the 1993 Punchestown festival and would love to have ridden him as he reached the pinnacle of his career. At the time, I thought it was normal, that the yard was entitled to have at least one great steeplechaser at any one time. Now, knowing a bit more, I realise how lucky we were. In racing, you are fortunate to come across one horse with the attitude and ability of the Duke's three two-milers.

Charter Party deservedly won the Gold Cup in 1988 and then there were the horses not good enough to win championship races at the Festival but who made us competitive on the big days throughout the jumps' season – Long Engagement, French Union, Springholm, Cottage Run, Another Coral, Bigsun, Against the Grain and many others.

Linking up with Nicky Henderson was going to work because he wanted me primarily for a select group and was sympathetic to my position with the Duke. Within a year or so of joining Nicky, I was riding Remittance Man, Brown Windsor, Wont Be Gone Long, Mutare, Sparkling Flame, Tinryland and Calabrese. At the same time I was also riding the top-rated staying chaser Desert Orchid and the top-rated hurdler Kribensis. On top of all this, the Duke and Nicky were paying me two decent retainers.

In terms of winners, my career progressed steadily but not spectacularly. In my first season as a professional I rode 46 winners and that increased by around ten winners every season for the next six years. As long as my total continued to rise, I wasn't too unhappy. I tried to put thoughts of the jockeys' title to one side. That was Peter Scudamore's, every year. In 1986 Scu began riding for the West Country trainer Martin Pipe who was setting out on the journey that would take him to the summit of the sport. Most seasons Scu was so far in front that the race was over by Christmas. In my mind, it was never a contest in the first place. Backed by Martin's never-ending supply of winners, Scu set off in the lead and in the tradition of good front-runners, he improved his position.

I tried not to worry, and reminded myself about the horses the Duke, Nicky and others were providing. In terms of quality, Scu couldn't compete. As a consequence, I tended to earn as much prize money as him even though I might ride half the number of winners. My retainers with the Duke and Nicky meant I was earning more money than Scu, no matter how many winners he rode. I should have been perfectly content and I was content, but not perfectly. I wanted to be champion jockey, and knowing that it wasn't possible didn't mean it didn't matter. I wondered how long Scu would keep going. Back then he seemed unstoppable. It would be an age before he retired and all I could do was keep improving, keep up my standards and make sure that whenever he did go, I was ready to take over.

Those hopes and ambitions make me smile now. How conveniently I ignored the threat of serious injury. But, as I've said, it is something jockeys can't afford to think about. Consider these four days in the life of an 'invincible man'.

On Wednesday, 25 October 1989, I was booked to ride three northern horses at Ascot – Sir Jest and Slieve Felim for Arthur Stephenson and Red Procession for Peter Liddle. W.A. Stephenson earned respect throughout the length and breadth of the racing industry for sending out an impressive number of winners year-in, year-out. Not a man for convention, W.A. had a reputation for doing it his way, and it worked. Offered a couple of rides on W.A.'s chasers, you knew there was a chance of winners but you had to expect the unexpected, especially on his novices. His schooling techniques over solid obstacles were certainly different from the Duke's and some of his chasers would take a little time to get the hang of it. But these were experienced handicappers and when I spoke to the stable jockey, Chris Grant, he told me all he knew about them. No one, however, could have prepared me for what actually happened.

Sir Jest was my first ride. He jumped stickily and was just plodding on for second place when disaster struck. Peter Scudamore was clear on the Martin Pipe-trained Huntworth but they jumped the last fence so far to the left that the horse ducked the wrong side of the wing of the hurdle on landing and was out of the race. Sir Jest had only to jump the fence to win but, distracted by Huntworth's antics, he dug his toes in and refused to rise. Headin' On and Tony O'Hagan came from a long way behind us to take the prize and, more than that, they were able to come home in their own time. It was not an auspicious start to the day and there was plenty more to come. W.A. wasn't there, so I had to explain on the phone how I'd managed to lose a race that was at our mercy; not the easiest call I've ever made.

Slieve Felim, a decent two-mile chaser, was next and once

the tape went up he was away with me. It was his usual style but going that mad gallop there was little time for manoeuvre and at the second fence down the hill he somersaulted. I walked away winded and seeing stars but the poor animal broke a leg and had to be destroyed. You kid yourself on days like this that it has to get better.

Red Procession, my final ride of the afternoon, was in a four-runner novice chase, and was well beaten going to the last fence. For God knows what reason, I drove him in at it and like Slieve Felim, he somersaulted. This time the horse was all right but I was badly concussed. Concussion results from bruising to the brain and mine must have taken a heavy bang. I remember nothing from the second the horse fell; it's a complete blank.

The fall happened in the fourth race and about a half an hour after the last, Simon McNeil found me in the sauna. How long had I been there? I hadn't a clue. Simon and I were good friends and used to change alongside each other.

'What are you doing here?' he asked.

It was a good question. Couldn't answer that, either. The races were over and though I sometimes liked 10 or 15 minutes in the sauna at the end of the day, I had no notion why I was there at that time. Simon, of course, recognised the symptoms and drove me home. That evening I watched a video re-run of the day's racing from Ascot and was amazed to see footage of myself talking to the racecourse doctor after the last fall. I had no recollection of this whatsoever, although it is standard practice for the doctor to examine a rider who has hit the deck. It was quite unnerving watching yourself doing things only four hours previously that you couldn't remember at all. Within seconds of Red Procession falling, I was on my feet. By the time the doctor arrived, I appeared normal. He asked me questions and I still don't know if I subconsciously concealed my concussion by answering them or if I was actually OK at that moment and the concussion was delayed. Whatever was the case, the doctor accepted my assurances that everything was fine and passed me fit to ride the next day.

Watching this bizarre scene on television, I thought how lucky I had been. Had the doctor picked it up, I would have been stood down for seven days or longer. Secondary concussion, that is a second case of concussion soon after a first, can lead to serious problems. While there is still bruising on your brain, the slightest fall or even violent shaking of your body will bring on more concussion, or, as one of the lads once put it, 'You fall on your arse and you're away with the fairies again.'

So that night Richard Dunwoody, an averagely sane and so-called mature 25 year old, considered his situation. Another fall in the next few days could cause a serious problem. The next day, Thursday, I had a few rides at Wincanton and little chance of a winner. Friday, I had three good spins at Newbury and Saturday was Highland Bud in the Breeders' Cup at Far Hills in New Jersey. Being mature, I skipped Wincanton but returned to action at Newbury the following day where there was the prospect of another winner. My first ride back was Royal Cedar in a three-mile chase and along with John White on Solidasarock, we went like bats out of hell on lightning quick ground. Royal Cedar won by 12 lengths and broke the track record. Even though my third mount at Newbury, the John Jenkins-trained Balasani, fell and floored a massive gamble, the fall had its good side. I got up, shook myself down and was still in one piece, physically and mentally fine. I could have cheered but there was no time for it and an hour or so later I was at Heathrow checking in for a flight to New York.

Having ridden Flatterer in the Breeders' Cup two years before, I was determined to ride in the race again and was particularly keen to renew my partnership with Highland Bud whom I'd ridden when the Duke trained him for Sheikh Mohammed. I travelled out with Ronnie Beggan who was to ride Polar Pleasure, another Jonathan Sheppard runner. Twenty thousand people crammed into Far Hills, a track that resembled a point-to-point course rather than a big-race venue. The Breeders' Cup offered the biggest monetary prize I had ever competed for. On his American form, Highland Bud had an excellent chance.

Down the back on the second circuit, Ronnie and I tracked the leader. He was on the inner, I was upsides. Highland Bud was jumping well and travelling easily while Ronnie had to escape from behind the leader who was beginning to tire. As he tried to ease out, I moved slightly in to make sure he didn't. 'Oh no you don't. You're not coming out of there yet.' We bumped slightly but what I did would not have raised an eyebrow in Britain or Ireland. Round the bottom bend, I set sail and the little horse bolted up. In the back of my mind I sensed there might be a problem. The stewards in America will disqualify anyone who causes interference in a race, even at the start. There had been such a case earlier in the afternoon and I was nervous. Winning by half the track would not save Highland Bud if the stewards believed I'd broken the rules. Yet we were stable companions and I couldn't see that I had done that much out of order.

'Look Ronnie,' I said, 'look after me here.'

Ronnie asked Jonathan if he should object.

'Do what you think,' Jonathan replied. 'If you want to object, do it.'

Ronnie objected. Jonathan, I suppose, had to consider the owners of both horses and we went to a tall wooden stand beside the track and gave our accounts to the stewards. Ronnie laid it on so thick he almost had me thinking the result should be changed. It's amazing how convincing a man can sound when all those dollars are dangling in front of him. I was thinking of the dollars too, but my horse had won the race by ten lengths and Ronnie knew I had done little wrong. The ten minutes I waited for the result were about the worst ten minutes of my career. I was trembling before the announcement. Highland Bud kept the race. I kept my sanity.

As the seasons change, so too the older horses move on and are replaced by younger ones. West Tip ran another fine race to be fourth in the 1988 Grand National and then came out a year later to finish a brave second to Little Polveir and Jimmy Frost. For a few strides going to the last, I thought we might win and I again had that almost electric buzz of anticipation. What a National horse he had been. I will always believe he was on his way to victory when hitting the floor at Becher's in 1985 and then for the following four years he was never worse than fourth. When as a 13 year old in 1990 he ran in the race for the last time, I was riding the Duke's Bigsun. He was a great National horse, West Tip, but by then maybe too old, and finished out of the frame.

Kribensis was one of the talented younger brigade and I went to the 1989 Festival believing he could win the Champion Hurdle. After the disappointment of Celtic Chief the previous year, this was a chance to put that further behind us and establish Kribensis as the best hurdler of his generation. At the top of the hill, Tommy Carmody kicked on the Irish horse Condor Pan and I reacted quickly, not wanting to allow him too much leeway. It was perhaps a kneejerk reaction to Mercy Rimell's criticism the previous year but Condor Pan's challenge soon petered out, and I was in front a lot sooner than I wanted. Hywel Davies passed us on Mole Board going to the last and then Celtic Chief, Celtic Shot, Floyd, Vagador and the eventual winner Beech Road. We finished seventh, beaten 11 lengths and even though I had taken it up too early, it hadn't affected the result.

Michael Stoute, Kribensis's trainer, was a pleasure to ride for. The horse was a short-priced favourite for the Champion Hurdle and was well beaten. Michael would have been justified in saying I had made my move too soon but he is a big man and was able to see the bigger picture. The horse wasn't on his best form and, even if he had been, it is asking a lot of a five year old to carry 12 stone against the older horses and win a Champion Hurdle. Michael is meticulous about how he prepares his charges and yet when it didn't go well in that Champion Hurdle, he took it on the chin. 'We'll look to next year,' he said.

Eighty-nine was also the year of Desert Orchid's Gold Cup. Charter Party returned to the scene of his previous year's triumph and ran a noble race in deplorable conditions to be third, nine lengths behind Desert Orchid. Walking down the shute in front of the stands on the way back to the winner's enclosure, the scene was one of wild delight. Dessie was the favourite, on the bookmakers' boards and in the public imagination. Hats flew in the air, a huge cheer greeted his arrival in the winner's enclosure and everyone was happy. Back in the changing room, Kevin Mooney sat in a quiet corner and was in floods of tears. Ordinarily Kevin was one of the toughest jockeys but he had just lost his best horse, Ten Plus, a faller when in the lead at the third last in the Gold Cup. A multiple fracture to Ten Plus's near hind leg meant he had had to be put down.

As Kevin's tears flowed just inside the entrance to the

changing room, Simon Sherwood was on the other side of the room receiving congratulations.

'Buck,' Simon said to valet John Buckingham, 'can you get a case of champagne in here?' Looking at the scene, you could see how fickle a game it was. Ten Plus had been Kevin Mooney's outstanding ride, his great chance to win the blue riband of steeplechasing. For two-and-a-half miles he had done everything right and when he and Ten Plus hit the front at the top of the hill, it was going to take a great horse to pass them. Then one mistake and it was all over. Kevin Mooney went back to Lambourn that evening with no Gold Cup and no horse.

Simon Sherwood retired at the end of the 1988–89 season and I inherited Desert Orchid. For Dessie's final three seasons we were together, except on one occasion at Sandown when I had to ride Waterloo Boy and Graham Bradley took over. It was a thrill to ride a horse that had so much power and was such a favourite with the public. His extraordinary popularity had its downside, though. When I rode Dessie my performance was more closely scrutinised than ever. I never experienced any-thing like it with another horse. You really had to do everything right and not make an error because even if you won, the mistake would be what people talked about afterwards. He became public property and ordinary people regarded him as they might a family pet. The morning after the 1990 Gold Cup, in which Dessie finished an honourable third to Norton's Coin, I was sweating in the bath when the phone rang. I didn't know the voice, didn't know the woman.

'Is that Richard Dunwoody?'

'Yes.'

'What did you mean by hitting Desert Orchid yesterday?'

'We were trying to win the Gold Cup. I don't think I was hard on him.'

'You butcher. You're so cruel. How could you?'

The woman was very upset about the few smacks I gave Dessie and I pointed out that at that stage in a Gold Cup, with his blood so warm, he would hardly have noticed my use of the stick. He was a very strong and tough horse and the object of competing in the race was to give our all. But, ultimately, the woman felt I had no right to hit Desert Orchid and we were always going to end up disagreeing. We spent about ten minutes talking about it. I did manage to calm her down and the discussion at least remained polite.

I twice finished third on Dessie in the Gold Cup. Cheltenham just wasn't his track. But when I rode him at Kempton it was like a great football team playing at home. I was lucky enough to be on board for the third and fourth victories in the King George VI Chase. In the first year, he made a hell of a mistake at the first ditch second time around and the photographer Alan Johnson was blamed because he was visible on his stepladder as we approached. I don't believe Alan had anything to do with it. Dessie just launched himself at that ditch and even though he only got a little higher than the take-off board, it didn't stop him.

What was striking was how well the horse knew the course. You would encourage him to take a breather going down the back but it seemed he had already thought of that. Then as you turned for home, he would move up a gear as if he knew that from there, his kick could be sustained to the finish. Another particular memory is of the moment in the 1990 King George when Sabin du Loir fell. He led us by four or five lengths and Dessie wasn't enjoying it as he usually did. But as soon as his rival went on the floor at the first in the back straight, he perked up and began to race more keenly. He performed best when he had the centre of the stage.

When all the memories have dulled, the one that will stay vivid is of the first morning I sat on Desert Orchid. Simon Sherwood and Brendan Powell, who used to ride out with him, warned me. 'Look,' they said, 'he's keen, very keen.' It was a Sunday morning early in November 1989, and we were down at trainer David Elsworth's stables at Whitsbury in Hampshire. Television cameras had come to film Dessie's first date with his new rider and one thing was certain, the jockey was more nervous than the horse. The first thing I noticed was his neck. Compared with other horses, it was bigger, harder and gave you a sense of enormous strength. That was truly exceptional. With the reins in your hands and Dessie pulling against you, you could only harness his power. Controlling it wasn't an option.

That Sunday morning, he took off on the all-weather circuit.

Simon and Brendan hadn't been having me on. We went down one side of the gallop, up the other and after we'd done a circuit, we went back downhill before beginning to climb again. As we went up for the second time, Elsie, as David Elsworth is called, stood in the middle of the gallop and put his hand in his pocket for a Polo mint intended for Dessie. Simon had told me this would happen – Elsie would stand on the all-weather gallop, reach into his pocket and Dessie would begin to pull himself up. Pity no one had consulted the horse. Desert Orchid kept going and if Elsie hadn't moved nimbly to his left, the television cameras would have filmed a lead story.

After the all-weather gallop, we went down to the schooling fences where David had sensibly arranged for Ross Arnott to give me a lead on one of the other good chasers in the yard. There were five fences and, of course, we were flat to the boards before we got to the first. With fences in front of him, Dessie was unstoppable. He was that quick and jumped them so spectacularly, the five fences almost seemed to merge into one that he just sailed over. Thankfully, the plan was for the horse to do a bit of work after the schooling and that saved me the potential embarrassment of having to try to pull him up. He carried straight on, did his work and eventually pulled himself up. That first experience was awe-inspiring. I had gone there to school him but it felt more like I was being schooled. He was the greatest horse I rode.

Twelve days later, I rode Nicky Henderson's Remittance Man for the first time. For a horse born to jump fences, he had done well over hurdles and we actually beat Scu and Regal Ambition in a tight finish at Cheltenham a couple of months later. There were many times when Scu had the upper hand in finishes so I savoured the times when I got the better of him. He was always the target, the standard, the man to beat. It said something for Remittance Man's potential that he should have beaten Regal Ambition over hurdles as Martin Pipe's horse became the top-rated novice hurdler that season. It was coincidental that my first experiences of Desert Orchid and Remittance Man should have come in the same month because they were two outstanding horses. If asked what was the best jumper of fences I've ridden, the choice is between them. Dessie had extraordinary scope, he could take off at the wings of a fence and get as far the other side. Remittance Man was different, less raw power but a real athlete and very precise. When he jumped, he felt as if he was on springs.

Nicky Henderson further improved the quality of the horses I was riding and also increased the number of winners. At the 1990 Festival I had Desert Orchid, the short-priced favourite for the Gold Cup; Kribensis, second favourite for the Champion Hurdle and 12 other good mounts. In jump racing, a jockey's status can often be measured by his book of rides at the Cheltenham Festival.

Two years before I had been unable to sleep on the night before the Champion Hurdle but now I was more experienced; I knew where to find the sleeping pills. After the gracious manner in which Michael Stoute accepted defeat a year before, I was willing Kribensis to win as much for him as for myself. Michael had prepared the horse differently this year, giving him an extra run in the Kingwell Hurdle at Wincanton less than three weeks before the race. It worked.

He was a straightforward ride and jumped well although he could get a bit too much height at the odd one. I settled him in early on, gradually improved my position and was just behind the leaders running down the hill. Going to the second last I switched in behind Scu on Nomadic Way who I knew stayed well and wasn't going to stop. We took a lead from them almost to the last, and jumped it marginally in front. Kribensis stuck his head down and ran all the way to the line. Nomadic Way kept going to finish a good second.

After that, the meeting didn't quite live up to my hopes. Waterloo Boy ran probably the best race of his career in the Queen Mother Champion Chase but was just beaten by Barnbrook Again and Hywel Davies. Before 1990, Hywel had never ridden a winner at the Festival, which is probably why he hated it so much, but his luck changed. He won the Grand Annual Chase on Katabatic on the first day, and then our battle in the Champion Chase. The race was run at a very fast gallop and turning into the straight, it was down to Hywel and me. As I challenged on his outer, Barnbrook Again hung to his right up the run in. We straightened and in the final surge to the post, I would like to think it was Barnbrook Again's strength that made the difference. They won by half a length.

There was a stewards' enquiry and I argued that Hywel had taken us well off a true line and could have cost us the race. Although I didn't say it, I felt that the better horse had won and it would have been unfair to have taken it off him. As for Hywel, whatever chance you had of outriding him in a finish, you had none of out-talking him in the stewards' room. The result stood. We also both received what I thought were undeserved whip bans. It spoilt a fantastic race.

Desert Orchid was taken on from a long way out in the Gold Cup but ran a smashing race anyway. From the second last he couldn't find the pace of Norton's Coin and Toby Tobias. The disappointment of the horse not winning was countered by the fact that he had given everything he had. He was not only the greatest but the most competitive horse I ever sat on. Put to the task, he would give everything.

In the next race Bigsun won the Ritz Club Handicap Chase to give me my second winner of the meeting and allow me to pip Hywel for the Ritz Club's award to the most successful rider at the meeting. I felt sorry for Hywel, but only slightly.

We moved into our new house on 13 October 1989, a Friday. Carol and I had lived in Bampton since getting married in June 1988, but it had always been the plan to find a house with more space, and so that Friday, we moved into our new place in Sparsholt, near Wantage. Hyperion House, as it was called, had enormous potential but it needed time and money. Foolishly, I imagined the work could be done almost without my noticing. Give Carol the money and after a long day at the races, arrive home to find everything straightened out – that's how I thought it should be. I just didn't understand what was involved. On the day we moved, I had to go to Market Rasen for two rides, one of which won. While I was there, Brendan Powell and his then girlfriend Lorna Vincent called round to wish us well in our new home. Lorna took one look at how much had to be done and said to Carol, 'This place will be the end of you.'

That first evening I got home to Sparsholt and was disappointed. Somehow, I'd expected that things would be different and as Carol often said, I didn't like muddle. My previous house in Bampton had been new and all I needed to do was buy the furniture and the place was fine. Not so here, and though Carol was a natural homemaker and looked forward to turning it round, I hated the upheaval. After a couple of losers and a long drive home from the races, I would be pissed off to find the house like a building site.

Essentially, I was becoming more and more single-minded. Even though we were a young married couple, I began to dislike going out, and almost completely stopped going anywhere in the evenings during the week. In the end I hated going out at all. Part of the reason was that I was riding out for the Duke, Nicky Henderson, Terry Casey, John Costello, Bryan Smart, lots of people. That meant being up at 6 to 6.30 almost every day. Late nights didn't make sense and I was always tired. Once I decided that I had to ride as many winners as I could, nothing was going to get in the way. Ambition became fixation. I can trace it back to 30 December 1988, a Friday afternoon when I was scheduled to ride a couple of horses for the Duke at Newbury. Terry Casey's Celtic Barle was running in the first at Hereford and if I could be there, the ride was mine. The thought of giving up the ride on Celtic Barle, who was likely to win, was too much.

So I ordered a helicopter that would allow me to ride in the first at Hereford and get me to Newbury for the third and later races. Celtic Barle won easily. I moved swiftly, weighed in, sprinted to the chopper and as we climbed into the sky and headed east, I could see Celtic Barle and the connections just leaving the winner's enclosure. We arrived safe and in time for my rides at Newbury. Both Springholm and Highland Bud won. Two racecourses, three rides, three winners and for me, the perfect solution to a difficult situation. I wasn't bothered that chartering a helicopter to ride Celtic Barle in Hereford was in some respects daft. The race was worth £680 to the winner. With the percentage of prize money added to the riding fee, I received something around £130 for winning on Celtic Barle. The helicopter cost £350 and although the owners contributed some, it was not a profitable expedition. But this wasn't about money. It was never about money.

Another example of the ever-rising need for winners came right at the end of the 1989–90 season. It was the first time I had a chance of riding 100 winners in a season and that became a huge thing in my mind. Graham McCourt was also on for riding his first century and he too was very keen. Both of us were vying for second place in the jockeys' championship behind the runaway winner, Scu, but for Graham, it didn't much matter whether he was second or third, he just wanted his 100 winners. I wanted both but with the Duke's and Nicky's horses long gone for their summer break, I was struggling for good rides. On 99 winners, I was desperate for the 100th. I scoured the racing papers and reckoned the John Upson-trained Mandray would win at Stratford. Martin Lynch, an Irish jockey with whom I got on well, had the ride.

I rang Martin and explained how much I needed one more winner. Basically, I asked him to allow me to ride Mandray and if the horse won, he would get the jockey's percentage of the prize money. Martin was pleased that I had gone to him and not to the trainer and he agreed. I squared it with John Upson, Mandray won and I had my 100th. I am still in touch with Martin who is now back in Ireland. When recently reminded of Mandray and how much I wanted that winner, he remarked that 'there was always a reason why R. Dunwoody needed one more winner'. Graham ended that season with 100 winners, I finished with 102; both of us got what we wanted.

The pursuit of winners took over my life. I organised my travel to the courses to ensure I got there and back at the times that suited me and some days I went alone as I wouldn't wait for the others riding in later races. The disruption caused by the renovation of the house at Sparsholt antagonised me and subconsciously I blamed Carol. I didn't accept that if you changed windows in a house, redecorated, built a garage and an extension, there was going to be some inconvenience. Carol was beginning to find out I wasn't easy to live with. Our first serious row happened on a Friday evening, 24 November 1989. Seventeen months had passed since our marriage and six weeks since the move into Sparsholt. We argued and it was more serious and more intense than anything that had gone before. No matter what Carol said, I put her down.

We didn't resolve things before going to bed, didn't speak the next morning and the bad feeling festered. I went to Newbury with the row on my mind. It was Hennessy Gold Cup day and I rode the favourite, Brown Windsor. During the race I thought about the falling-out with Carol, wondering had we done the right thing moving into this house that needed so much work. I told myself to concentrate on the race, this was the Hennessy Gold Cup, the most prestigious pre-Christmas race on the calendar. Up the straight, we were up against it with Hywel who rode Ghofar. We pinged the last and got an advantage but halfway up the run-in, Brown Windsor began to tie up and wander and Hywel got up to beat us by a neck. Afterwards I was distraught, not just because I'd been beaten but because I had not been properly focused.

Carol and I made up that evening and went together to the Amateur Riders' dinner at Newbury where we had a good night. But there was one thing I had to tell her.

'During the race, I was worrying about our relationship and the row we had. I wasn't concentrating on Brown Windsor and we ended up losing by a neck. That was totally wrong. It was so unprofessional.'

From that day on, I would never let an argument with Carol affect my riding. If we disagreed about something at home, I would blank it out before I got to the races. The day after the Hennessy, I made a vow to myself. 'Yesterday you showed weakness. You will never let it happen again.'

11

NOTHING PERSONAL

In the beginning it was a sort of love affair. Devoted to the pony, I rose and fell with him, laughed and cried. I held the reins but it was he who led. When my parents told me of the move from County Down to England, I knew it would be all right. Tony was coming as well. I was eight then and it didn't really matter where we lived as long as I had my pony. But young riders grow, the pony gets too small and we move on to bigger ponies or even horses. Some of us become jockeys and end up riding racehorses morning, afternoon and evening. Over 17 seasons, I had close to 10,500 rides on maybe 3,500 different horses. It is natural, then, that the once simple bond between horse and rider becomes more complex. You can't fall in love with every animal you ride, and the joy of riding horses is overtaken by the business of riding horses. Jockeys learn that racing is a hard sport, it takes its toll. And so, like a man on a tour of one-night stands, we try to keep the emotional attachment to a minimum.

There were, of course, a few I thought the world of, grand old warriors that might not have been the quickest or the most athletic but who gave their best. That's all you ever sought. Then there were the characters, those thinkers who tried to dupe us and you got to like the odd one because of its personality. The really talented ones, it was always easier to like them. But the relationship between jockey and horse is nothing like that first boyhood love. How could it be? You spend your young life with the pony, maybe an hour a year with the racehorse.

I remember some of the times early on when a horse I was riding suffered a fatal injury. I would wait for the vet to arrive and hold the poor animal until it was put out of its misery. The walk back to the weighing room was miserable, saddle under one arm, the horse's bridle in the other hand. The part I hated was meeting the stablelass on her way to the scene of the fall. She saw the bridle and never needed to ask. The tears always followed and there was nothing you could say. That horse was part of her life but, for you, there was the next race and it wasn't good to spend too long thinking.

So, as time goes on, the jockey learns to get away from the stricken horse as soon as help arrives, and detach himself from the upset. There were even some horses that were difficult rides, uncooperative, a few downright dangerous, and when one of them met an untimely end, you thought it was a case of good riddance – 'at least they won't get one of us now'.

As jockeys, we all know and have ridden against colleagues who have been killed or seriously injured riding horses. I think of Philip Barnard, Jayne Thompson, Michael Blackmore, Richard Davis, Vivien Kennedy who all died as a result of falls; and of Shane Broderick, Sam Berry, Nigel Coleman, Sharon Murgatroyd, Rebecca Hewitt, Jessica Charles-Jones, John Cardon and Scott Taylor who have suffered injuries that will severely affect them for the rest of their lives. The worst days in the weighing room are when news filters through of serious injury to one of your colleagues. Even this we must soon blank from our minds and carry on. I remember the day in Fairyhouse when Shane Broderick was so badly hurt at the last ditch down from Ballyhack; flying to Southwell and hearing the news of Declan Murphy's terrible head injuries back at Haydock; and the afternoon in Perth when Scott had his awful fall. The mood in the weighing room was bleak and still we carried on.

Over the 17 seasons of my career, about 70 horses that I rode were killed or had to be put down following falls. It averaged out at four, maybe five, each season and inevitably some of the most talented horses never realised their potential. What might Mighty Mogul, Thetford Forest and The Proclamation have achieved had they been given the chance? Tragically, other high-class horses died prematurely but got the opportunity to show how good they were – One Man, Sound Man and others. But it is the ones who go before they reach their prime that you lament even more. Mighty Mogul began the 1992–93 season as a handicap hurdler, but by Christmas he was short-priced favourite to win the Champion Hurdle. In his final prep race at Cheltenham, I pulled him up lame after jumping the third last and he had to be put down within a week. He could have made it to the very top.

In terms of raw ability The Proclamation was also right up there with the best. But he was a keen, almost manic horse who ran on his nerves. I first sat on him at the Punchestown festival in 1989 in the big two-mile novice hurdle when Paddy Prendergast Jr was training him in Ireland. He was incredibly strong but won in good style. He was owned by Michael Buckley and the following season moved to Lambourn to be trained by Nicky Henderson. He went novice chasing immediately and won easily first time out at Ascot. Next time at the same course we decided to hold him up and get him to settle. Maybe we were foolish to believe we could tame such a wilful beast. That day he was more wound up than ever. I tucked him in behind the leader and tried to persuade him to relax. All he wanted to do was fight me and even though he wasn't concentrating on measuring his fences, he accelerated as soon as he saw one. Powerful, headstrong and aggressive, he never gave himself a chance. We left Ascot that evening with one less good horse. The notes I wrote were succinct – 'Tracked leader, blitzed second, fell fourth, broke back, dead.'

If only The Proclamation had had the head to go with the talent. I felt particularly sorry for Michael Buckley who had been largely responsible for me being offered the job with Nicky. Sadly, two of Michael's best horses, The Proclamation and Mutare, were both killed at Ascot. He deserved better.

Luck is such a big factor in racing. If you walk away without serious injury after a long career, you've been one of the lucky ones. How many times are we fired into the ground and knocked senseless with no guarantee that we'll come round? More than any of us wish to recall. From all of the near misses, there is one that stands like a lighthouse in my memory. It was a February afternoon in 1992 at Ludlow. Twelve days before the

Cheltenham Festival, the most important thing was to leave Ludlow in one piece.

Tug of Gold, a handicap chaser trained by David Nicholson, was my first ride. We took the lead jumping the trappy third last, were headed at the final fence but he gallantly got back in front on the run-in. It was an all or nothing finish – head down, driving with my right arm, waving the stick in my left and going to win. Then, not far from the post, I felt my horse falter slightly and heard the crowd screaming. Unknown to me, a riderless horse, Ben Ledi, was racing towards us and a collision looked inevitable. Eventually I sensed something was wrong and lifted my head. Ben Ledi was about 20 yards away and making directly towards us at over 30 m.p.h. With one hand on the reins and the other in the air, there was no time to do anything. I braced myself for the impact.

At the last second Tug of Gold took evasive action. It was the most brilliant sidestep I've ever experienced – Barry John and Phil Bennett, the great Welsh fly-halves, rolled into one. Tug of Gold at the very least saved me from serious injury and, eight years later, I am still grateful.

Afterwards people remarked how ashen-faced I was. One of the things that unnerved me was the thought that if I had lifted my head a few seconds earlier and had the time to get my hands on the reins, I could have pulled Tug of Gold right into Ben Ledi's path. Tug of Gold, acting instinctively, had produced the neatest, deftest manoeuvre you have ever seen. The swerve cost him a couple of lengths and Ronans Birthday, ridden by Chris Maude, got up to beat us in a close finish. We were unlucky to lose but lucky to be alive.

The worst falls I've seen have happened in this way. On more than one occasion it has occurred at Sedgefield and the collision has been sickening. Horses have been killed and jockeys very badly hurt.

Less than two weeks later, Tug of Gold, partnered by Marcus Armytage, won the Kim Muir Challenge Cup at the Cheltenham Festival. No horse deserved it more.

I tried for the most part to keep my emotions on a tight rein. If you didn't get high on the good days, you were better protected on the bad days. More Lester Piggott than Frankie Dettori, I played everything down. Whatever you say, say nothing, was once the prevailing advice in Northern Ireland and I understand the sentiment. I enjoyed the lads' company but there were times when I preferred to sit with the *Racing Post* and concentrate on the job in hand. They were friends but they were also rivals and on the racecourse, business came first. The part that came easily to me was channelling all my energy into the pursuit. Once I truly committed myself to something, the commitment was total.

It was always the same for me. At school it was examinations and I had to study hard. When my weight was a potential problem I dieted manically – not a man for half-measures. In my early days at Captain Tim Forster's, I needed rides and frantically made phone call after phone call to owners and trainers whom I had never met. Then as my career began to take off, winners became the be-all and end-all. Each season's total had to be greater than the last until, eventually, the winners put me on the trail of the jockeys' championship. Each level brought with it greater demands but I never minded that. The higher you climbed, the thinner the air. No matter how hard I pushed myself, I didn't mind if next season I had to push myself further. What was I prepared to do? Whatever it took.

The ambition worked best when it was narrow and focused. Distractions had to be eliminated, things that softened my attitude had to be avoided and, ultimately, all that mattered was the next winner. Celebrating successes didn't interest me, reviewing good rides was generally a waste of time but if something went wrong, I tortured myself with the video. I had to know how and why we'd lost. Carol says that one of her abiding memories of our marriage was the sound of the video recorder rewinding. For days after the 1996 Champion Hurdle, I re-ran a video recording of the race many, many times as I worked out how it had gone wrong. I froze the picture, went forward frame by frame, measured how far behind we were at the third last, then the second last and finally the last. Basically, I had to know if I had given the horse too much to do. Despite what the trainer Kim Bailey believed, I actually hadn't fallen asleep and the video showed what I felt throughout the race, namely that Alderbrook had not been the horse he was the year before.

When Nicky Henderson offered me a retainer to ride his best horses in 1989, it put me in a very strong position. As well as being stable jockey for the Duke, I was also top jockey for one of his rivals. The Duke wouldn't have been enthusiastic about the arrangement but while I always tried to be diplomatic and accepted that compromise was inevitable, there was a point beyond which he couldn't push me. Had the Duke said, 'No, you can't ride for Nicky,' we might have seen where that point lay. There were also going to be questions in the weighing room when some jockeys would lose rides on horses they thought should have been theirs. I had to remain immune because if I worried about it, I'd be less inclined to go after the best rides. Had someone accused me of being ruthless, which they didn't, at least not to my face, I would have said it was a ruthless business.

One weekend in December 1990, we had Cheltenham on the Friday but then were snowed off on the Saturday. On that day, Nicky had a couple of horses running at Lingfield that John White was due to ride. John worked for him and was a great horseman. Under the terms of the deal I had with Nicky that year, I was stable jockey. So that Saturday morning, I rang him.

'With Cheltenham off, Nicky, I'd like to ride at Lingfield.'

'You're the stable jockey. That's fine. I want you to go down and ride Pendennis but John will ride the other.'

'I'd like to ride Sparkling Flame too.'

'No. John has ridden him a lot at home and I can't take him off.'

I liked John but I was very unhappy that I wasn't riding the two. John and I did a lot of schooling together at Nicky's and we got on well but if I didn't go after those rides I wasn't doing my job. I was taking the soft option. Sure, it was tough on John if I took over but I didn't make apologies. The bottom line was that trainers and owners decided who rode their horses and if someone felt hard done by, there was no point in coming to me.

There were, of course, times when I sensed resentment in the weighing room. On the morning of the 1993 Gold Cup, Another Coral was lame in his box and the Duke decided to pull him out. That left me without a ride in the race. I had been speaking with Martin Pipe on and off over the previous three weeks

A bad day at the office. End of the first day at the 1993 Cheltenham Festival – one fall, two winners missed and a couple of hours in the sauna to do 10st 1lb for an unplaced ride in the last. *(Gerry Cranham)*

Plenty of room for improvement – Game Trust carries me over the last at
Cheltenham in May 1983 to give me my first winner under National Hunt rules.
(Bernard Parkin)

Tracking Chris Grant on Young Driver at the last in the 1986 Seagram Grand
National. Steve Smith Eccles and Classified are back in third. *(Gerry Cranham)*

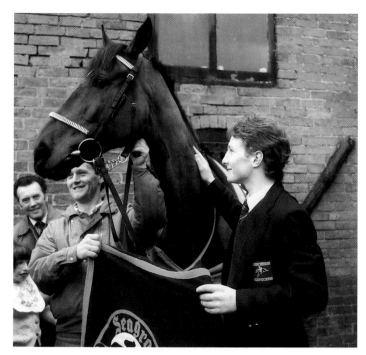

At Michael Oliver's after the 1986 Seagram Grand National with West Tip and Andy Easton. I don't think I'd taken the team blazer off since our trip to America in June 1985. *(Les Hurley)*

At our wedding in July 1988 in Oxfordshire. West Tip makes another guest appearance.

On the 'banana' in Zante, Greece, June 1988. Left to right: Nick Deacon, me, Paul Croucher, Martin Bosley, Jamie Osborne, Marcus Armytage, Dave Deacon, Ray White, Sarah Whitaker and Tarnya Davis, Paul's girlfriend at the time. Just over a month later Paul was killed in a car crash.

With David 'the Duke' Nicholson after winning the 1988 Cheltenham Gold Cup on Charter Party. The Duke had taken to wearing a red jumper to match his lucky socks. *(John Crofts Photography)*

With Nigel Day, Marcus Armytage and John Francome after my first polo match, against the trainers near Newmarket, in September 1991. It is a brilliant sport, especially on board an international horse as I was that day.

Waterloo Boy flies the last alongside Sabin Du Loir and Scu in the 1989 Arkle Challenge Trophy. The main threat to us came from out-of-shot Southern Minstrel and Chris Grant.

My Ultimate Driving Machine – Highland Bud clears the last on the way to providing me with my most profitable win to date when taking the Breeders' Cup Chase at Far Hills, New Jersey, in October 1989.

Kribensis comes up with me at the wings in the 1989 Top Rank Christmas Hurdle. Graham McCourt is upsides on Osric. I enjoyed reminding him of the race. *(Gerry Cranham)*

Desert Orchid pops the water alongside Solidasarock and Luke Harvey in the 1990 Racing Post Chase. I always felt it was his best performance while I was riding him – we were giving Delius (in black colours behind us) two stone. *(George Selwyn)*

Catching up with the form at Stratford in 1998.

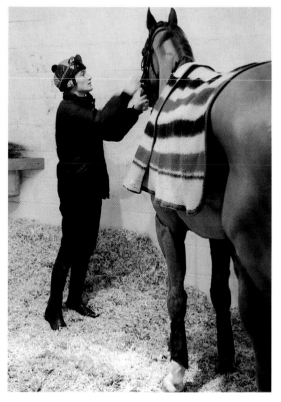

Despite what some people might say I could put a bridle on – tacking up Wonderman at the Duke's in 1992.
(Gerry Cranham)

Miinnehoma on his knee at Becher's in the Martell Grand National in 1994. And I thought they should never have levelled off the drop! *(Gerry Cranham)*

Hands off, Martin, it's mine! Raising the jockey's trophy after Miinnehoma's 1994 National success. *(George Selwyn)*

because he had wanted me to ride his second string, Rushing Wild. He knew there was a doubt about Another Coral making it, though when it seemed he would, Martin booked his second jockey, Jonothan Lower. His name was alongside Rushing Wild's in the morning papers but as soon as we heard the news I told Robert to ring Martin and ask for the ride.

Martin jocked off Jonothan and Rushing Wild gave me one of my most exhilarating rides in the race. He made most of the running, took the fences in his stride and lengthened from the top of the hill. Jodami, the winner, ranged alongside turning in but we were the only ones to make a race of it. Jonothan woke up that day looking forward to a ride in arguably our most prestigious race and by breakfast, he was without one. There wouldn't have been too many of the lads in the weighing room cheering us on.

In the same way, One Man didn't have too many supporters in there when starting favourite for the 1996 Gold Cup. One Man had been Tony Dobbin's ride, injury allowing, until the owner John Hales asked me to become his rider. Tony had done little wrong on the horse and many would say didn't deserve to be replaced. But once I was asked, I couldn't say no. The northern lads particularly would have felt for Tony and you can be sure they weren't shouting for One Man. I don't think they held me responsible. If some did, then that's life, but on occasions I'd also lost rides and believed each one to be fair game. If there was resentment, I couldn't let it get to me.

To understand how much each and every ride meant to me, consider Acre Hill at Newton Abbot in May 1992. That afternoon I had been at Hereford and won the sixth race on Tinryland for Nicky Henderson. It was about 12 minutes after five o'clock when I weighed in and if I could get to Newton Abbot before 7.30, I would take the ride on Acre Hill who had a walk-over in the handicap chase. Johnny Kavanagh was down to ride him but as he was one of Nicky's, I was entitled to it provided I could be there on time. Horses with a walk-over, that is, having no opponents, must still show up and canter past the stands, and the jockey must weigh in afterwards. Hywel Davies came with me from Hereford. I had to be quick and coming down a hill on the A312, I spotted a police car in the distance and slowed down. They still pulled me over. I had been doing 102 m.p.h. Down at Newton Abbot, the lads had little sympathy. Served me right for taking a winner off Johnny. But it was one more on the scoreboard.

There wasn't time, nor any inclination, to worry about what others thought. I had to work non-stop to keep the Duke and Nicky happy and I had to deal with a marriage that was beginning to founder. Maybe because it was racing that truly mattered to me at this time, I handled my rival guv'nors better than I coped with the problems in my relationship with Carol. During the first season of the arrangement with the Duke and Nicky, the Duke was in charge and Nicky used me whenever it was feasible. That was the 1989–90 campaign. The following season, Nicky had better horses and the deal was more 50–50, he and the Duke having almost equal rights. I say almost because the Duke was the Duke, if he didn't get what he wanted, there was trouble. But there was a pragmatic side to him, he understood that Nicky had a very good team of horses and to take on Scu I needed to ride them as well.

Throughout, I tried to be diplomatic. Nicky would tell me where he intended running his best horses and I would suggest changes based on where I felt the Duke would be going with his. Then Nicky would ask me to encourage the Duke to run his horses at meetings that allowed me to ride for both. Of course that was to my advantage but it was hard approaching the Duke with too many requests. 'Why don't you speak to the Duke your-self?' I would say to Nicky, but they would rarely communicate with each other. It was like a chess game where the pawn was trying to control the kings. And, to be fair, there were times when they ran horses to suit me. I was lucky to be in that situation.

I was less able when it came to dealing with the difficulties in our marriage. There were lots of good times. In the summer of 1990, we went to America with Aiden Murphy, Anabel King and Michael 'Corky' Caulfield and had a terrific time. During the stay we visited Useppa Island where John F. Kennedy supposedly liaised with Marilyn Monroe, and the romance between us blossomed as strongly as ever. Soon after that, we went on our own to the Portuguese island of Madeira. It seemed that when-ever we could get away from racing and I stepped off the treadmill, things between us were fine. Carol and I have talked about it and we both agree the pressures of the jockey's life cannot be blamed solely for our break-up. They just made the situation far worse. I'm not sure any woman could have lived with me during the years that were about to follow.

It was sad that as the house at Sparsholt began to come together, the cracks widened in our marriage. Carol had devoted a lot of time and energy to the house and turned it into a lovely home. It was spacious inside, had three boxes at the back where we could keep horses and it was set in beautiful surroundings. Once I tried to become domesticated and began to cut the lawns and trim the edges but it wasn't me. I hated it. Peter Terry, a sports psychologist whom I visited from autumn 1993 onwards, considered me 'a sensation-seeker, addicted to speed and danger'. The lawn-mower and the strimmer just didn't do it for me.

Three years before, I had decided that my messing days were over and proposed to Carol. How little I knew myself. Fidelity was like the lawn-mower, it didn't work for me. It was very tough for Carol. She could see that with success, things changed in my life. Women were attracted to a successful jockey and I was not exactly discouraging the attention. In a way it is part of horse-racing's culture. At the jockeys' dance, the majority flirted with everyone except their spouses. A lot of jockeys live on the edge and when they circulate in normal society, they find it hard to play by the rules.

It comes back to the essence of our lives – every day we risk our necks and in a way, we are attracted to the danger. Many of us could not leave that part of ourselves in the weighing room. On 5 March 1991, exactly a week before Cheltenham, I went to Warwick and, pre-occupied with choosing my Festival rides, I was feeling the pressure. I rode Shamana for the Duke in the first race and then didn't have rides until the seventh and eighth races. Spending three hours with nothing to do in the weighing room at Warwick races didn't appeal, so I arranged a discreet meeting with a girl in a nearby hotel. As I tried to slip quietly out to the car park, I bumped into Shamana's owner, Lord Northampton.

'Ah, Richard, where are you off to?'

'Just off, ah, to do a bit of shopping,' I replied, producing what may have been the most feeble lie of my life. Checking into the hotel, hoping no one would recognise me, I made off for the room. The encounter was swift, it had to be, and I returned in time for the last two races. A good horse of Nicky's, Everaldo, was expected to win the finale. He started 5 to 4 favourite in a 23-runner maiden hurdle and fell at the first. Either my mind wasn't properly focused or the gods were telling me something. My rationalisation was straightforward – in the week before Cheltenham I was feeling the strain; I had to have something else, some risk, to drag my mind away from the sport. It may have been some sort of explanation for my behaviour but it certainly didn't excuse it.

By now our friends Aiden and Anabel, Corky, Richard Phillips, Martin and Sarah Bosley and Mel Fordham were concerned about our relationship and discreetly tried to help us. What was obvious, I think, to everyone was that Carol was blameless for the deteriorating state of it. Once Mel Fordham came round to our place and tried to convince me of what I had – a beautiful home, no financial worries, devoted friends and everything to live for. Mel turned to me and said, 'Richard, that woman standing there would do anything in the world for you. Very few people ever find someone like that.' And Carol and I would try to make things right. On the rocky road to break-up, there was some fun, too – an evening at the cinema, three days in Paris, four days in Vienna. Any trip that took us far away from racecourses had a chance.

Having edged out Graham McCourt for second place in the 1989–90 jockeys' championship, it occurred to me that if Peter Scudamore had a mishap, I might be the one to benefit. Three months into the following season, Scu went to Market Rasen to ride Black Humour for Charlie Brooks. Black Humour fell at the fifth hurdle, Scu remained in the saddle too long and broke his left leg. It was 9 November, he had 54 winners at that point, I had 37 and there was the certainty that he would not ride for at least two months. I didn't allow myself to believe it gave me a chance. I knew he would get back sooner rather than later and even though November, December and January were busy months, he would have plenty of time to make up whatever he lost.

So rather than concentrate on the battle with Scu, I focused on the class horses that I had to ride, the aim being to better last seasons 102 winners. Remittance Man was setting out on his chasing career, Desert Orchid was preparing for his fourth consecutive victory in the King George VI Chase and for me to start focusing on the championship would be asking for trouble. In racing, you don't need to tempt Fate. It happens anyway. Christmas at Kempton was extremely profitable; Sparkling Flame, who had now become my ride, and Remittance Man won the two novice chases and Desert Orchid was brilliant in the King George. The good run continued through the last week of the year. Then on New Year's Day Mulloch Brae absolutely buried me at Cheltenham. At the first ditch in a two-and-a-half mile chase, she dragged her hind feet, caught the take-off board, her head went up, her hind quarters went into the fence and she torpedoed me into the ground. The force of the impact cracked some of my teeth. Happy New Year.

Medical people say that if you hit the ground at a particular angle, you break your neck. I probably deserved it for the way I was behaving at home and in over 600 falls that was the closest I got. My neck was very sore, I was badly concussed and I accepted the need for the ten-day rest stipulated by the racecourse doctor. Mulloch Brae wasn't my favourite mount that evening but three months later she would be my 100th winner of the season. Scu returned to action on 24 January, a little over ten weeks after breaking his leg and by then I led by 20. With Martin Pipe's strong team in April and May, I didn't give myself much of a chance. It developed into a skirmish rather than a full-blooded battle. It was right to be pessimistic.

The Festival came and went, promising more than it delivered. Remittance Man proved his class in the Arkle Challenge Trophy and sprinted right away from Uncle Ernie on the run to the last to give me a perfect start to the meeting. Then Nomadic Way ran a cracking race, leading Morley Street into the straight in the Champion Hurdle before again finishing runner-up. But, for me, that was the end of the good news. Even though second again in the Champion Chase, Waterloo Boy was beaten seven lengths by Katabatic. A problem with his wind had worsened and affected his performance. Desert Orchid ran very bravely in the Gold Cup. At the top of the hill he was out of gas and I thought we may even have to pull up but the old horse, now 12, kept going and won the race for third behind the two principals, Garrison Savannah and The Fellow. When a horse runs as honestly as Dessie did that day, you admire him as much as, if not more than, on the days he won. Thirteen rides at the Festival and just one winner, I would have left Cheltenham feeling a bit down. Not for a second could I admit to that, though, because I'd had one winner when so many others went away empty-handed. But you build yourself up for the meeting, you choose what you believe are 13 good rides and you're thinking two or three winners. As I left the course on Thursday evening, Remittance Man's race in the Arkle on Tuesday seemed a long way away.

Liverpool was better. I won on Aquilifer for Martin Pipe and then on Nicky's Sparkling Flame. At this stage I was more comfortable with my riding than I had ever been and felt I did well enough on Aquilifer to beat Norton's Coin and Graham McCourt. Revenge, though, is sweet and Graham had it when Norton's Coin and Waterloo Boy met at Cheltenham a few weeks later. It was one of the most unusual steeplechases ever to be run – a four-runner race over two-and-a-half miles. The Duke told me to be the last to challenge. Jamie Railton made the pace on Pegwell Bay but went so sedately, we were hardly out of a canter. I waited for Graham to make his move, he waited for me. Knowing Norton's Coin well, I felt it could be the wrong tactics but the Duke had been adamant, and so both of us sat without twitching a muscle all the way to the last fence. We jumped it in unison and fairly sprinted from there. In the history of racing at Cheltenham I don't imagine two chasers ever surged up the hill to the line faster than we did. It was Graham's turn to brandish a toothless grin. Norton's Coin won by a head.

I stayed ahead of Scu until 26 April, five weeks before the end of the season. But the fight for the title effectively ended the previous day at Wincanton where I partnered Ron Hodges' chaser Came Down. We led going into the last but I wasn't as

tight to the wings as I should have been and there was enough
room for Kevin Mooney on Kilbrittain Castle to push up on the
inside. The rail after the last jutted in towards us and when my
horse jumped right-handed, Kevin was squeezed for room and
his horse lost momentum. Still we won easily by two and a half
lengths and though there was a stewards' enquiry, we held on to
the race. That, I thought, was the correct decision but Colonel
Whitbread and Cath Walwyn, owner and trainer of Kilbrittain
Castle, appealed to the stewards of the Jockey Club at Portman
Square. I had ridden for both and pleaded with them not to,
knowing that a suspension would cost me whatever chance
there was of winning the championship. Kilbrittain Castle was a
15 year old, he had been a great servant and this was his last
race. The connections were keen that he ended his illustrious
career with a win.

The appeal went ahead and even though the Wincanton
stewards and stipendiaries were on my side, the Jockey Club
upheld the appeal, the result was reversed and I was given a
five-day ban. The championship race ended. It devastated me
because I felt other forces were at work. Our case was heard
after the appeal by the connections of Cahervillahow against
his disqualification in the Whitbread Gold Cup. I felt the
Sandown stewards were wrong to demote Cahervillahow and
award the race to Docklands Express. Many racing people
shared that view. But the Jockey Club backed the racecourse
stewards and Docklands Express kept the race. I feared then
that the Jockey Club would want to prove they were prepared
to overturn the decision of their local stewards and I believe
we were the victims of that. Trouble often arises with racing's
system of justice and what I remember from that episode was
the friendship between the Jockey Club chief steward and
Kilbrittain Castle's connections. I also thought that he didn't
much care for me. Of course, there is no suggestion that this
affected the findings of the committee but when you're a
jockey, it is easy to feel the odds are stacked against you.

Newspapers carried the story that I accepted that the
championship race was over. I had spent several days agonis-
ing over a further appeal and those headlines destroyed me.
Good advice indicated that it would be futile to visit Portman

Square again. Of course I didn't accept that the race was over –
the stewards had forced me out of it. I ended with 127, 14
behind Scu's 141 winners. It was by far my biggest tally but the
title remained a long way off. Scu had broken a leg and still
beaten me.

For the following season, 1991–92, I tried to settle for the
attainable again and concentrate on improving on my total.
The retainers with the Duke and Nicky meant there would
always be plenty of good horses, so I had to stay focused on
keeping the volume of winners high. It went well. Another Coral
won the Mackeson Gold Cup at Cheltenham after a gripping
duel with the Irish-trained Toranfield and his young jockey
Adrian Maguire. It was Adrian's first season in England and it
was clear that he had precocious talent and a fierce will to
win. That battle for the Mackeson was our first serious rendezvous but there would be many more.

That Christmas, Desert Orchid tried to win his fifth King
George VI and even though Remittance Man might have had
the better chance, I couldn't forsake the grey horse. We had
twice won the King George but my favourite memory at
Kempton was his performance when carrying top weight in
the 1990 Racing Post Chase. That day he was brilliant. His leap
at the second last was out of this world. Jamie Osborne got the
ride on Remittance Man and for Christmas, to keep his mind
on the job, I sent him a tape of the Queen and David Bowie
hit 'Under Pressure'. As it turned out, neither of us won. Dessie
just didn't have it any more and fell heavily at the third last
after I unwisely lengthened him into it. Remittance Man didn't
stay the three miles. I was reunited with Remittance Man for
the Arlington Chase at Newbury in February and later that
afternoon rode Waterloo Boy in the Game Spirit Chase. Both
horses won impressively and there was a chance they would
clash in the Queen Mother Champion Chase.

Hardly had I slid off Waterloo Boy when the Duke said,
'You're going to ride mine in the Champion Chase.' We weren't
sure if Remittance Man would even go for the two-mile race so
I tried to evade the issue. 'Yeah, OK, maybe,' I said. Had we
known at the time that Remittance Man would be running, I
might still have gone for Waterloo Boy as Nicky's horse wasn't

proven against the 'big boys' at two miles. The Duke played it cleverly by using every opportunity to remind people that I had committed myself to his horse. At times like that, you understood why he was called The Duke.

You wouldn't have had to be a fortune teller to work out the ending to this little tale. Remittance Man with Jamie on board won the race that I wanted to win more than any other, barring the Grand National, but never did. That wasn't the end of it. New York Rainbow was my choice in the Supreme Novices' Hurdle and Flown was left for Jamie. Corky Browne, the head lad at Henderson's, told me I was mad. I was. Flown flew, New York Rainbow finished fourth. Then in the Stayers' Hurdle, Jamie won on another of my rides, Nomadic Way, because Nicky insisted on me riding Rustle. I tried to get off Rustle but he reminded me a good retainer was being paid and I couldn't have it both ways. He was right and Jamie rode three of the first four winners on the opening day of the Festival. He ended up riding five, three of which were mine. What had Jamie done to deserve so much generosity?

Thetford Forest and Montelado were winners for me, so it wasn't a bad meeting. Again, Liverpool was better. Although Jamie had won the Champion Chase on Remittance Man, Nicky repaid my loyalty at Cheltenham and I was reunited with the horse for Aintree. He was one of my four winners. The Duke's Carobee, a brilliant horse who never fulfilled his potential due to leg problems, won the first race of the meeting and I enjoyed another fantastic spin over the big fences when riding The Antartex in the John Hughes Memorial. He won at 33 to 1, bravely hanging on up the lengthy run-in. Remittance Man and Morley Street picked up two of the more valuable races on Friday and Saturday. With Remittance Man the pressure was back on me. Had I made a semblance of an error I might not have been given the leg-up again as Jamie had got on with him so well at Cheltenham. Fortunately, I didn't but I did on Morley Street. He was running away with me at the second last in the Aintree Hurdle and I let him cruise to the front well before the last – big mistake. He tied up badly on the furlong and a half run-in, treading water in the closing stages to hang on from Minorettes Girl at whom Tony Mullins had thrown everything bar the kitchen sink. Four winners, leading rider at the meeting – could it have been better? In racing, it can always be better.

In the three days there were also six crashing falls, from Shamana, Calabrese, Gambling Royal, King of the Lot and my last two rides at the meeting, Brown Windsor in the National and Thetford Forest in a novice hurdle. Travelling well to Becher's first time, Brown Windsor jumped to his left, collided with another horse in mid-air and came down. He was wearing blinkers for the first time, had very little lateral vision and just wasn't aware of the horse on his inside. Worse was to follow as Thetford Forest fell at the third hurdle in his race, injured a leg and later had to be destroyed at the local veterinary hospital. It was a terribly sad end to such an up and down meeting. Though I could barely walk from the course on that Saturday evening, the only thing that concerned me was that I be passed fit for Ascot the following Wednesday.

I made Ascot and made it to the end of the 1991–92 season with 137 winners and though almost 40 behind Scu, I was a clear second and determined that one day I would win the jockeys' championship. The skirmish of 1990–91 had whetted my appetite for something more serious and now I had improved on that. One hundred and thirty seven winners – how many more did I need before I seriously worried Scu? Like a shark that sensed blood in the water, I was homing in on the title.

12

THE KING AND I

I f I had a hero in the weighing room, it was Peter Scudamore. People talk now about how fast A.P. McCoy accumulates winners, how he will leave the sport with a heavily rewritten record book and it is wholly impressive. A.P. is an extraordinary jockey and, in terms of attitude, not unlike Scu. But I was weaned on Scu's hardness. In the weighing room of my youth, he was the epitome of the great jockey. It is hard to admit somebody else might be better. For as long as he was there, Scu set the standard. To beat him, you had to need winners as badly as he did. Losing had to hurt you as much as it did him and you had to be just as dedicated. What I became was just a dream of him.

There is a hierarchy in the weighing room and it can be traced by the position of the pegs used by each man. The senior and most successful jockeys get the top pegs. Steve Smith Eccles and Scu had the No.1 and No.2 pegs. As I began to ride more winners, I moved up the pecking order. By the early nineties, I was changing close to Scu, sometimes alongside him and at other times two pegs away. The closer we got in the championship, the closer we were in the weighing room. At the beginning of the 1992–93 season, the championship was *the* ambition in my life. Second to Scu for three consecutive years, it was time to put aside my admiration and see if there was any way he could be dethroned.

He still rode for Martin Pipe who, in an average year, trained more than twice the number of winners of his nearest rival. That gave Scu a significant advantage over the rest of us but I was now desperate to get even closer than I had in the past. In the early months of the new season, Scu wasn't the man of old. He was still competitive and professional but not as driven as before. Little things added up to something greater. A novice chase and a horse that he could have ridden would have another jockey's name where his should have been; another time, he would return to the weighing room vexed because his horse hadn't won, swear and say, 'What's happening here?' and although it was normal for him to be upset, this was different. It wasn't just anger but frustration, tinged with a little resignation. Later Scu would say he just wasn't as brave at 34 as he had been at 24.

There were other factors. Martin's horses weren't running that well and some of the pressure that comes when a big stable is going through a lean time was being transferred to the jockey. Not long after, I experienced the difficulties of riding for M.C. Pipe when the stable wasn't performing and then I knew what Scu had gone through. Pressure like that chips away at your enthusiasm and Scu wasn't enjoying it. We would talk about things. He was president of the Jockeys Association, I was on the committee and we were both striving to improve the jockeys' lot. Occasionally, I would rib him about the championship. 'I'm going to get you this year, Scu,' I'd say. 'We'll see,' he would reply, but you could tell that his heart wasn't in it the way it had been a couple of years previously. But while he was still riding, he was competing and that meant hiding all of the inner turmoil from his rivals in the weighing room.

Although I suspected Scu wasn't as happy as before, it didn't please me. There was too much respect for that, and years of trying to match his intensity had made me mentally hard. Had I believed Scu was on the way out, I may have taken my foot off the accelerator. Instead, I drew encouragement from his disenchantment. 'Scu is going through a lean time, you've got a chance this season, you've got to make the most of it,' I'd think. But I never truly believed he would retire. He had been champion for seven consecutive years and even though I led by ten or 12 for most of that season, the lead was nothing. If Scu rediscovered his old hunger or Martin's horses hit top form, the positions in the jockeys' championship would quickly change. I kept thinking that no matter what, he would catch me in the end. To believe Scu was gone, I needed to see him laid out, his eyes closed and a stake driven through his heart!

November was extraordinary. Through a very competitive month in the National Hunt season, it rained winners for me – 33 in 26 days of racing and by the end of that month I had ridden my highest ever total for that time of the season, 61. On the first Saturday in November, I went to Chepstow to ride five horses, two for the Duke, two for Nicky Henderson and the fifth for Kim Bailey. They were all good rides and in the sauna that morning, checking each race in the *Racing Post*, I reckoned all five had good chances. Two out of five would have been acceptable, three would have been a very good day and four a dream. Freeline Finishing, Mighty Mogul, Shahdjat, Travelling Wrong and Thumbs Up all won and my one-winner deficit on Scu turned into a four-winner advantage. As early as this was in the campaign, it was significant. A message had been sent to Scu – this was going to be a long winter.

To everyone else in the weighing room, mine was an enviable position. Before the season began my retainers had been renegotiated with the Duke and Nicky to ensure that, ultimately, I decided which horses I rode. If Remittance Man and Waterloo Boy clashed in the Queen Mother Champion Chase again, the choice would be mine. The important change was that the Duke had to accept that Nicky now had an equal claim on my services. With the pick from two outstanding yards, I was certain to win a fair share of the more valuable races. As well as that, I had built up relationships with a lot of smaller trainers who, along with the Duke and Nicky, would help me to compete against Scu in the numbers game. It wasn't just the Duke, Nicky and the others in Britain, there was also the association with Jonathan Sheppard in America. In the middle of October, I slipped away to New York for the weekend, won my second Breeders' Cup Chase on Highland Bud at Belmont Park on the Saturday and was back in England for Fontwell on Monday.

That second win in the Breeders' Cup was an impressive

testimony to Jonathan Sheppard's ability as a trainer. Highland Bud had been off injured for most of the past two seasons but Jonathan nursed him back patiently and had him spot on at Belmont on the day. After the Breeders' Cup, November brought that avalanche of winners.

It was not, however, a coincidence that as my career soared, my marriage plummeted. That summer I had ridden in Ireland, one week at the beginning of July, another week at the end of the month and in part I was staying there because I didn't want to be at home. I rode at Bellewstown for two days, made the journey south for one ride at Wexford and remained in Ireland for two rides at Roscommon three days later. Whenever I got home, Carol would be there and even though I sensed her disappointment, there were no recriminations. She wasn't that kind of woman.

We spent our customary weekend in Jersey, staying with owner Paul Green and his wife Jenny, and rode at Les Landes racetrack. Carol and I actually rode in the same race for Paul but neither of us managed to make the frame. The few days in Jersey went well for us both, as it invariably did. It didn't seem to matter how things were beforehand, once we were there, they improved. But back with the unrelenting grind of the National Hunt season, the strains in our relationship resurfaced. Disagreements over the smallest things flared into full-scale rows and even though Carol had no desire for conflict, she couldn't escape it. I don't regret anything about my career, in fact there is little in my life that I would change, but I deeply regret how I treated Carol and what she went through before our marriage ended. We remain friends but nothing that I say or do will properly make up for what happened in the past. I never needed to ask for Carol's forgiveness because it was always there. She knows how difficult it was to live with me during the bad years and, better than anyone else, she also understands how troubled and immature I was.

There is a line in Oliver Goldsmith's poem 'The Deserted Village' about the relationship between the schoolchildren and their master and how they knew full well the day's disasters in his morning face. On a run-of-the-mill afternoon in October or January or April, Carol would keep an eye on the racing results so that she knew what to expect when I arrived home. If there were no winners, there could be no peace. If things had gone well, there was every chance of civility. Once home, I would go to the sauna and spend maybe an hour wasting, then supper, and afterwards I would retreat to the living room and review that day's racing. Sometimes Michael Caulfield and Richard Phillips came round to watch 'A Question of Sport' and we fought like cats to answer the most questions. Corky and Richard were both bachelors and Carol reckoned I enjoyed their company so much because I hankered after the single life. They did ease the tension in the house but I feel what I most needed was to be able to go through this part of my life alone.

The pressure was immense. Try to imagine the madness that had me at Market Rasen on a Friday afternoon in November 1992. I went to ride the unfancied outsider Lover's Moon for Nigel Tinkler; three and a half hours there, three and a half hours back. Lover's Moon was feeling the pace after three hurdles, well behind after five, and finished ninth of 14 having been beaten by 34 lengths. Nowadays I say to A.P. McCoy, 'You're bloody stupid. What are you going there for? He's got no effing chance. Are you mad?'

'No madder than you were,' he replies, and he's right.

Though addicted to this never-ending journey, it didn't make me happy. I hated time spent in the sauna, disliked the travelling and always having to watch my weight. Yet, at the time, there seemed no choice. To what was I addicted? Recently I spoke to Scu about it and he recalled a dream he'd had a few nights before. It was unusual, he said, because he never dreams about racing but in this one he is again a jockey. The horse he is riding is young and promising but still unproven. In the race they jump well and coming to the second last the horse quickens, he clears the last two hurdles perfectly and stretches away from the opposition. In the winner's enclosure, the excited connections lean towards Scu as he undoes the saddle. This horse can go on to big things, he tells them. Then he woke up. He didn't find it hard to work out the significance of what he had dreamt.

'It's the adrenalin buzz of a good horse quickening in your hands that hooks us,' said Scu. 'As a top rider, you've got a chance of that almost every day and it's what makes the jockey's life special. No one else in racing gets that thrill. I'm part of a training operation now and in some ways training is more fulfilling than riding. You have a greater involvement. But the buzz, that's the jockey's territory. That's what you dream about.'

For me, the addiction wasn't all. I had to learn from every mistake and needed to feel I rode as well as I possibly could. Winning wasn't enough, I wanted to believe I was as good as the best, to look around the weighing room and not feel inferior to any rival. The turmoil in my life had its source in mistakes that I could not accept. How did I fall off that? What went wrong there? Why didn't I win on that?

Scu went home after a bad day and had his two boys to sort him out. Young Michael didn't give a damn about dad's riding career and Tom just teased him about me – 'Hey Dad, Richard rode another two today.' And so Scu wasn't allowed to dwell on winners that had got away. But I couldn't let them go. Why did you do it? What made you lengthen and throw that tired horse into the fence? Ultimately, the endless recrimination would improve my riding but it came at a cost. Routinely down on myself, I could be pretty miserable – a horrible bastard when in bad form is how one of the lads used to put it. Yet that's the way it was. Addicted to the buzz I may have been, but it was the compulsion to improve that I brought home in the evenings.

As the 1992–93 season gathered momentum and the title loomed as a real possibility, I really did need to be alone. The intense introspection would have been the same, I certainly would have been no less hard on myself but, at least, I would have been hurting only me. Not getting on with Carol, I suggested a trial separation in late October and even though she didn't want to leave our home, she agreed to spend some time with Aiden and Anabel. Now when we recollect this time, Carol reckons she was away for about three weeks but I remember it as maybe a week or ten days. Although she got on well with Aiden and Anabel and rode out every morning, Carol hated the separation.

In contrast, I liked it and used the freedom to immerse myself totally in racing. It didn't matter how much I beat myself up about a missed winner or that I came from the races in foul humour, I had only to contend with myself.

During her stay at Aiden and Anabel's, Carol received just one phone call from me. That came on the Saturday evening of my day at Chepstow. Having had five winners from five rides, there was nothing to be reproachful about. Because Carol had seen so much of my darker side, I wanted to speak with her that night. Soon afterwards she came home and we agreed to work hard to make a go of it. Through Hilary Kerr, an almoner of the Injured Jockeys' Fund, I arranged to visit a psychotherapist who would help me to understand what had gone wrong in our marriage and whether we could get it together again. I was also curious to find out things about myself. What made me behave this way? Why should I treat a good woman so badly?

The image of the swan moving serenely across the surface of the water while its feet paddle furiously underneath is an appropriate one for how things were in my life. To the outside world, things could hardly have been better. There were so many good horses to ride and, for the first time in my career, I had the chance of becoming champion. In my dealings with the racing world, I tried to be polite and rational. Trainers had no problem putting me up on their horses and even though some of the lads in the weighing room would have regarded me as much too intense, there was some respect for my professionalism. To all of them, I was the one who had it made. No one saw the paddling and the fury beneath the surface. For the sportsman there is no escape from this; people want the poise not the paddling, the successful jockey not the struggling husband. So I kept the best side out, went to Cheltenham for the Mackeson meeting in mid-November and rode Morley Street against his full brother Granville Again in the Coral-Elite Hurdle. Granville Again was ridden by Scu and even though Tyrone Bridge and Oh So Risky were in the race, this was a showdown between two talented brothers. With such a small field, tactics were always going to play a part. I tucked in behind Scu and waited for him to move. When he did, I waited some more and asked Morley Street to go halfway up the run-in. We won by a length and I won an award for the riding performance of the meeting. When you are perceived to be good, a straightforward ride sometimes earns more credit than it deserves. In fact, most jockeys would have won on him.

Beating Scu always meant something. Even now, thinking back, the narrow wins over him are easily recalled because they were the most important. He says the only guys in the weighing room he didn't want to see riding winners were John Francome and myself. I know what he means and it is the highest compliment. I felt the same about Adrian Maguire for two seasons. The challenger you don't want to see riding winners is the one you fear.

All through the winter of 1992–93 I stayed ahead of Scu but never by that many. It was a good time for me – six winners over the two-day Hennessy meeting at Newbury and then three winners on the second day of Kempton's Christmas meeting. For The Grain was the second winner at Kempton and one of the best rides I ever gave a horse. Flat to the boards at halfway, I had to stoke him up a mile from home to get him into contention and even though we were all out going to the last, we got up to beat Mark Richards and Calapaez by a neck. Tinryland, whom I could have ridden, finished less than a length behind in third and had he beaten me, a good day would have been greatly diminished. It seems ridiculous now, this preoccupation with always having to pick the right horse, but that is the way it was.

Mrs Buckley was the therapist who agreed to help us with our marital difficulties and we talked regularly about how things might be improved. Carol, she thought, needed to become more independent. Arising out of that observation, Carol started working as a racing photographer with Mel Fordham. That was good for her as it got her away from the house and allowed her to do things on her own. In January she and her friend Mary Ann 'Mouse' Clark went skiing together and even though we continued to have our bad times, there were also times when we got on well. But it didn't matter what advice I got, as long as the jockeys' championship remained a possibility, it was the priority. Everything else had to take its place in the queue behind that. On Monday, 8 February, I went to Wolverhampton for six rides and for the following 27 consecutive days rode without a break. That was 110 rides and 32 winners; I was around 20 ahead of Scu as we moved towards the Cheltenham

Festival. I should have been feeling good having achieved 129 winners by the end of February and happy with the way I'd been riding. Relaxed? I didn't know the meaning of the word.

Cheltenham meant hassle and important decisions – could I get the Duke to allow me to ride the Irish-trained Montelado and not his Dreamers Delight in the Supreme Novices' Hurdle? Should I try to get on Travado for Nicky Henderson in the Arkle? I thought Travado might just be better than the Duke's Wonder Man but Travado's owner Michael Ennever wanted Jamie Osborne who had ridden the horse in his previous race. Then there was the muddle of the bumper. Offered different rides, I had narrowed it down to a choice between the Irish pair, Rhythm Section and Diplomatic. 'This one will win,' Homer Scott kept telling me about his horse, Rhythm Section.

These were important issues because even though things were going well, there were no guarantees at the Festival. After Desert Orchid's fall in the King George at Kempton, the Burridges retired him and even though Kribensis was in the Champion Hurdle, he was not the horse he once was and I would ride Flown to finish unplaced. As game as ever, Waterloo Boy was having trouble with his wind and by now he was also bursting blood vessels. He would struggle in the Champion Chase. At this particular Festival, I needed things to go right.

The Duke insisted I rode Dreamers Delight. We fell heavily at the second last. I was OK until I got up.

'What's winning?' I shouted to commentator and journalist Brough Scott whom I'd noticed among the crowd.

'Montelado's hacking up,' he said.

I could have cried but settled for silent damnation of the Duke. Since winning at the Festival a year earlier, I had been Montelado's rider. As bad starts go, this was right up there. I had my doubts about Wonder Man being good enough to beat Travado but thought he just could. On the wrong horse again; Travado beat Wonder Man. Two races and I was two winners down.

Over the years at the Festival, there were times when the place just got me down. Because it's the biggest meeting of the year, it came laden with pressure. I would get to the course around 10.30 or 11 a.m. to beat the traffic but in the evening there would be no escape, and to a man who has never been really comfortable in large racecourse crowds, it was claustrophobic. Over the past few years at Cheltenham, I've done some corporate hospitality work for Guinness, speaking to their guests before racing. While I was appreciative of the remuneration, it wasn't something I really enjoyed doing and if jockeys were better paid it's not something they would do. Can you imagine footballer Sol Campbell entertaining corporate guests two hours before the start of an FA Cup final or rugby player Jonny Wilkinson amusing the captains of industry at lunchtime prior to an England v. France game at Twickenham? I don't think so.

I can't remember or imagine what I said to the corporate guests on the Wednesday before the second day's racing but it can't have been too convincing. At that point, I was sore and tired and seven races later, despair had set up camp inside my head. Waterloo Boy finished down the field in the Champion Chase and Barton Bank, who should have run well in the Sun Alliance Novice Chase, burst a blood vessel. How lucky for his pilot that humans are not as vulnerable to the same condition. Then, after six races and no sign of a winner, came the bloody bumper. It had preyed on my mind for two weeks – Rhythm Section or Diplomatic? Homer Scott continued to ooze confidence about his horse, Mick O'Toole said Diplomatic had better form and Ciaran, his son and my agent in Ireland, agreed. As both horses were trained over there, I spoke to friends who knew the Irish form inside out and, after much deliberation, I made my choice: Diplomatic. The young and gifted Paul Carberry got the ride on Rhythm Section and yeah, the rest was predictable. Rhythm Section won, Diplomatic finished fifth, beaten ten lengths.

I had known Ciaran O'Toole a long time, and he usually stayed with us for Cheltenham. When I was an amateur at Chepstow, he had booked me for my first ride for the Duke on Sir Gordon after Niall Madden had been injured. Ciaran was working as assistant trainer at the yard at this time and we've been great mates ever since. I used to meet him back at Newmarket during the summer when he worked for Tom Jones and when in Ireland in the early nineties, I would stay with his parents, Mick and Una, until I rented my own place over there in 1995. Ciaran knew how to handle me as well as anyone, and his mickey-taking would, more often than not, pull me out of a dark mood.

On this occasion, nothing he said could lift me out of despondency and the majority of the drive home that Wednesday evening took place in funereal silence. It wasn't Ciaran's fault but to miss a winner at the end of two bad days was too much. This was one of those times at the Festival when I would willingly have fast-forwarded to Wolverhampton on the Friday. Just beam me out of here.

Thursday began as Wednesday concluded. Favourite for the Triumph Hurdle, Beauchamp Grace ran disappointingly and Baydon Star was another beaten favourite in the Stayers' Hurdle. Then there was a break in the clouds. Even though beaten by Jodami, Rushing Wild ran the race of his life in the Gold Cup. God, I can only imagine how sickening that must have been for Scu as well as for Jonothan Lower. Scu rode Martin Pipe's other runner Chatam and when we kicked at the top of the hill, it must have been hell for him. Afterwards Martin asked me if there was anything we could have done that might have made the difference? I felt I'd given the horse a decent ride and we had been beaten two lengths. No, there was nothing. But it was clear to me even then that only winning interested Pipey. No matter how fine a performance, second place was never good enough. Rushing Wild's performance had, however, given me a lift.

Shamana ran a great race for me in the Grand Annual but we were beaten by Adrian Maguire on Space Fair. Just as I had given up all hope of riding a winner at the 1993 Festival, Thumbs Up came to the last in the County Hurdle so full of running you would have thought he had just entered the race. When I asked him to quicken, he streaked home and we won by six lengths. Of all the tales of the unexpected from Cheltenham, running away with the ultra competitive County Hurdle may be the most unlikely. Thumbs Up was bred in County Antrim by Peader McCoy, a man now much better known for having bred a jockey. Thumbs Up was a talented horse and the jockey would turn out OK too. After three days of losers, it was amazing what that one winner did for me. 'Thank God I'm not leaving here empty-handed,' I thought.

In much better form, I checked to see what I was riding at

Wolverhampton the next day – three rides, one of which looked certain to win. That Thursday the traffic out of Cheltenham didn't seem half so bad.

Wolverhampton Racecourse, a gloomy place in March, was a dream – two winners out of three and my lead on Scu was back up to 20. But then on the Saturday, Red Amber fell at Uttoxeter and I fractured the metacarpal bone in my right hand. Of course, I tried to kid myself that it was a bad sprain, rode Windy Ways in the following race, the Midlands Grand National, and went to Plumpton for two rides on the Monday. Both finished second and after another runner-up at Fontwell the following day, the pain and the frustration of not being able to use my hand led to an X-ray and the hand was encased in plaster. I was told not to ride for two weeks. This, I thought, would give Scu the incentive to reel me in. Every day I studied the entries and the results. What was Scu doing? How many was he riding? But it wasn't happening for him. Martin wasn't having many runners and I could tell from his rides that Scu wasn't chasing the spares as he had.

On the last Sunday of my enforced break, Carol and I went to the Lesters, the awards night for jockeys. The function was held at the Hilton in Park Lane and was the usual jockeys' get-together; great camaraderie, some drinking, some flirting and a lot of fun. Music, or at least the entertainment, was provided by Bob Marley. But that part came after sensible people were safely in their beds. Many of the jockeys were staying at the Plaza on Hyde Park and after the Lesters ended a few of us were having a drink back at our hotel. Roger Marley, known to all of us as Bob, and myself and a few others were keen to extend the night. Alas, the bar staff were keen to close up and get off to bed. As residents, we felt entitled to a few drinks. When the fire alarm went off, one of the lads behind the bar accused the jockeys of being responsible for it. They were smiling, didn't seem too concerned, and Roger and I were convinced they had set off the alarm as a means of clearing the bar. We told them as much. 'What did you that for?' we said. 'You're trying to empty the bar but everyone here is a resident.' Weary, maybe, after a long evening and tired of our abuse, they decided they'd had enough and called the police. Minutes later, the boys in blue were swarming all over the place and they approached Roger first.

'If you don't go to bed now, we're going to arrest you.'

'You can't do that, I'm a resident.'

'OK, you're arrested.'

They carted Roger off.

'I don't believe this,' I said as sobriety quickly returned. I went after the police.

'You can't do that. You can't arrest him for not going to bed.'

'If you don't go to bed, you'll be arrested too.'

I turned away and banged my plastered right hand against a pillar in frustration. A female constable grabbed one arm, her male colleague got hold of the other and they pulled me in opposite directions. Anyone looking on would have thought I was putting up a fight. They said I had been unruly and had tried to resist arrest. Two fellow jockeys, Johnny Kavanagh and Simon McNeil, saw me being taken away.

'Don't arrest him, you can't arrest him.'

Neither Johnny nor Simon had quite as much influence with the Metropolitan Police as they'd hoped. By now I was very sober and tame as a lamb, no backchat, no insolence. As they were arresting me, one of the constables knocked over a glass and that too would be on the caution sheet. Even though I tried to behave well, they pushed me around outside and I began to get angry again. They slapped me down on the bonnet of the paddy-wagon.

'Why don't you do that again?' I said. So they slammed me on to it a second time and then handcuffed me. Now I was starting to get abusive. 'You continue doing this and I'll bloody sue you.' They pushed me round to the back of the van. 'Don't bother opening it,' I said and they banged me hard against the closed door. Eventually I was inside, lying on my stomach, hands cuffed behind my back with one of the policemen standing on my head. We were taken to Paddington Green station and by now Roger and I were all meekness and timidity – yes sir, no sir, three bags full sir.

'Name?'

'Dunwoody.'

'First name?'

'Richard.'

'And you, name?'

'Marley.'

'First name?'

'Bob, Bob Marley.'

One of the constables who had arrested us had to turn away to prevent his colleagues seeing him laughing. And though I was beginning to worry about what I had got myself into, I still found Bob hilarious. Bob Marley, the reggae king from Malton in Yorkshire. Bob Marley and the Jailers.

'What's your proper first name?'

'Roger,' he said. 'Roger Marley.'

'Why didn't you say Roger the first time?'

'I did. It must be me Yorkshire accent. You guys down here don't understand me.'

All it lacked was for Bob to break into 'I Shot the Sheriff'. Sadly, the officer on duty didn't share Roger's sense of humour and had him carted away to the cells. I was asked if I accepted a caution for being unruly, drunk and breaking glasses. If I didn't accept I would be in court. The thought of what the media would make of that convinced me to accept the caution. I spent the rest of the night in my cell, one blanket, no pillow but it was comfortable and I slept well. As I was dropping off, one thought struck me – I could be the first jockey to win the championship and be arrested in the same year. But what would the Duke say? I could square it with Carol and my parents but I imagined the Duke would flip. I rang him first thing the next morning and even though he pretended to be annoyed, he was actually quite good about it.

The newspapers were full of the story. As well as being arrested, they said I had been in a fight with Vinnie Jones, who had been drinking at the same hotel after attending the Professional Footballers' Association awards, and whom some of the jockeys had met. Me and Vinnie fighting? Even though I had once entered the stablelads' boxing championships, Vinnie wasn't my type of opponent. We hadn't said boo to each other all evening.

A day later, I went to Sandown where I had a ride for my first boss in National Hunt racing, Captain Tim Forster and two for the Duke. Amari King won and, of course, the Captain was asked about his headline-making jockey. 'Well,' said the Captain, 'when he was with me, he was a nice young boy who was always tucked up in bed at eight o'clock in the evening with nothing more than a glass of milk and the form-book.' Then I rode the aptly named Musthaveaswig who skated home and the day ended with Shamana giving me three winners from three rides. If the coppers could have guaranteed that every time, I would have lived in the cell, pillow or no pillow.

A week later I stayed on the right side of authority but it didn't get me far. Liverpool had been a bad meeting for me anyway. My right hand was still quite sore and the Duke's horses were at the end of a long season. But the disaster of the three days at Aintree was the Grand National itself. Thirty-nine lined up at the start, animal rights demonstrators gathered down at the first fence, and from there all hell broke loose. The demonstrators were moved away, we lined up again, they returned and we were turned away again. Nine minutes after the scheduled start of the race, the starter Captain Keith Brown, who later and extremely unfairly became the scapegoat for the whole affair, pulled the lever but, weighed down by rain moisture, the tape rose slowly and many of the horses became entangled in it. Four minutes later the starter tried again and this time, after one horse had caught the tape, it wrapped around my neck and, with some of the runners treading on it, I thought I was about to be pulled off my mount, Wont Be Gone Long. This had to be a false start and I gambled that it would be. Nine of us remained on the sensible side of the first fence as the other 30 galloped away towards Becher's. Fearing he would be mown down, the recall man had scarpered. I was worried to death that I'd done the wrong thing. 'Oh no,' I thought, 'there's thirty horses disappearing into the distance and I've pulled up. What if it isn't a false start?'

'It's definitely a false start,' said Jamie Osborne. 'I was on the outside, I heard it on the loud-speaker.' A lot of the lads didn't hear the starter and seeing no recall man and no red flag, they kept going. From there, it was a farce. Half of the 30 starters pulled up after a circuit, a few fell, but a hard core kept going. They were mostly Irish jockeys and I could imagine them –

'Keep going lads, this isn't our cock-up. Maybe they'll let us away with it.' I suppose it was worth a try. Afterwards they were telling stories in the weighing room and apparently Norman Williamson had suggested to Adrian Maguire that they pull up. 'I'm not bloody pulling up,' said Adrian, 'I'm going too well.' You could see it from their point of view. They knew something was wrong but they decided to take the chance and hope that a line in the rules would allow the result to stand.

My disappointment at not getting to ride in the world's greatest race was tempered by my lack of enthusiasm for Wont Be Gone Long. He wasn't jumping as well as he had been when winning the John Hughes in 1990 and a week before the race had fallen heavily when schooling at Towcester racecourse. I should have ridden him that day but as my hand was still in plaster, I had had to cry off. My old friend Martin Lynch, who had voluntarily given me one of his rides so that I could achieve my first century of winners, deputised for me at Towcester. The carrot for Martin was the National ride on Wont Be Gone Long if my hand didn't heal in time. The old horse buried Martin, he injured his back badly and never rode in a race again. Remarkably, we're still mates.

The next day Michael Caulfield came round and we sat down to watch the BBC's coverage of the aborted National. It made a great comedy. There was the Duke out on the track flagging the riders down and he didn't even have a runner in the race; Roger Farrant, a racecourse official, was helpless as the field made out on to the second circuit; and afterwards Richard Pitman rushed round doing all sorts of interviews and someone had squashed his hat. Looking back, maybe the funniest thing of all was that there I was on the day after the race, knowing it had been declared void, watching the re-run to see what had happened to Scu. He was riding Captain Dibble for Nigel Twiston-Davies and I followed his progress until he pulled up after a circuit. I gave a sigh of relief. No matter what happened, Scu wasn't going to get a winner out of it. Pathetic, I know. It was really that bad.

I was driving home from the physio when the telephone rang. It was Robert Kington.

'Scu's retired,' he said. 'It's all over. Well done.'

'I don't believe you.'

'I'm not taking the piss,' he said. 'It's true. He has retired. You're going to be champion.'

'Sorry Robert, I'm finding it hard to take in. Scu's retired?'

I put the phone down and cried; supposedly the coldest fish in the weighing room and the tears rolled down my face. There was relief that I would now be champion, but there was no elation, no joy now that I had what I desperately wanted. Instead, I felt sad that Scu had called it a day. The weighing room would be a lesser place without him. Afterwards he said he had seen Michael, his father, injured late in his career and he didn't want that to happen to him. I could see his retirement only from my own point of view. Scu had been the jockey I tried to emulate, the one who showed me what toughness was and, in the end, he became my rival, the man I had to beat. Maybe it was that by retiring, he had denied me the true victory I craved; in the photographs taken in the days following his departure, I am not smiling.

Late in the season, Martin Pipe's horses began to find their best form and the winners came with the regularity that only Martin knows. And as it happened, I thought to myself, 'Jesus, I'm glad Scu is gone.'

13

FIRST IMPRESSONS

I have always tried to be a good timekeeper. Doesn't matter what the circumstances, if I agree a time I do my utmost to stick to it. Less than two weeks after Peter Scudamore announced his retirement, Martin Pipe invited me down to his yard at Nicholashayne in Somerset. He wanted to talk about the job and the possibility of us working together. This was as close as racing gets to a job interview. It was a Monday morning, 19 April, and if ever I wanted to be on time for an appointment this was it. I left Sparsholt in good time, quickly got to the M4 and headed west. Leaving the M4 to link up with the M5, I had a puncture. Having left early, there was time to deal with this small problem and I pulled in on the first slip road on the M5 to change the wheel. But the nuts had corroded and I couldn't prise the wheel free.

No need to panic. I called the AA and told them I needed help. I also phoned Martin to say I would be a bit late. The AA car turned up but although I saw the driver circling the roundabout about a hundred yards away from where I was stranded, he couldn't see me. Then he disappeared, came back around the roundabout 15 minutes later and after what seemed like an age, he eventually found me. But the wheel still wouldn't budge and in the end he was forced to use a mallett. Two and a half hours passed before I was on the road again and by the time I pulled into Martin's yard, I was two hours late.

I did wonder if the gods were, once again, trying to tell me something.

I wanted the job. Martin trained far more winners than anyone else and unless something unusual happened his stable jockey would be champion. 'You've become champion riding for me. I don't see why you have to leave,' David Nicholson said, but my success in the championship owed more to Scu losing his true appetite than any other factor. Even in my first championship season, Martin trained 194 winners to the Duke's 100 and that was nothing more than an average year for Martin.

When Scu left the Duke to join Fred Winter in 1986, there was bad feeling because the Duke had not been kept informed about what was happening. As I was about to make an approach to Martin, I spoke to the Duke. We had been together for eight years and if I was moving on, it had to be on good terms. 'Look, I've got to talk with Martin,' I said to him. In an interview with the *Sporting Life*, Martin mentioned seven possible replacements – Adrian Maguire, myself, Charlie Swan, Graham McCourt, Mark Perrett, David Bridgwater and Carl Llewellyn. I reckoned it was down to Adrian and me.

I was keen to know what Scu thought. It had been reported that Martin would consult with Scu and I hoped he would be on my side. While stable jockey to Martin, Scu won the title without hardly ever seeming to get into a battle for it. That appealed to me. Scu was also a fan of Martin's and said he was more relaxed with him than with any other trainer he had ridden for. It was Scu who made the important point.

'If you want to be champion,' he said, 'you've got to go there, you've just got to go.'

Robert Kington felt the same. 'If you're going to go for the championship again, you've got to consider this.'

I thought of what I had been through to win my first championship, the constant fear that Scu would just click into gear and overtake me. I'd agonised over that jockeys' title for six months. There was no way now I would decide that it wasn't the most important thing to me.

My best-of-all-worlds deal with the Duke and Nicky Henderson also could not continue much longer. The Duke had moved into Jackdaws Castle near Temple Guiting in Gloucester-shire at the beginning of the 1992–93 season and his team of horses was getting bigger. Nicky was also improving his string and gradually moving towards a situation where he would have his own stable jockey. Mick Fitzgerald was coming through and it was clear he would eventually become Nicky's retained rider. Even though it had worked for me up to now, it hadn't been easy to keep both the Duke and Nicky happy at the same time. I believed if I was given Martin's job, Adrian would take the rides at Jackdaws Castle and I would be able to continue riding some of Nicky's horses.

There were, of course, downsides to this proposed move. Was I prepared to leave all those good horses the Duke and Nicky trained? They tended to have well-bred National Hunt horses with even temperaments and many with the potential to go right to the top. Riding for the Duke and Nicky, I had got used to having fancied rides in most of the big races throughout the season. That would not be the case with Martin who had quite a high percentage of less expensive, ex-Flat racers that won plenty of races. Although there were some top-class horses in the yard, they would not keep me as busy at an Ascot or a Newbury on a Saturday. There was also the realisation that even though I might ride twice as many winners for Martin as I did for the Duke and Nicky combined, I would earn less. Martin didn't believe in giving his stable jockey a retainer whereas the Duke and Nicky agreed to generous and fair deals, but it was a price I was very willing to pay.

Ultimately, it didn't matter how many times I tossed it round, the conclusion remained the same. Being champion jockey was what mattered. I had come through the battle with Scu and had no wish to go through another. I had served my time, finished second for three consecutive years before finally win-ning the title. Did I want another fraught campaign with whoever rode for Martin? No. Was I prepared to hand the initiative to another rider? Definitely not. If Martin's job was offered, I was going to accept.

But there were still six weeks of this old season remaining and, knowing I was going to be champion, I was a little more relaxed. Martin also put me up on a few of his horses and I rode a lot of winners in those closing weeks. Topsham Bay finished second to Givus a Buck and Paul Holley in the Whitbread Gold Cup but we'd been taken a good way off a true line after the last and were awarded the race in the stewards' room. Three days afterwards we were in Punchestown and by now the word was out – I would ride for Martin Pipe next season. I looked forward to the challenge and it helped that there was very little acrimony with the Duke. He was able to announce Adrian as his new stable jockey before it was publicly known I would ride for Martin and this was important to him. After eight years, I wanted to leave on good terms. The test came at Punchestown where the Duke agreed I should ride Viking Flagship on the opening day. He won easily and was starting to show the potential that would later take him to the very top. It was clear from the Duke's attitude that there were few hard feelings. Viking Flagship, probably the toughest horse I ever rode, turned out again two days later and won a valuable novice chase. Anne Marie O'Brien's Bayrouge and Nicky's Thinking Twice helped provide me with the four winners that were enough to make me leading jockey at Punchestown. In those years when I was able to ride there for three days, it was an enjoyable trip. Coming towards the end of the season and being in Ireland, it had a welcome social dimension to it. I stayed with Brendan Powell's parents, Benny and Sheila, and was extremely well looked after.

Through the month of May, Martin's horses were returning to form. My reign as his stable jockey would not formally start until the beginning of the 1993–94 season but during that month, I rode 12 winners for my boss-to-be. It augured well for the future. But before that could begin, there were some loose ends to be tied up.

Simon McNeil and I had talked about letting our hair down and the idea of a party was mooted. We both were trying to achieve important goals. I was going for my first title and Simon, after years of toil, was on target to ride his first-ever half century. 'If we both do it,' said Simon, 'we'll share a party at the end of the season.' It was a great idea. Both of us had many of the same friends and from my point of view, it would be good to share a party with one of the most popular lads in the weighing room. At Fontwell a few days later we talked again. 'Look,' I said, 'let's have the party anyway. Win or lose, let's just do it.'

The planning began. We set the bar high, deciding to get the famous Irish band the Saw Doctors to provide the music. Among a number of us, the Saw Doctors are heroes and I thought why not? Obviously, the fee was going to be a bit of a problem. We couldn't pay what they would get anywhere else but we thought it worth a shot. Through John Durkan and the Irish trainer, Mouse Morris, we got in touch with their agent, Ollie Jennings, and begged.

'We're thinking of the middle of July, maybe Saturday the tenth?'

'The boys are actually playing Slane that day.' Slane is Ireland's biggest pop concert, attended by 65,000 people.

'Oh.'

'Let me talk to the boys and I'll come back to you.'

The Saw Doctors agreed and were very fair about their fee. One of the band members, Leo Moran, was the son of a bookmaker and they had a soft spot for racing. They came directly from Slane and travelled by ferry to keep the expenses down. While in England, they slept at our house and generally left us all mightily impressed by how down-to-earth they were. This was a band who had appeared on 'Top of the Pops' and on the night before the party they were down in ex-jockey Martin O'Halloran's pub in Uffington, living it up with the rest of us. Davy Carton, Leo Moran, Pearse Doherty, John Donnelly, Tony Lambert and Anto Thistlethwaite – a great bunch of lads.

We set up a marquee at the Farmhouse Restaurant near Frilford and about 350 people came. It was a brilliant night. Carol had done the organising and the success of the evening was mostly down to her. The Saw Doctors were themselves – informal and great fun – and the music was outstanding. At one point they got Simon, Michael Caulfield and me up on stage to back them. I don't know about the other two, but I certainly had no right to be there. Years before when I rode out at the Captain's, David 'Taff' Rossiter described my singing voice as the worst he had heard in a lifetime of listening to bad singers. After that, Taff never called me anything other than 'The Voice'.

That summer Carol and I went to Barbados with a big gang of mostly racing people – Scu and his wife Maz were there, Steve Smith Eccles, Graham McCourt and others. Although Carol and I were having our ups and downs, we got on fine as usual on holiday. Then we went to Jersey for the weekend and again it went well. By now, I suppose, we realised our marital problems were not going away. There were rows and then periods of silence followed by a temporary patching up of differences. But even when we were getting on OK, it wasn't like it had been. Our house was now the home we wanted, we had just added a conservatory and the place had been transformed. Sadly, we weren't able to rebuild our relationship in the same way.

As the first days of the 1993–94 season dawned and my reign as stable jockey to M.C. Pipe began, I should have been hugely excited. This was the start of a new era. Scu's time had gone, now it would be my turn to dominate. Yet something bothered me, a slight worry that maybe Martin and I would not hit it off as I had with the Duke and the Captain. That April visit to Nicholashayne hadn't entirely reassured me. Martin understood why I was late; that wasn't a problem. But there was something in the chemistry between us that didn't seem quite right.

I had read a piece written by David Ashforth in the *Sporting Life*. David wrote about the succession race for the Pipe job and asked Martin what factors were important. 'Personality comes into it,' Martin replied. 'I'm a funny old devil, aren't I? Who would want to work with me? And then who is available? Who do the owners want?' I had ridden many times for Martin before going down to Nicholashayne on that Monday but two minutes in the paddock before getting on a horse or the snatched conversation as you dismount in the unsaddling enclosure are not the same as sitting in a man's living room for two hours. Scu got on very well with Martin, A.P. McCoy enjoys a good relationship with him but I didn't hit it off with him in quite the same way. Even though I was champion jockey, I was intimidated, almost overawed, and I did not find him the easiest to talk to. Intimidated or not, I asked about a retainer.

'I don't give my stable jockey a retainer,' Martin said. 'You

come here to ride my horses and be champion. That's it really.'
I didn't think I'd succeed but I had to try.

Maybe I had been too sheltered during my years with the
Duke, where all I had done was ride, get the odd holiday in the
summer and not really have to think too much beyond that.
With Martin, I had a sense of entering the real world where I
would have to look out for myself and develop a tougher skin.
The Duke could bark but he was always more bark than bite
and, generally speaking, you could work things out with him.
Martin didn't have the Duke's authoritarian presence but there
was an intense hardness, something that put you permanently
on your guard.

We talked a lot that day, he showed me around the yard and
yet I don't believe we were really at ease in each other's
company. I tried to play down my reservations. 'Come on,' I
thought. 'You can handle this. The winners will come and
everything will turn out fine.'

14

TO THE WIRE

E ven with my talent for suppressing the more unpleasant memories, there are some that don't go away.

It was the first day of the New Year, 1994. I was riding Richard Hannon's Supreme Master at Newbury. Supreme Master had reasonable form on the Flat and was favourite to win this extended two-mile hurdle. One of the dangers, Winter Forest, was ridden by my arch rival, Adrian Maguire. We were getting close to halfway in the season and Adrian was 39 ahead in the jockeys' championship – almost out of sight. At the beginning, the championship was deemed a non-event. As stable jockey to Martin Pipe, I was expected to walk away with it. It hadn't happened and now Adrian was in control. Adrian was everyone's favourite; journalists wrote about him, television commentators praised him and the public warmed to him. Who was I? Last season's champion, yesterday's hero. I followed Adrian's progress closer than anybody; I had to know where he was riding, how he was doing and, if we were in the same race, I kept an eye out for him. I didn't mind who rode winners as long as it wasn't him. To be beaten by Adrian in a finish was unbearable.

I settled Supreme Master in behind the leaders, came with a steady run up the straight and was upsides Adrian on Winter Forest as we went to the last. My horse was travelling well and provided he jumped it reasonably, he would win. Maybe it was because I was neck and neck with Adrian, who knows, but I asked Supreme Master to lengthen his stride and really ping the last. It was too much. The horse didn't get high enough, hit the hurdle hard and stumbled. On another day, I would have stayed in the saddle. This time I was unseated. The race was Adrian's. I hated myself.

One of the advantages of Newbury was that it was so close to home. Thirty-five or 40 minutes and I was there or back. This evening, the last thing I needed was to get home early. The fall that afternoon stayed with me, festering like an infected sore. How could I let it happen? A bloody televised race and I had fallen off. Made a present of a winner to Adrian Maguire. By the time I got home, I was fit to be tied. Carol only had to ask how the day went and I exploded. The row was vicious but one-sided; all the aggression, the malice and the anger came from me. Carol doesn't have a mean bone in her body. She just happened to be with the wrong man at the wrong time.

I could never just leave it. After rowing with Carol, I went to the video and replayed it over and over. I must have watched it a hundred times. What had happened? How had I cocked up? Why hadn't I reacted quicker to the horse's mistake? Mentally and physically, I was exhausted but that was no reason. I couldn't see that sometimes you want to win so badly, you try too hard and that makes you lose. There was no excuse that was acceptable, no way that I could allow myself even one mistake. I tormented myself because that was what I deserved. Anything Carol tried to do didn't help. I didn't want to be cheered up, didn't want to feel better about myself. I'd messed up. The row simmered, then erupted again. 'That's OK, I'm getting out of here,' I said. I threw a couple of things into a weekend bag, grabbed my passport and headed for Heathrow. I didn't know where I wanted to go except that I had to get away from England and this miserable contest with Adrian. Halfway to Heathrow along the M4, I knew I couldn't run from it. Unable to cope with failure, I couldn't quit either.

Looking back on the irrational rage, it seems milder, calmed by the passage of time. But I know what I was like then and there was nothing mild about it. I was out of control, a danger to both Carol and myself. That evening I loathed myself. Full of rage and frustration, I literally knocked and banged myself against doors and walls in our house. I wanted to damage myself, punish myself for a stupid and costly mistake. By doing so I eased the torment inside my head.

Later in the month, I won four races at one of the big Cheltenham meetings. There was a photograph of me coming back in on Flakey Dove. Sometime later I saw that picture and tried to remember how I got the black eye. It didn't take long. Two days earlier I had ridden Punch's Hotel for Richard Rowe at Huntingdon. He made a mistake at the ditch in front of the stands and unseated me. That evening the self-recrimination was as bad and as violent as it ever was. The black eye and bruising had been self-inflicted.

It was the best of times and the worst of times, the 1993–94 season. At the end I would have 197 winners, my second success in the Grand National and my second jockeys' championship. I achieved what I set out to achieve, but at what cost? There is a saying about it being better to travel hopefully than to arrive, that somehow the journey is superior to the arrival. This was a journey through hell and one I never wanted to go through again. Adrian Maguire put up an unbelievable fight for the championship and to beat him, I had to demand more of myself than I had ever done in my life.

The championship began at Bangor on 30 July and ended over ten months later on 4 June. In between I had 890 rides in England alone and 47 falls. It was easily the most rides I'd had in a season and my falls-to-rides ratio wasn't that bad, one in 17. But the statistic that stands as the ultimate tribute to the campaign was that I didn't have one red entry in my medical book, not one missed ride through injury. Of course, there was a certain amount of luck involved but it wasn't just that. Why was it that Adrian hardly missed a day either? The fact was we wouldn't allow ourselves to be injured.

Sometimes we reach deep into the well and draw so much that we end up with less for future campaigns. When the season ended at Market Rasen on 4 June, I was glad still to be champion but sick of the battle. It had been too long, too punishing and, in the end, too cruel. Adrian rode 194 winners and lost. I was glad it wasn't me but I also knew it was ludicrous to speak of a winner and loser at the end of a race in which both riders had reached into God-knows-what reserves to surpass themselves. My 197 winners to Adrian's 194 didn't make me a better jockey. He too had achieved his highest-ever number of winners and had ridden as well as he ever would. But the following season and for some time after that, we would pay for what we spent in 1993–94. It would be a long time before the well returned to its old level.

What made it so tough for me was that the hassle began right at the beginning or, to be precise, four days into the new season. The first three days had gone fine; I'd ridden six horses for Martin, three of them winners. That was the kind of strike rate you expect from M.C. Pipe, the most phenomenal producer of winners the sport has known. Celcius was my seventh ride for him, a 6 to 1 on shot in a three-horse selling race at Exeter and a virtual certainty to be my fourth winner for the stable. Martin suggested I drop Celcius in behind the other two and make my challenge late. Sometimes a trainer gives specific instructions because he believes his horse needs a certain type of ride. Implicit in the relationship between trainer and jockey is an understanding that if the race rides differently from expectations, the rider has to be able to change the plan.

As my two opponents in this three-runner race were deter-mined not to make any sort of pace and Celcius was racing quite keenly, I thought it counter-productive to fight with him. In a race run at a crawl, lesser horses usually have a greater chance. So we bowled along in front, setting a sensible pace, confident we would be much too good for our two rivals. Coming to the second last David Bridgwater and his mare Emma Victoria cruised up and within a few strides had gone clear. We were beaten eight lengths. I didn't feel riding the horse from the front had made any difference. Celcius didn't feel right and his wind wasn't good. I put it down to one of those things; it happens in racing. Martin and his right-hand man Chester Barnes thought differently and when I got back to the unsaddling enclosure, I could tell they were not in the best of humour.

Martin said I definitely should have waited with the horse and then went silent. Through the afternoon he hardly spoke to me. Chester agreed with Martin and a couple of days later he referred to my performance on Celcius as 'the biggest cock-up since Scu got beat on High Knowl', a race that had taken place six years before. This riled me. Who was Chester Barnes to judge how I rode? I also had a sense that they enjoyed putting me down. I had been the Duke's and Nicky's boy, and they were going to show me. I hadn't impressed them with my riding performance, not one bit. And they hadn't impressed me with their reaction. It really bugged me when Chester went on about Celcius but I didn't have the front to tell him where to get off. They said they always slated Scu about High Knowl, and expected I wouldn't mind. Well, I did. Celcius was my fourth day into the new job and I wasn't ready for that.

Eight days later Celcius ran at Newton Abbot and finished a well-beaten fifth of nine. This time I dropped him in and tried to come late. But the horse found nothing when asked to quicken, just as he hadn't at Exeter.

From the beginning, my relationship with Martin was, shall we say, never that close; professional and businesslike but lacking any real warmth. I discussed the situation with Robert Kington and we agreed it made sense for me to keep my options open. So I continued to ride out for Nicky Henderson, Terry Casey, Charlie Mann, Chris Nash and my neighbour Matt McCormack. I was not going to become a part of the Pipe team as Scu had and so couldn't afford to sever the connection with other trainers. I didn't want to be owned by Martin and if things ever went wrong and I had to jump, I needed lifeboats. Also, I wanted to keep my independence and, although nothing was said, I got the impression Martin would have preferred me to be totally devoted to the yard.

A few months after joining Martin, I suggested that maybe the woman who blood-tested the horses would do the same for me. I was down in Pipe's riding out every week and it would be no hassle to give a blood sample weekly or fort- nightly and have it analysed. Because I had to keep my weight unnaturally low, hours were spent in the sauna and occasion- ally I became anaemic and felt drained of energy. I had always thought it would be useful for jockeys to know if their blood was deficient in iron or anything else. Humans are different from horses but in a physiological sense, they also have much in common. I went to Martin.

'Look, ' I said, 'I thought it might be a good idea for me to have my blood tested, give a sample when I'm here and get the results the next time I'm down.'

'Don't want you to do that. No, don't want you to do that.'

'But as I'm here a lot . . . I wouldn't be able to get it done as easily anywhere else.'

'No, don't want you to do that.'

He may have thought I should be going elsewhere for a blood test. But I wasn't sure it was appreciated that I had spoken to the woman who did the horses' tests. Martin didn't like his vets to speak to the jockeys and there was a secretiveness about the operation that I had never experienced. But that was part of Martin's nature; he's a secretive person. The stable liked to have a bet and that meant they often preferred to keep things quiet. Sometimes even the jockey didn't know what was happening. You looked for guidance: which one's right, which one's not? You didn't always find out. In the end I didn't ask any more, I didn't want to know. 'I'm trying to give as much feedback as possible and I'm not receiving any in return,' I thought. At the Duke's and Nicky's, everything was discussed.

The tensions would have been more easily dealt with if Martin's horses had been on better form and Adrian not been flying. By his own incredibly high standards, Martin was having a lean time and I rode just 11 winners in August, six of which were for outside yards. Riding for any other trainer, 11 winners in August would be fine but I wasn't riding for any other trainer. September was the same, another 11. This time five of the winners came from outside rides and by the end of the month I was trailing Adrian in the championship by 22 to 34. This wasn't how it was meant to be. I had left the Duke and Nicky so that I would be guaranteed the championship with Martin and it wasn't happening. As for the bigger prizes later in the season, Adrian had the Duke's good horses to look forward to.

October was another lean month. I had 14 winners, four of which were trained by Martin. Had I not continued riding for other yards, Adrian would have been out of sight. Martin's horses were suffering from a virus with no knowing when it might disappear but as his horses struggled, I started doubting my own ability. What was I doing wrong? Scu had no trouble winning on Martin's horses. I could sense Martin didn't appear to have much confidence in my riding and the endless newspaper interest in why the Pipe/Dunwoody partnership wasn't firing only added to the tension. Because he had been so successful, the media could not conceal its enthusiasm for this apparent failure.

By the end of October I was close to despair, believing I was on the verge of losing everything. What could I do to improve my performance? 'What about talking to a sports psychologist?' Michael Caulfield suggested. Corky helped me get in touch with Peter Terry who had worked with all sorts of sportsmen and women. We first met at Bisham Abbey and Peter's initial assessment of my character was interesting. I was compulsive, a perfectionist with intrapunitive tendencies, i.e. I needed to punish myself if I didn't live up to my own expectations. This intrapunitive factor caused me to be hard driving and self-critical. Another side of my personality was that I was attracted to speed and danger, characteristic of most jump jockeys. Peter kept notes of our first meeting:

'Tell me about your recent rides.'

'Well, Adrian got the better of me in that one . . . I just held Adrian there . . . Adrian's a good rider all right.'

'Did I ask you about Adrian?'

'What do you mean?'

'Every time I ask you a question you tell me about Adrian Maguire. What do you think about during a race?'

'If Adrian's riding in it, I'll be watching for when he makes his move. Have it covered.'

'What do you think of that strategy?'

'What do you mean?'

'Thinking about what your closest rival is doing rather than what you're doing.'

'I've never thought about it. Is it wrong?'

'Most people in sport try to focus on what they are doing because that's the only thing you can control. It's called controlling the controllables. You can't do any more than get your bit right can you?'

'I suppose not.'

'But if you focus too much on what someone else is up to, you may make mistakes, miss a stride, something like that?'

'I think that happens sometimes. I need to change.'

Peter was also concerned that so much anger was showing in all the profiles he did, and that related to Adrian, too. I was the champion but he was the one everyone wanted while I struggled to get outside rides. Adrian had this agent, Dave Roberts, who was doing my head in. Dave was the cool Londoner and very good at what he did. Occasionally I would look for a ride only to be told, 'Dave Roberts was on already and Adrian rides our horse.' It was torment. I put a lot of pressure on Robert Kington – 'Why weren't you on before bloody Dave Roberts?' I'd say, and Robert would reply, 'Well, Pipey had several horses entered in the race and I couldn't guarantee you would be free.' Of course Robert was right. Martin entered his horses and then when the blood tests came back, he could take them all out. Still, I was worrying not just about Adrian but about Dave Roberts as well.

But you don't train as many winners as Martin Pipe does without doing a lot of things right. His operation is professional and well run. He schools his horses well, arranging the fences so that horses can move progressively on to bigger obstacles. Once David, his father, made the point that horses make a lot of bad mistakes at ditches and so Martin put up a line of them. It made sense. If a horse can jump a ditch, he can jump any fence. He was also building an excellent loose school. Without wishing to be unfair to the horses, some of them needed education. I had been warned by more than one of his rivals that if I went to Martin I would end up riding little rabbits and free-running beasts that would be difficult to steer.

Some of them weren't nice rides. They were bought off the Flat and weren't typical jumping horses. There were good ones, such as Chatam and Granville Again, but a good percentage wouldn't help you. On the racecourse the problem was compounded because so often the tactic was to make the running. Martin got his horses really fit and it made sense to set a good pace but, by God, his first-timers could run around in front. I've

OBSESSED

got to admit, what I'd left behind at the Duke's and Nicky's played on my mind.

The better days from this time were spent away from the grind of chasing Adrian. In the middle of October I went out to New York to ride Highland Bud in the Breeders' Cup at Belmont Park and again he ran bravely to finish second behind Lonesome Glory. A week later I went to Navan and had my first experience of Paul Carberry. I was there to school Flashing Steel for John Mulhern and Paul was on Noel Meade's Mubadir. Paul showed up half an hour late, claiming he had been out late the night before with Graham Bradley. Well, as excuses go, that was plausible enough. Although a good hurdler, Mubadir had yet to begin his steeplechase career and Paul cantered him down to the first fence along the back. Showing the horse the fence and feeling the effects of the previous evening, he whispered into Mubadir's ear. 'You better take a good look at this,' he said, 'because I can't see it.'

Before we started, I said, 'OK Paul, take it easy. It's Sunday morning and we don't want to go too quick.' Paul, of course, started at a million miles an hour and Mubadir jumped from fence to fence. More experienced but taking time to warm up, Flashing Steel jumped deliberately. We raced down the far side, then turned into the straight and I had to really grab hold of my horse to stay within three or four lengths of Paul. In the straight I had to give him a good few slaps down the shoulder and only then did I get upsides. He was riding a novice that had hardly jumped a fence; I was riding a horse that was nearly Gold Cup standard. Seeing Paul in action reminded me why his dad had once been a hero of mine. Abiding memories of the times when my parents took me to Galway races as a young child include the swimming pool on the fourth or fifth floor of the Great Southern Hotel in Eyre Square and Tommy Carberry. Time had moved on.

Adrian was moving further ahead. By the end of November, he was 27 clear and the bookmakers were quoting him a 1 to 5 favourite to win the championship. I was easy to back at 3 to 1 against. Nothing was working for me. My relationship with Martin continued along its unmerry way. I won the Gerry Feilden Hurdle on Bold Boss at Newbury and that was our first important win of the season. A couple of races later, Rolling Ball crashed to the floor at the third fence in the Hennessy and the gloom returned. On the following Friday, 3 December, I went to Exeter to ride four for Martin and Lake Teereen for Richard Rowe. I was beaten a neck on the first of Martin's, the second pulled up lame, the third was beaten a distance and the fourth fell when upsides at the last. My ride for Richard won in a tight finish.

Martin knew I was unhappy and, in hindsight, I'm sure he wasn't enjoying the silent pressure I was putting him under. There would have been plenty of owners expressing disappointment at how the horses were running and the last thing Martin needed was a disgruntled jockey.

'Do you want to continue riding my horses?' he asked me that afternoon in Exeter.

'Look,' I said, 'I'm your jockey, you're the guv'nor. Of course I want to ride your horses.' Martin wouldn't have been too worried if I had walked away. At times I felt I was being invited to.

The following day at Chepstow I rode Riverside Boy in the Rehearsal Chase. 'Watch this fellow,' Martin said beforehand. 'Keep your stick in your right because he could try to duck out.' I thought, 'Now he's giving me riding lessons,' and I was fool enough to listen. Maybe if I had been more laid-back I could have laughed it off or made some joke to defuse the tension but that wasn't me. Some of the owners were giving him a hard time and he took it very personally. He gave me a hard time and I took it very personally. I had the feeling I was clinging on to the job by my fingernails.

At the time, the lack of outside rides bothered me as much as the form of the Pipe horses. Three days after Exeter, I went to Ludlow to ride Celcius for Martin but had only one ride in the other five races. It was only the first week of December, a long, long way from the end of the season but I was at the end of my tether. One spare ride in five races – Adrian didn't have to cope with this. Desperate, I telephoned Robert Kington.

'Robert,' I said, 'it's just not working. I can't go on like this. I've got to make a change here.'

'Yeah, I understand. It's not working.'

And that's how I split with Robert Kington. I'm not happy

about how it ended. Robert did a lot of good work for me. We got on well and when it came to assessing how I rode, I valued his judgement greatly. I should have called to see him and not ended our relationship over the phone but I was wound up to the eyeballs and felt I didn't have the time. He was going through a tough time with his marriage and the last thing he needed was me on his back. I haven't spoken to Robert since that telephone call but from time to time I have asked Maz, his sister, how he is getting on. It was sad and bad that I didn't end things properly.

My split with Robert, especially in circumstances where I did not have a replacement lined up, was going to look bad – panic-stricken Dunwoody sacks his agent. So when my two rides at Ludlow, West Monkton and Celcius, both won, I quietly told Bob Davies, clerk of the course at Ludlow, that I had just ridden my 1000th winner. It was true but it was 1000 winners worldwide, including Ireland, Belgium, the US and Australia. In the strict sense, it was not my 1000th because such landmarks are based on winners ridden in Britain. But everything over the previous two months had been so negative, everything about Adrian was so positive, I didn't need more bad publicity. Bob Davies presented me with a bottle of champagne to mark the occasion and, hey presto, it was in the newspapers the next day. They also carried a piece about my break with Robert but the news of my 1000th winner diluted that.

Monty Court, writing in the *Sporting Life*, criticised me for including winners from around the world in my 1000. His view was that two winners in a racing country like Belgium, where the sport is so small, should not count. How could I celebrate the proper 1000th winner when it arrived asked Monty. I understood the argument but at the time I was desperate.

Through December, Adrian's good run continued and the gap between us widened. I wasn't yet in the basement but I was getting there. A week before Cheltenham's two-day December meeting, I spoke with Martin about the Tripleprint Gold Cup in which he intended to run the former Jimmy Fitzgerald-trained horse Fragrant Dawn. Jenny Pitman was keen for me to ride her horse, Egypt Mill Prince. I had won on him at Newbury two weeks before and Jenny was pressing me to make a decision.

Fragrant Dawn had been off the track for some time and I spoke with Mark Dwyer and Paul Holley who had both previously ridden the horse. Neither thought Fragrant Dawn would stay two and a half miles around Cheltenham. Martin reckoned the horse would stay but as I had a slight preference for Jenny's horse, I needed Martin to be more positive.

'Jenny needs to know whether I'm riding her horse or not,' I said. 'Should I ride yours?'

'If you want to ride hers, do,' he said. 'I think our horse will get the trip and he seems well. But the other horse is going to be favourite. It's all right if you want to ride him.'

'You're not going to get upset about it?'

'No, not at all.'

Fragrant Dawn was having his first run for the stable and even though the horse had worked well, how could Martin be sure when so many had run so badly? I told Jenny I would ride her horse and Martin got Declan Murphy to ride Fragrant Dawn. Declan gave the horse a peach of a ride – cool, patient and very stylish – and won comfortably. It would have been hard for any jockey to have looked as good as Declan did on Fragrant Dawn that day. It shattered me, left me gutted. I've no agent, Adrian Maguire is thirtysomething winners ahead and I've voluntarily got off one of the biggest winners of the season. Trying to find a reason for carrying on, I told myself it couldn't get any worse.

Two days later I won on Bold Stroke at Newton Abbot and Martin's biggest owner, David Johnson, joked afterwards, 'You're just as good as Declan Murphy.' Short of a sense of humour at the time, I didn't take the comment well. Normally I wouldn't have responded but I had to say something. 'I'm still champion jockey. I've had a few winners, you know.' Insecure, I quietly tried to reassure myself – 'Come on, don't mind that. You're better than Declan.' But I wasn't yet part of the team at Nicholashayne; there was Martin and Chester Barnes and I was on the fringe, not excluded but not fully involved either. My relationship with Martin at one point got to the stage when he didn't even want me down to school. It was clear we needed to give each other some space.

Christmas came but brought no cheer. I still had no agent

and was killing myself trying to do all the ringing around. Rolling Ball jumped badly in the King George VI Chase and was well beaten before I pulled him up. To make matters worse, Adrian won it on Barton Bank. The experience of being my own agent showed me just how difficult it was. My winners strike-rate didn't improve one jot under my auspices and I realised what an incredibly difficult job Robert had had to do. The day after the King George, I won the Welsh National on Martin's Riverside Boy and that might have suggested things were about to get better. No chance. Five days later the year turned but my luck stayed exactly the same. Supreme Master ranged upsides Adrian on Winter Forest at the last hurdle, made that mistake and unseated me. My whole world fell around me.

The next morning, Robert Parsons called round to see me. I needed an agent, he wanted the job. Straightaway, I felt he was the man. He asked for more money than the other agents but that didn't worry me. If I didn't employ an agent soon, I would be calling for the men in white coats with a straitjacket. There was no time for niceties with Robert.

'I want to be champion, but it's not working. I'm forty behind Adrian. Are you good enough for this?'

'I believe I'm good enough. I'll do a proper job for you,' he said.

'This will be very hard work,' I said.

'I don't mind that.'

'There's Dave Roberts. He's the best at this. We've got to take him on.'

'We can put Dave and Adrian back in their boxes.'

Robert's quiet confidence was exactly what I needed. He had proved himself working for Richard Quinn on the Flat and there was no reason he couldn't do the same job for me. I needed to concentrate on my riding and leave the phone calls to Robert.

There was a final low before things began to improve. The next day I had one ride for Martin at Cheltenham, Gay Ruffian, and it fell. Falls happen in racing but such was my relationship with Martin I felt there was no margin for mishap. And the next day, it got worse. Doualago was hacking up at Southwell and went to the last a distance clear. This time I let him go in close, wanting nothing more than a safe jump. But he dragged his hind legs and tipped up. This was an unlucky fall; I couldn't believe it. It felt like the most violent kick between the legs.

I think it was David Richmond, Martin's second travelling head lad, who came down and met me as I walked back from the last hurdle. He had his mobile in his hand and Martin, who had watched the race at home, was anxious to speak. David passed me the phone and Martin was clearly upset at the other end of the line. Ironically, the race had been won by a horse named It's Not My Fault and there was I saying to Martin that while I was sorry about what happened, I didn't think there was anything I could have done. I doubt if a word registered with him, so I just switched off. 'OK,' I thought, 'you do what you want. The horse fell, it wasn't my fault. I don't give a damn any more.'

God knows why luck changes but it does. Three days after that unlucky fall, I went to Warwick to ride four horses for Martin. The first three, Prerogative, Honest Word and Gay Ruffian, all won and it was as if someone waved a wand and changed everything. Two days later I was at Southwell – five rides for Martin and again three won. Six winners in two racing days and I thought, 'This is why I joined Martin Pipe.' Adrian's lead had been at an all time high of 43 when I went to Warwick but leaving Southwell on that Monday evening, the deficit, still great, no longer seemed insurmountable.

If the winners proved Martin's horses were coming into form and that my luck had turned, so too it had turned for Adrian. Winning the King George on Barton Bank was close to the high point of his season but the win came with a small sting in the tail. Adrian got a two-day ban for misuse of the whip and it was the beginning of a bad run for him. He incurred a further two suspensions in January, four days for careless riding at Folkestone and six days for misuse of the whip at Warwick. On that day at Warwick, there was another indication of how the pendulum had swung my way when Adrian rode Waterloo Boy in preference to Viking Flagship in the re-scheduled Victor Chandler Chase. The Duke, who may have twisted Adrian's arm in Waterloo Boy's direction, offered me the ride on Viking

Flagship and we won well. Gurgling as he nearly always did, we just got up on the run-in to beat Jamie Osborne riding my Tripleprint partner Egypt Mill Prince.

Our race for the championship had become *mano-a-mano* – we began to ride not against every jockey in the race but more and more against each other. Adrian's six-day ban at Warwick happened because both of us felt impelled not to lose to the other. It was a two-and-a-half-mile novice chase. I rode Castle Diamond, Adrian was on Ramstar, and from the second last, we had the race between us. Both our horses were hardy partners and from the moment Ramstar drew alongside Castle Diamond, no one could foretell the result. We would each rather have died than let the other win. Adrian knew, with me having ridden nine winners in the previous week, that at last I was on his trail. And in the blistering intensity of this fiercely fought finish, everything but the desire to win went out the window. People will say Adrian should not have hit Ramstar as often as he did. In the cold light of day no jockey would but this wasn't the cold light of day; this was man against man, two jockeys prepared to fight to the end.

I might have used my stick more sensibly than Adrian did but I was eight years older. At 22, how would I have dealt with that kind of pressure? I wasn't even good enough to get into that position at that age. Castle Diamond won a titanic race by a short head, Adrian got a six-day ban and even if I couldn't defend his use of the stick, I fully understood it. The last thing I would do is criticise him for it.

Before all of this, Adrian and I hadn't known each other that well. There was an age difference and we didn't change near each other. We had different valets – Adrian's was Pat Taylor; the Buckinghams sorted me out. We had gone racing together a few times but he was fairly quiet and although he had achieved a lot in a very short time, he was a relative newcomer to the weighing room. He certainly could ride and he was popular with the other Irish lads who knew him better than I did. Even from a distance, he wasn't someone you could dislike and there was never a lasting grudge between us. But this campaign made us rivals and it was inevitable that it became personal. I didn't want him to ride winners, he didn't want me riding them, and like two live wires, sparks flew when we touched. Whether I agreed or disagreed with Adrian's ban was irrelevant. I saw it simply as my opportunity.

Over seven racing days from 29 January, I rode 18 winners. Ten of the 18 were on Martin's horses and, significantly, four of them were on horses trained by the Duke. Every winner I rode for the Duke was like two because it was one Adrian should have had. As happens in sport, winning sorts out problems. Martin and I began to get on much better and I sensed that, at last, he was beginning to have confidence in me. He was certainly being more supportive. I had 29 winners in January and when Adrian returned to action on 7 February his lead was down to six. By the end of February it was down to four and Martin's talent for producing winners on spring evenings in April and May meant the odds now favoured me. It could even have been enjoyable had I occasionally been able to step back from the blinding search for the next winner, but that wasn't possible.

Things were happening in races between Adrian and me, little skirmishes unnoticed by everyone except us. He would come up my inside and I would shout, 'Adrian, where are you going? Don't try it.' Having grown up on the pony-racing circuit in Ireland, Adrian knew the rules. You went up somebody's inside at your peril. We're talking the ethics of the weighing room, not the rules of racing. Adrian was just proving he didn't fear me. I had no doubts on that score. He wasn't the aggressor. I would try to get up his inner, too. It was a matter of putting one over on the other and if you let someone up your inside, you were soft and you weren't doing your job. Though Adrian and I were different characters, we could both be volatile. And so, almost inevitably, along came Raggerty and Mr Geneaology.

It was a hurdle race at Nottingham on an afternoon in early March that would normally pass the racing public by. With three hurdles to jump, I pushed Raggerty into the lead aware that Adrian was right behind. A bit earlier he had shouted at Willie McFarland, riding Mr Geneaology's unfancied stablemate Manon Lescaut to move out so he could come through on the inside. That would have meant Raggerty being pushed wider than I wanted and I tried to keep Willie pinned where he was. I jumped the third last on the inside but then drifted off the inner going to the second last. With no running rail to guide us, I wanted to stay just a little off the inside to make sure Raggerty didn't run out.

Unintentionally, I'd given Adrian the opportunity to push up on my inner and he seized it. In my eyes, what he attempted was unacceptable. He wasn't simply trying to win the race, he was trying to put one over on me. I wasn't having it and pulled Raggerty to the left, closing the door on Mr Geneaology. Had he been a braver horse, he may still have jumped the hurdle but he ducked out and we went on to win by 15 lengths. Steve Coathup, Raggerty's trainer, thought as I did that Adrian had no right to be poking his nose up the inner. The stewards, we felt, would see it that way but, in fact, we were the only two people in Nottingham who took this fairly uncompromising view.

In the weighing room, Norman Williamson suggested I would be in trouble and Jonjo O'Neill advised me to tell the stewards that I hadn't seen Adrian coming up on my inside. They might have believed I was stupid but I don't think I could have convinced them I was blind. Outside the stewards' room I sat, Adrian stood.

'What the fuck were you at?'

'Where the fuck were you going?'

The stewards replayed it on video, from one angle and then another. I went into the stewards' room angry but the red mist evaporated with each viewing. I had left a gap through which Adrian could have driven a small car. When Geoffrey Forster, the stewards' secretary, started to acknowledge that Adrian had every right to go where he went, my approach changed. I wasn't looking for justice any more. Mercy would do. I was given a 14-day ban for causing intentional interference. That meant no Cheltenham. For the first time in my career, I would miss jump racing's biggest meeting. Not a word passed between Adrian and me until later in the afternoon when he said, 'I'm sorry you're going to miss Cheltenham.'

That evening I suggested to Adrian we should stop for a drink at TGI Fridays, just off the M6 near Coventry. Five or six of us stopped; maybe the lads thought it dangerous to allow us to meet alone. I bought Adrian a drink and we laughed about it –

well, sort of. I joked about him needing to look where he was going. He said I'd better keep watching my inner. We smiled and left it at that.

A couple of days later I went to Peter Terry's office to discuss my latest escapade.

'Tell me what happened,' said Peter.

'Adrian tried to take liberties up the inside. I didn't let him.'

'Do you remember we spoke about you being more aggressive?'

'Yes, I do, but this wasn't what we agreed was it?'

'How long is the ban?'

'Fourteen days, starting next week.'

'How do you feel about life at the moment?'

'The championship's over for me I think. He'll be too far ahead. And I'll miss Cheltenham. All in all, I'm very low.'

'What are you planning to do for the two weeks you're banned?'

'I haven't really thought about it.'

'What have you always wanted to do but couldn't because racing stopped you?'

'I've always wanted to go skiing.'

'Is there any reason why you shouldn't go skiing next week?'

'No, there isn't.'

The next day I booked a week's skiing in Val d'Isère in the French Alps and went there with Mark Low, a friend who had ridden as an amateur. What a week! Philippe Brabant was our ski guide. Yes, of course, we can ski, we told him when what we meant was that having ridden over fences, skiing didn't worry us. Going down was fine, pulling up was the difficulty and without the orange netting surrounding the ski-lifts, we mightn't have done it. In the evening we told tall stories of hair-raising descents, tales fuelled by countless rounds of tequila slammers. Don't ask how many but I can tell you what they did – they obliterated Cheltenham. Next morning a glance at *Paris-Turf* was as much real life as I could cope with. I read that Flakey Dove and Mark Dwyer won the Champion Hurdle, Viking Flagship became another Adrian winner in the Queen Mother Champion Chase and I was relieved to see The Fellow had won the Gold Cup. If Adrian had won on my intended mount Miinnehoma, it would have been too much. And so off we went for another day on the slopes, Mark, myself and Philippe who, being a fairly mad Frenchman, warmed to our crazy antics. By the end of the week we'd discovered that courage only gets you down the slopes; it takes something more physical to stop you.

Peter Terry believed the skiing break would rekindle the fires and it did. My last ride had been on 9 March and by the time I returned at Wincanton on 24 March, Adrian had increased his lead to 25 but the deficit didn't faze me. Instead it gave me a target and I felt ready for the next nine weeks. From Hexham to Huntingdon, Worcester to Wetherby, Cheltenham to Cartmel, I was available for every ride. Adrian did the same and though neither of us enjoyed the last leg of our rollercoaster ride, we didn't have a choice. We did, however, go through our end game without ill-feeling. The Raggerty–Mr Geneaology collision at Nottingham had brought simmering hostility to the surface but once expressed, it vanished. From now to the end, there was hardly a hint of rancour.

It must have been a terrible time for Adrian. At least, I was getting the winners and constantly eating into his lead; he was making the same effort, travelling the same distances but not getting the rewards. Four weeks from the end of the season, at a time when Adrian desperately needed winners, the supply line ran dry. Over a two-week period he rode 49 consecutive losers and as much as the winners I rode, his losing run determined the destination of the championship.

On the last Monday in April, I went to Hexham for one ride, Peter Beaumont's Skircoat Green. Hexham is as close to Scotland as makes no difference and I overnighted in West Auckland before travelling on to Wetherby the next day. I rode two there, then flew south to ride four at that evening's meeting at Ascot. Next morning I flew to Punchestown and after riding three over there, I caught a flight back to Staverton airfield to make Cheltenham's evening meeting. Next day it was back to Ireland for six rides at Punchestown. That was Thursday. On Friday I was back in England for Newton Abbot and then Bangor in the evening. The madness of the week ended the next day with four rides at Uttoxeter followed by five that evening at Plumpton.

From Uttoxeter I travelled to Plumpton on a private helicopter hired by the owner Colin Smith for Adrian. It was normal for Adrian and I to share helicopters when it was convenient and even though some journalists believed there was enmity between us, there wasn't. We each knew what the other was going through. During those six days from Monday to Saturday I'd had 34 rides at ten different race meetings. The eight winners were the immediate compensation but the toll would come much later. The footnote to the week came with my last ride that Saturday night at Plumpton, Musical High for Martin. Running in a hurdle race, Musical High shattered a hind leg and had to be put down. Momentarily I wondered what it was all for and then I got on with it.

April was bad, May was even worse. On one manic day, Adrian and I rode at three different race meetings – Hereford, Southwell and Huntingdon. Even though the pair of us should have been on our knees, the adrenalin fizzed through our veins and over the last two weeks of the campaign, we both rode a stack of winners. When our battle was at its most intense, we were both more committed and more concentrated than we would ever be in our lives. We persuaded horses to win that in normal circumstances would never have got there. Whatever credit I deserve for surviving ten months on the trail of the jockeys' title, Adrian deserves just as much.

Even though I hated it, the battle had become all consuming, difficult to live with, impossible to live without. For me, the hardest day was the first Wednesday in June, three days before the end of the season. There was no National Hunt racing that day and I didn't know what to do. Sit at home and relax? Impossible. Go to the Epsom Derby and deal with all those questions about the championship? No thanks. In the end I went down to the Queen's pub in Lambourn, where the jump racing clientele knew not to ask the usual questions. There, I watched the Derby with a mate, Tom Butterfield, and waited for the day to pass. Butters, an Aussie, did his best with his humour and sharp wit to take my mind off things.

Next day was Uttoxeter and I thought I could win the first on Ghia Gneuiagh. I did but Adrian rode a treble and reduced my lead to three with just two days to go. On the second last day,

Adrian won the first at Stratford on Southampton and although not listed to ride in the third, he got the call for Res Ipsa Loquitur when Dean Gallagher's car broke down and he failed to get to the course in time. Had Dean deliberately given Adrian the chance of a winner? Perhaps he did but so what? We had to get winners any way possible. Res Ipsa Loquitur won and halfway through the second last day, I led by just one. That became two when I won the last on a very willing partner, Ron Hodges' Take A Flyer.

It was only right that it went to the wire. Martin, who had continually helped me plot and plan in the closing weeks, had foreseen that it might. His horses had been a godsend in the latter stages of the season and he sent four to Stratford on the final day. Three of them won, extending my advantage to five. Barring the bizarre, the title was mine. Then at the final venue of the season, an evening meeting at Market Rasen, Adrian won the first two races and the crowd were thinking of the most improbable finish – another three winners and he could tie. He would have deserved it but it didn't happen. I felt no elation; spiritually drained, I wondered what Adrian must have been thinking.

Next day was Brendan Powell's wedding. Adrian was best man and had to make a speech. I tried to get in the swing of it but didn't feel much like it. On the Tuesday we went down to Shepton Mallet in Somerset to see the Saw Doctors in concert and had a good evening. A few days later, I happened to be driving to Swindon and pulled into a McDonald's. The burger and milkshake were the first I'd had for many months. They were the best. That was my celebration.

Of the 36 runners who walked round the paddock for the 1994 Grand National, Martin Pipe trained five. I had chosen Miinne-homa, a past winner of the Sun Alliance Chase at Cheltenham and a horse of undoubted ability. I rode him earlier in the season when he won at Newbury and got the impression he did not like to be in front for very long. With four other runners, I didn't spend long talking tactics with Martin.

'If we're in contention, I won't be hitting the front too soon. Is that all right?' I said.

'Yeah, fine, fine,' he replied.

We both knew Miinnehoma was a high-class horse on his day but the heavy going might be against him and there was no guarantee he would like Liverpool. He went off at 16 to 1, a price that tallied with our view.

I'd had a good Liverpool. Docklands Express and Cyborgo had won on the Thursday and Friday and after my week's skiing at Val d'Isère I felt refreshed. First thing I noticed on Grand National morning was the snow on the ground, as it had been the year West Tip won. Miinnehoma's number was eight, as West Tip's had been in 1986. And I knew that if Miinnehoma took to the Aintree fences and went on the ground, he would have a big chance. After the fiasco of 12 months earlier, we first had to get started. This time there was no trouble and Miinnehoma flew down to the first, faster than I wanted, and for most of the first circuit, I tried gently to restrain him. The trick was to relax him, not disappoint him. Then, there was the problem with his jockey – such was the ease with which the horse was travelling, I was finding it hard to believe. I could feel the tension, the excitement, the irregular breathing – we have a chance here! At the time there were still three miles to go. At Valentine's, I took several deep breaths and soon I began to relax. Miinnehoma made things easy for me, his sure-footed jumping kept him out of danger and his natural class allowed him to race as close to the pace as I wished.

After a circuit, we were cruising in third place and my greatest concern was to make sure we didn't end up in the lead. But as horses fell, got knocked out of the race and others tired it was proving impossible and Miinnehoma found himself in front going to the huge ditch, the nineteenth. With nothing to follow, he was trying to stop and I roared at him to get him to jump. Ebony Jane, the Irish mare, then came past us and everything was all right. At Becher's second time, Miinnehoma pecked on landing and dropped to his knee, his head on the ground, but he righted himself and away we went. Luckily, I sat where I was. It was one of those recoveries that looked dramatic but he kept straight and I was able to stay on board. From there to the finish, I had so much horse underneath me it wasn't true. All I had to do was bide my time.

Crossing the Melling Road and going to the second last, Adrian loomed up beside me on Moorcroft Boy. 'I suppose you're going to win this one as well, you little bastard,' I shouted half jokingly across at him. But I hadn't moved a muscle on Miinnehoma and only when Adrian quickened away from the last, did I have to give my horse a smack. He picked up immediately and overhauled Moorcroft Boy effortlessly; then came the shock. Aintree's run-in is notoriously long, the noise of the crowd can stop horses and I sensed Miinnehoma trying to pull himself up as we rounded the elbow. As I tried to kid him, not using the stick but just loosening the reins, a black head suddenly appeared alongside. My heart missed a beat. 'Jesus, we're stuffed,' I thought. To have been beaten on a horse that had hardly been off the bridle would have been mortifying. But the sight of Just So galvanised Miinnehoma, he picked up again and won decisively by a length and a half. Chester and Martin ran up like lunatics as we pulled up. None of us could believe it.

Carl Llewellyn and I had long decided that if either of us won a second Grand National, we would celebrate even more than we did first time round. In many ways, Miinnehoma's win was better than West Tip's; it was unexpected and it came so soon after my return from the 14-day suspension. The victory was savoured. Yet when I got home after the second or third party, the thought did strike me that success in the world's greatest steeplechase was just another winner in the battle against Adrian. It was that kind of year.

15

NO TWO PEOPLE

B y the early months of 1994, Carol and I knew our marriage was nearing its end. The realisation came gradually and painfully. We married in July 1988, both young, both sure of the commitment we were making. For two years it was fine, then little disagreements became rows, the rows became more frequent and no matter how many times we made up, we couldn't return to the easy harmony that had been there in the first place. We both tried and Carol did everything she could to make it work. In the end I think we accepted we weren't meant for each other. During the final years with Carol, I knew it would be better to be on my own. This wasn't so much a reflection on her, more a need to give myself completely to my career. It wasn't that I didn't want Carol getting in the way; I didn't want anybody in the way.

Consider the morning in early May 1993 when the letter came from Buckingham Palace. Basically, it said that if the Queen of England did not find any reason to do otherwise, she was including me in her honours list. Within weeks I would be champion jockey for the first time and now this award of an MBE that transcended racing. I was amazed. Sometime later, a date for the investiture was chosen – 7 December. I checked the racing fixtures – Plumpton. 'Damn,' I thought, 'Martin will probably have runners at Plumpton that day.' So I said no, couldn't make it in December. It would have to be in the summer.

Nothing could justify missing the chance of riding winners. Even when it came to ending our marriage, we couldn't do it in mid-season. A few months before we separated, we knew it was over and I would move out. But at the time I was locked into that duel with Adrian Maguire for the jockeys' championship and didn't have time to leave my wife. How could I find another place to live, have a sauna installed, move my stuff, get a new home telephone number, fix up the new place and not let it affect me? I couldn't. I had to be champion and therefore I couldn't leave. I asked Carol if she minded my staying until I got the season out of the way and she agreed. Even though she had accepted we should separate, she was very unhappy about it. She later said that during those months she felt as if there was an egg-timer on our marriage and every day she watched as the grains of sand inexorably slid away.

It was early August, the beginning of the 1991–92 season and I had two rides at Market Rasen, Infeb and Mummy's Fox. Infeb was due to carry just 10st 6lb which meant I had to get down to 10st 2lb. Just returned from the summer break, I had pounds to shed before setting out for the day's racing. The prospect of two hours in the sauna to lose 4 or 5lb invariably put me in bad form and at times like that, Carol and I could argue about anything. That morning it was particularly explosive. Carol had found out that I had been involved with another woman and was desperately upset. She said she didn't mind being number two to racing, that she could accept, but she wasn't prepared to be number three or four. She insisted we talk but all I could think of was that 10st 6lb on Infeb. 'I'm sorry,' I said, 'I've got to stay in the sauna.' Carol couldn't take any more.

She went upstairs, came back down and got into her car. Seconds later I heard the car crash into the fence. I went outside. The car was moving at about five miles an hour down the driveway but not exactly in a straight line. I brought Carol back inside; it was obvious she wasn't well. She said she had taken 20 paracetamol. I rang for an ambulance and then rang Bob, her father. I said, 'Look, Carol isn't very good here.' Bob, who has since passed away, loved his daughter dearly. He was desperately angry. Of our two families, he more than anyone sensed our marriage wasn't good and knew instinctively that if anything had happened to Carol, I would have driven her to it.

The ambulance arrived first. I was still in my dressing gown because I would have to go back to the sauna. After examining Carol, one of the paramedics told me she was going to be all right. Then Bob arrived. He looked into the ambulance and saw Carol lying there. He was incensed.

'What have you done to her?' he shouted, pinning me against the wall of the house.

'If you want to hit, hit me,' I said. 'Go on, it doesn't matter.'

Whatever Bob did, I would have deserved it. Nothing could have made me feel any worse than I already did. I hated the way I treated Carol and yet I went on doing it. What was it? Frustration with the constant wasting? An inability to cope with bad days at the racecourse? Maybe something deeper? As I have said before, my behaviour could be explained but never excused. Bob knew there was no point in throttling me, taking out his anger on me wasn't going to help his daughter and she was what he cared about. The ambulance took Carol to the Princess Margaret in Swindon; Bob drove home, picked up Ann, Carol's mother, and followed on to the hospital. I went back into the sauna.

After about an hour I showered, got dressed and headed cross country to Market Rasen. Though favourite for her race, Infeb was beaten a distance as was Mummy's Fox. That evening I called in on Aiden Murphy and Anabel King on the way home from the racecourse and although I told them about Carol's hospitalisation, I would not have encouraged in-depth discussion. The following morning, Carol lay in hospital in Swindon waiting for me to come and visit. Her parents were there, my parents were there, but the one person she was desperate to see didn't come. My absence caused deep hurt. When it was time for her to be discharged later that day, I came and collected her. She asked me to drop her at her parents' house but I said no, we were still married and it would be better to go home. And I carried on as if not much had happened.

Carol felt guilty about the overdose even though she had absolutely no reason to. I'm not sure why I didn't visit on that Sunday morning; like a lot of things at the time, I'd simply blanked the previous day from my mind. I almost believed it hadn't happened. I didn't want us to separate. We put so much into building our home and for a long time, I half-hoped our problems were caused by the torturous demands of racing and by my immaturity and that once they were behind us, our relationship would improve. Carol, I imagine, nurtured the same hope. There wasn't a thing Carol wouldn't have done to save our marriage and it survived for another three years. It wasn't good but neither was it always bad. Saturday was our night out and we would link up with the Bosleys, Martin and Sarah, Simon and Sarah McNeil, Carl Llewellyn, Luke Harvey and others. I would fall asleep at the table and Carol, always sympathetic to how hard the life could be, would drive me home.

The difficulties in our marriage were at their worst during the more pressurised periods in my career. I could never relax. There was always some race to review on the video, another hour to do in the sauna and important telephone calls to make. A quiet evening watching TV didn't interest me. Where was the importance or the thrill in that? A clandestine relationship, that was something else. Carol heard about some of the liaisons and once confronted me about a woman with whom we were both friendly. I admitted it was true. Carol felt betrayed. A few years later, she found herself standing next to her former friend at a funeral. Not much was said until the congregation was asked to recite the Lord's Prayer. At the point it says 'and forgive us our trespasses', Carol gently nudged her in the ribs and as their eyes met she said aloud, 'as *we* forgive those who trespass against *us*'.

No matter how difficult or impossible I was being, Carol continued to be a devoted wife. Supper was always ready, the sauna was on before I got home, the racing had been recorded and the more Carol did for me, the more I resented it. I needed space, not devotion. In the end I was almost asking to be kicked out. But the worse I behaved, the more Carol tried to appease me. During our marriage and after it ended, the tabloids tried to get her to tell sensational stories of our life together. In all there were three or four approaches and, of course, she would have been well paid. Another woman might easily have been tempted but Carol had too much dignity for that. She has also said that seeing the strain I was having to deal with, she could forgive me anything. Only she could take so charitable a view.

Although not as committed to our marriage as Carol, I did try. With Hilary Kerr's help, I began visiting Mrs Buckley, the psychotherapist who was qualified to advise those with marital difficulties. We met at her office a number of times. I spoke honestly about our relationship and how I could lose my temper when we argued. Plates could fly, pictures could be smashed and reason went out the window. Realising how dangerous I was in that state, I would turn the anger on myself and beat my fists and head against the walls and doors. Mrs Buckley asked me to bring Carol along for a consultation and having spoken to us individually, she then spoke to us together. She concluded that our relationship was too combustible and we should separate.

Leaving Mrs Buckley's that day, Carol was dejected but prepared to go with the advice. Again, she asked me to drop her off at her parents'. But I still wasn't prepared to give it up. We'd been together for five years and if I sorted myself out, maybe everything would be OK. But Mrs Buckley had also said that no one, not a marital counsellor nor anyone else, could make people love each other and there just wasn't enough love to hold us together.

We tried different things. On Mrs Buckley's advice, Carol thought it would be good for her to develop her own life and she started the photography with Mel Fordham. Even though our marriage was on its last legs, I was proud of her when the *Sporting Life* used photographs taken by her of my jumping the last on Miinnehoma in the Grand National. Once the photograph was taken, Carol abandoned her professional responsibilities and cheered us home. She did well behind a lens and it was a pity that after our separation, she stopped doing it. She found it hard to be at the races photographing her ex-husband. Five years later, injury forced me out and now I prefer not to attend race meetings. So both of us have different reasons for feeling the same way about the sport.

As soon as the 1993–94 season ended, I looked around for someone to do some secretarial work and Liz Simmons came to help me. She had once been Fulke Walwyn's secretary and also worked for Jamie Osborne who recommended her highly. Carol had done much of my office work and she resisted Liz because it was another step along the separation road. Liz was actually a pillar of strength during the separation and sometimes acted as a go-between. She kept me in check, insisted I always treat people fairly and was like a second mother. 'Make sure you send Robert and Ciaran decent presents,' she would say. 'My God, they deserve it!' Liz, sadly, passed away in 1997.

Despite the fact that our relationship was in terminal decline, Carol and I agreed to go on holiday together in early June. There was a racing group going out to Barbados again and the previous year we had been able to put our troubles behind us. This time, it wasn't possible. We hadn't left the country before we were rowing.

'Look,' I said eventually as we drove down to Mel Fordham's. We were leaving our car at Mel's and he was taking us to Gatwick. 'We don't want to be going on holiday together.'

Carol agreed, saying she didn't want to go either. But the holiday was booked and it seemed too late to turn back. On the flight we had our second row and I moved to the rear of the plane. The flight attendant asked me to move back and we endured the rest of the journey in silence. At the airport in Barbados, we continued to argue.

'You can take the next flight back, if you like,' I said.

'Fine. I'll do that.'

Carol was in tears, I was wound up like a coil and it just went from bad to worse. Some nights we managed to go out for a couple of hours together, other times I got a takeaway from the nearby petrol station and spent the evening alone. I don't remember much about the holiday. I've removed most of it from my mind. I thought back to the holidays we had once enjoyed together and finally understood that our marriage was over. Carol knew it too.

Back in England, I began to make arrangements for the separation. Carol and I agreed she should continue to live in our home because she wasn't the one wanting to leave. Liz helped me find a small cottage in the nearby village of Great Coxwell and Carol and I agreed to use this period away from each other to see how we felt. During our marriage there had never been another man in Carol's life and at that time there was no other woman in mine.

Racing marriages, they say, are conceived in stables and dissolved in horseboxes. On the last Tuesday of August, sandwiched between Monday and Wednesday racing at Newton Abbot, Martin Bosley came with the horsebox to move my belongings. Martin was a good friend to both of us and had been my best man. He knew this would be a much less happy occasion, so he tried to lighten the mood. 'I was there at the beginning,' he said, 'and it's only right that I'm here at the end.' We went from room to room, taking what I needed to set up a new home. Carol was there throughout. When we got to our bedroom and I started to take my clothes out of our wardrobe, she broke down.

'You can't go, you just can't go.'

'Carol,' I said, 'we agreed I would move. It's best.'

'I know,' she said and let me go.

Almost immediately Carol wiped her tears, drove into Wantage and bought all the provisions you need when moving into a new house – sugar, coffee, tea, cereal, bread, milk, butter and lots of other essentials. They were packed into a box and when she got back Martin and I were almost ready to move.

'This is your Red Cross parcel. You'll be needing it,' she said with a smile.

Leaving home that August afternoon, I knew it was over but I had no wish to make it official.

'We won't get divorced,' I said, 'we'll sort this out some other way.' Five years passed before we accepted there was no other way.

In the meantime, it was important to work out a separation settlement. Carol had been my wife for six years and she had to be properly taken care of. I wasn't that rich and I felt I'd rather give the money to Carol than it end up in the pockets of solicitors and barristers so I asked her if we could work matters out without the help of the legal profession. There were times when it became a little stressful but, by and large, we sorted things out. We were both satisfied. Carol remained at the house for about a year and then we sold it.

After I moved out, we would meet regularly, sometimes for coffee, sometimes for lunch and we usually got on great. People would see us together and suggest that maybe a reconciliation was on the cards. We knew it wasn't.

After a while, Carol began seeing Gerry Hogan, a likeable and very popular Irish jockey who rode for the Duke and Jenny Pitman. They had a good time together and in the weighing room I was mercilessly teased by Adrian, Johnny Kavanagh and a few of the other Irish lads. I'd be after winning a valuable race and feeling quite pleased when Adrian would say, 'What's that Richard, your percentage of twenty grand, about eighteen hundred? Not bad, but then, of course, you'll have to give half of that to Gerry.'

'Look lads, don't be talking,' Johnny Kavanagh might say, 'sure, isn't it great that Gerry can have such a good day without having to be at the races?'

Well, I suppose it was good to be able to laugh. Five months after our separation, the Saw Doctors invited Carol over to where they lived in Tuam, County Galway. Leo Moran said she could do with some R and R, rest and recreation. She didn't get much of the former but there was plenty of the latter as Carol discovered Tuam's livelier pubs. She stayed with Leo's father Jimmy who is one of nature's gentlemen. Jimmy must be in his eighties now but he took Carol under his wing, showed her the local sights, drove her out to Connemara and let her take in some of Ireland's most breathtaking countryside. A lot of people told Carol how wise Jimmy was, a great family man and a great one for traditional values. Seeing herself as a separated English lass, Carol was a little fearful. The subject of our separation had to come up.

'Carol,' Jimmy said, 'no two people are meant to be together forever.'

16

BREAKING POINT

L uke Harvey changed my life.

On the morning of 6 January 1995, Uttoxeter was just another day at the office. It was halfway through my fourteenth season and having won two Grand Nationals, a Gold Cup, a Champion Hurdle and two championships, it had been a good career to that point. For the first 13 seasons, I had managed to ride more winners every year. On this Uttoxeter day I led the jockeys' championship with 111 winners and there wasn't much to complain about. For the first time in my career, the 200 winner mark looked reachable. After last season's battle with Adrian, perhaps I could win the title without drama. That was how I wanted it. But just when I thought things had been sorted, Luke Harvey came creeping up behind me and life would never be the same.

We were friends from ten years before when both of us worked at the Captain's at Letcombe Bassett. I was on the second rung of the ladder, he had just stepped on to the first, and we were very different characters – his cheese to my chalk. But you had to like Luke. He was witty, good fun and even if he took the mickey out of everyone else, he didn't take himself too seriously. We mixed in the same social circle and in ten years of friendship, there was hardly an angry word. Then came Uttoxeter. I can laugh now but on that January afternoon in 1995, it was hard to see the funny side.

The race was a novice hurdle for mares, an inconsequential

contest that catered for the less talented horses. Luke's was called Wadswick Country and mine G'Ime A Buzz. There were just six horses in the race and with four hurdles to jump, G'Ime A Buzz was on the outside of the leader, Gala's Pride. Luke was close behind us. Gala's Pride fell at that hurdle and I was left in the lead. I went to the rail but my horse was hanging slightly to the right, leaving a small gap. On the bend before the finishing straight, Luke saw the opportunity to sneak through. 'Oh no you don't,' I thought. I could hear him behind and edged my horse closer to the rail to stop him. As has been said, you shouldn't try to come through on the inner unless your horse is quick enough to get there. Luke had tried but not made it.

Once in the straight, there was no running rail to guide us and, suspecting Luke would attempt it again, I went inside the line where the rail would have been and where we normally would have raced. He shouldn't have even considered it but, probably annoyed at having been shut out on his first try, he went for it again. He was going a long way off the course. This was mad; neither of our horses was going to win. They were barely doing a canter at the time. Angry now, I bore further to the left in an attempt to stop Luke. G'Ime A Buzz was simply not up to it. Going that bit quicker, Luke got through. Anger turned to rage when we both had to pull quite sharply right handed to jump the first hurdle in the straight, the third last. Wadswick Country finished a ten-length second to Hops and Pops, G'Ime A Buzz struggled home an even more distant third and then the drama began.

I got to Luke as he pulled his horse up.

'What were you bloody well doing?'

'You left enough room on your inside.'

'You were totally out of order, you'd no right . . .'

'I had every right.'

The stewards, of course, wanted to speak to the two cowboys for whom the race had seemed a secondary concern. Outside the stewards' room, the argument raged on.

'What the hell were you trying to prove?'

'Who the hell do you think you are? Champion jockey, can't be touched?'

'Don't be so stupid. If you had brains you'd be fucking dangerous.'

'You're being stupid.'

Luke was actually among the more intelligent in the weighing room.

Had the stewards' secretary not called us in just then, there might well have been a punch-up. Luke insisted he had done nothing wrong, there had been a gap and he went for it. But, in my eyes, he hadn't got there and it was stupid of him to try again. He was putting one over on me. Walking into that stewards' room, I was as angry as I'd ever been in my life. Normally, jockeys don't criticise each other in front of the stewards but so fierce was the animosity, the normal rules didn't apply. Robert Earnshaw, the former jockey and stewards' secretary at Uttoxeter, asked the questions.

'Mr Harvey, what is your account?'

'Coming to the last bend neither Richard nor myself were going particularly well. I was content to track him. My horse got a second wind and started to run on again. Richard's horse was lying a horse's width off the rails and I've decided to go up his inside. I've gone to within a head or a neck of him and he's closed the gap.'

'Thank you. Mr Dunwoody, your account?'

'I've jumped the last down the back and have gone round the faller. I've gone on to the rail as soon as I left the back straight and all I know is Luke is trying to force his way up on my inner halfway round the bend. It was an absolute fucking disgrace. He had the whole of Uttoxeter racecourse to go round me.'

'There appeared to be a second incident, Mr Harvey?'

'I'm on the inside berth again and I've got enough horse to stay where I am. My horse was not beaten by any means but the gap has been closed again.'

'Mr Dunwoody, your account of the second incident?'

'I didn't know there was a second incident.'

'Would you like to add anything, Mr Harvey?'

'If I was to ride the race again, I would do exactly the same.'

'Mr Dunwoody?'

'If he was to ride the same race again, he would not be going out to ride in the next one.'

'Do you still feel, Mr Dunwoody, that Mr Harvey was forcing his way up your inside?'

'It was the most stupid piece of riding I've ever seen.'

'What, keeping on the inside?'

'Excuse me gentlemen, could we take this one at a time?'

After going over the same ground, Robert Earnshaw asked us to wait outside. Calling us back in, Mrs Ockleston, the Chairwoman of the panel, read the verdict – 'The stewards have found there was interference which was caused by you, Mr Dunwoody. As this is the second offence of this nature, the matter is referred to the Jockey Club.'

Sometimes the difficulty for jockeys is that the rules of racing do not tally with what *we* consider unacceptable. A panel of jockeys, I believe, would have ruled that Luke was not entirely blameless. It was said afterwards that I'd tried to kill him but that was never the case, at least during the race! Those two horses weren't going fast enough to keep themselves warm. There was no danger to either of us.

The visit to Portman Square fell on my birthday, 18 January. Experience in these cases convinced me it would be as well to conduct my own defence and I went there without legal representation. Luke was called, too, and having gone through the evidence, the Jockey Club cleared me of the careless riding charge in the first incident but agreed with the Uttoxeter stewards that I caused intentional interference in the second. They took a dim view of the fact that it was the second such offence in a 12-month period and handed me a 28-day ban. It came with a warning that a third offence would lead to a draconian suspension. Twenty-eight days seemed draconian enough to me.

There were a lot of media people at Portman Square but with seven rides at Windsor, I couldn't hang around. A number of photographers anticipated my escape through the back door of the Jockey Club's offices but we made the course on time. Out front they stopped Luke and asked about the outcome. Without divulging details, he said, 'Richard's been given a good opportunity to improve his skiing.' At Windsor, there were other media people on the case. Had there been a murder? Was there a pyscho in the weighing room? It felt like that. Rob

Bonnett interviewed me for the BBC News, six o'clock and nine o'clock.

'How do you feel about it?' he asked.

'Well, there are a lot worse things going on in the world,' I said.

Windsor – seven rides but no winner – was my last race meeting for 30 days. The next two days were lost to the weather and then my suspension kicked in. Such was the length of the ban, I had time to think beyond the next day, the next week, the next winner. It was a strange experience. Twenty-eight days this time, 14 for running Adrian out a year before, was I losing it altogether? The authorities clearly thought so. Chris Grant recalled a time at Cheltenham when the two of us were a long way off the pace, out of contention and I closed the door on him as he attempted a run up the inner. What struck me about the Granty incident was I couldn't even remember it. Was it happening so instinctively? Michael Caulfield said the rights and wrongs were secondary, what I had to get into my thick skull was that this was the last chance. Once more and the stewards would crucify me.

Martin Pipe was disappointed as it left him without a stable jockey for almost a month. Maybe he would have preferred me to stay around to help with schooling but there could be no question of that. Watching other people ride my horses for that length of time would have been too demoralising. This ban gave Adrian the chance to get right back into the championship race. We were now looking at the kind of head-to-head that neither of us wanted. I had four weeks to play with and the intention was to keep fit and to play.

Three weeks earlier Emma Heanley had walked into my life and this was an opportunity to spend more time with her. Emma had called round to my cottage in Great Coxwell, sent by our mutual friend Jez Webb, to pick up a copy of a book for her mother for Christmas. We got talking. Emma worked in Monaco but her parents lived in the neighbouring village of Little Coxwell. I invited her out for a meal, she agreed and our relationship developed from there. Although Emma had evented, she was not into racing and it was refreshing for me to be with someone who didn't have a clue who I was. For the previous 12 years, I had never stepped outside the boundaries of racing. Emma worked for Keke Rosberg as personal assistant to Mika Hakkinen, the Formula One driver, among others, and her world fascinated me. So three days after Portman Square, I began my sentence in Monaco. It was the start of a big turn-round in my life.

Monaco was more than a breath of fresh air. I found the new scene idyllic and stimulating, but on this particular visit, the joy was shortlived. A day after I got there, Ciaran O'Toole called from Ireland to say that Barry Kelly and his fiancée Sandra Clifford had been killed in a car crash the previous evening. Barry trained near Trim in County Meath. We knew each other through my riding his horses and, like so many people, I thought the world of him. Crowded House was second for us in the 1992 Triumph Hurdle at Cheltenham and Barry often tried to get me down to Clogher Head on Ireland's east coast where he had a summer home and liked to water-ski. It was impossible not to like Barry. He and Sandra were just about to marry and the thought that they had both been killed was devastating. Two days later I was in Trim and so big was the crowd for their removal that there was little chance of getting into the church.

A late flight out of Dublin got me back to Heathrow. I picked up my car there and it was well after midnight when I arrived back in Great Coxwell. I turned on the answer machine. The first message left on the Saturday morning I'd departed came through loud and clear – 'Richard, Barry here. You stupid prat, getting yourself banned. It's lucky for us. Now you can come along to our wedding next week. Make sure you do.' It was eerie, almost surreal. I couldn't take it in. The brutality of real life, one minute he was there, then he was gone. All I had ever worried about was the next winner. For the first time in my life, there was something else to think about, something more important. Where was the sense in my little world? Wondering what Martin would say when a horse got beat? Getting uptight about Luke going up my inner? Losing my mind because some owner preferred to use another jockey? There were more important things in life than riding horses around muddy fields. It had taken me a long time to see it.

The week before, showjumper Nick Skelton had invited me out to Austria where there was a chance of some skiing while he was competing, jumping on the snow. So the next day I joined him in the resort of Kössen and had a memorable four days. Nick is a top man, an exceptional horseman, and he and the other showjumpers certainly know how to live life. Their company was good for me. After Austria, it was off to Dubai where I spent two weeks riding out for Paddy Rudkin who used to be head lad at Henry Cecil's and at Al Quoz, Sheikh Mohammed's yard. A good group of British and Irish Flat jockeys was there. One of them, Johnny Murtagh, and I regularly played squash in sweatsuits to keep the weight down. I felt I had to make the most of my opportunity to travel and immediately after returning from Dubai, I went skiing in Valberg in the Southern Alps with Emma. We met up with David Coulthard, his girlfriend of the time Andrea Murray, and his manager Tim Wright, who worked for IMG (International Management Group). One afternoon there was a speed skiing competition and, with the practice run alongside open, we were tempted.

'Let's give it a go,' I said.

'I'm not going down there,' Tim said.

'Come on.'

'OK, but you first,' he said, giving me a push.

'Right,' I said. There was no way out of it now.

Seven days on skis, I felt, was enough qualification to go down a descent that would get me up to a speed of about 80 miles an hour. Because it was a practice run it was very bumpy and quite dangerous. Halfway down an old woman walked across the run and her life flashed before me – 'If I hit her, she's dead and I can't do anything here.' Thankfully, she stepped away at the last second. As lucky as she was to survive, I was even luckier to stay upright and make it to the bottom. Tim did likewise and we found it an absolutely incredible adrenalin buzz. Then Tim tried to enter me in the competition, telling the organisers they had 'Le ski champion de Grand Bretagne' in their midst. Adrenalin buzz or not, I didn't fancy showing off my recently acquired skills and, luckily, the late entry wasn't accepted.

Back in England, Adrian had closed the gap in the championship and the newspapers were talking of another

Dunwoody/Maguire battle. I dreaded the prospect. During the four weeks, despite having an eye on my weight, I'd gone up by ten pounds and the thought of how much time I would have to spend in the sauna depressed me. I arrived back in England on Saturday, 18 February and had five rides at Fontwell on the Monday. On Sunday afternoon, I called round to see my parents in Clanfield.

'I'm giving up, just don't have the desire any more,' I told them.

'If that's what you want to do, do it,' they said.

I spoke with Ultan Guilfoyle, the TV producer and a close friend for many years. Not wanting to stay in racing after riding, what was I going to do? He advised me not to do anything rash; maybe try to ease back into riding.

'Christ,' I said, I don't want to do these weights any more. And if I'm not doing the light weights, Martin's not going to want to know.'

I was all set not to appear at Fontwell but bad weather caused its abandonment and that gave me more time to think it through. I used the free day to go to see Peter Terry.

'I just can't do ten stone any more. It's becoming unbearable. I'm thinking of giving up.'

'Tell me what it's like.'

'It's murder. I seem to spend half my life in a sauna. It's dragging me down.'

'I knew of one jockey who kept a noose outside his sauna for the day it all became too much.'

'I know how he felt.'

'What are your options?'

'Well, I suppose I could carry on with things as they are or I could stop trying to make ten stone or I could stop riding altogether.'

'What weight could you make comfortably?'

'Ten stone six.'

'What would Martin Pipe say if you said you couldn't make anything under ten stone six?'

Next day on the way to Warwick, the call was made.

'Martin, I want to let you know that I'm not going to do ten stone any more. I'll do ten stone four or ten stone five but I'm not going to kill myself to get down to ten.' He just said, 'Yeah, yeah, if that's the way, that's OK, that's fine.'

It wasn't fine. Martin, the professional that he is, hates his horses carrying overweight, and if I couldn't do ten stone it was bound to be a problem. But with Martin things were never out in the open. Over a season and a half together, an Aintree Grand National winner and many other successes, our relationship had never got to the point where I felt that come hell or high water, Martin would back me. A new confrontation was brewing over the ride on Kissair in the Triumph Hurdle.

Four days before the suspension, I rode Kissair in a novice hurdle at Cheltenham and though a well-beaten third, the horse impressed me. That day we tried to ride him close to the front and I suggested being more patient next time and he would do better. His second run was at Ludlow while I was suspended and this time Jonothan Lower dropped him behind the leaders, went to the front before the third last and bolted in. He had been very impressive and was Martin's only horse for the Triumph Hurdle. About ten days before the Festival, Martin said the owner was keen for Jonothan to keep the ride, having won on him twice. I'd ridden the horse when the tactics were wrong and he had been green first time out over hurdles. I had pointed out how the horse should be ridden and was stable jockey. Martin didn't make it clear if he wanted me. Kissair had a genuine chance in the Triumph and from my point of view, I should have been riding him.

That Thursday afternoon at the Festival is one of the bleaker memories. Before racing began, I had to go to Martin's corporate hospitality box and speak to his guests. 'Well, ladies and gentlemen, we'll start with the Triumph Hurdle. Martin's Kissair has a very good chance although I will be riding Shoofk, a 50 to 1 outsider trained by Simon Dow. We will have run well if we make the first half dozen.'

Shoofk actually finished ninth but through the race, I watched with dismay how easily Jonothan was travelling on Kissair. This was all my nightmares rolled into one. Kissair won well and in the minutes after the race, I realised in terms of my attitude, nothing had changed. Missing Kissair hurt as much as any missed winner had ever hurt. I had given up a lot of good horses to join Martin. I did so because it would help me ride more winners than I could ride anywhere else but I had presumed I would ride the best horses in the yard. Had it been the Duke, he would have stood up to the owner and said, 'He's my stable jockey, he rides it.'

Before the next race, Martin legged me up on his Stayers' Hurdle horse Cyborgo. We didn't exchange a word. When things weren't right, there was little or no communication between us. Cyborgo finished second, Miinnehoma was third behind Master Oats in the Gold Cup, Cyphrate broke down in the Grand Annual Chase and Pridwell could do no better than seventh in the County Hurdle. They'd all been trained by Martin and after three days at Cheltenham there had not been one winner. Allegation did win the next day at the course but it wasn't part of the Festival and for the two seasons I'd been with Martin I hadn't had a winner there.

Kissair was proof that Martin and I hadn't connected. We had a lot of success together and no one could question his record as a trainer. It is testimony to a phenomenal talent for turning out winners. Yet the reality of our time together is that we never hit it off in the way that a trainer and his stable jockey should. We both probably found it difficult to cope with each other's intensity when things weren't going well. I also felt he didn't appreciate my keenness to remain independent of him. Without Martin, I couldn't have beaten Adrian in the 1993–94 championship but it is also true to say that I couldn't have done it without the 103 winners from outside trainers. As he says himself, Martin is a funny character and maybe I didn't have the skill to play him as cleverly as, say, A.P. McCoy now does.

There were other differences of opinion. Martin liked many of his horses to make the running and would often advise me to go as fast as I could for as long as I could. For a man who was so analytical and so bright about many other aspects of training, that wasn't the most enlightened approach to tactics and it didn't leave much to the jockey's skill and judgement of pace.

Aside from that, if the idea was to get from the start to the winning post in the fastest time, it had to be counter-productive to go all out from the beginning. Middle distance and distance athletes believe that to achieve optimum times, you need to cover the second half of the race quicker than the first. The reality is that you lose more time when tiring at the end than you gain by going very quickly in the beginning. In the early months, it upset me having to ride horses at a pace I was convinced was too fast for them. 'You're better than Pipey at this,' Graham McCourt would say. 'You go and tell him to bugger off.' It never came to that; over time I learned to listen to the instructions and not be ruled by them.

Even after A.P. took over at Martin's, it was clear he was getting similar instructions and occasionally it cost him. One of the best rides A.P. gave a horse in the 1999–2000 season was on Edredon Bleu in the Queen Mother Champion Chase. That day A.P.'s achievement was his judgement of pace; he didn't go mad in the first mile and ensured that over the decisive last half-mile, Edredon Bleu had enough in the tank. They easily broke the course record for two miles over fences at Cheltenham and did so by getting the pace right in the first mile. It was A.P. at his very best.

I wasn't comfortable with my involvement in Martin's telephone tipping service, the Pipeline. It was expected that the stable jockey would contribute and would do so for nothing. That was a minor quibble. The bit that bothered me was the presumption that I would discuss rides for outside stables on the Pipeline.

This and Martin's frustration when fancied horses were beaten could have been overcome if, at the end of the day, I felt he was being completely supportive. During that second season, we fell out over Encore Un Peu. The horse had his first run of the season at Chepstow on 1 October, having arrived from France during the summer, and as he wasn't fancied, Martin allowed me to ride Charlie Mann's Washington Heights. The arrangement with Martin was that if we thought his horse didn't have a good chance, he'd allow me to pick up a better-fancied spare ride. Washington Heights finished second and with Jonothan Lower on board, Encore Un Peu was fourth, having run keenly, beaten 14 lengths.

Almost four weeks later, at the end of October 1994, Encore

Un Peu was in a novices' hurdle at Stratford. I was on board and after his run at Chepstow, he seemed to have a good chance. Before the start, Martin said he didn't want the horse to have too hard a race as he wasn't quite right, and I was to look after him.

Martin fitted a net around the horse's mouth, which can sometimes help keen horses to settle better. With this, they tend not to pull as hard. Encore Un Peu didn't like the net. He was badly hampered by the fall of Sail by the Stars and Carl Llewellyn at the first hurdle. The lost lengths would have been hard to make up and, obeying instructions, I didn't abuse the horse. We finished fifth, beaten ten lengths, but nevertheless I had general misgivings about the approach adopted for the race. On the way back to the weighing room a brief encounter with one of the stewards gave me the opportunity to mention how badly hampered the horse had been at the first hurdle and really he had not been able to recover from that. The stewards accepted the explanation.

Five days later, Encore Un Peu was entered in a novice hurdle at Exeter and the only apparent danger seemed the Paul Nicholls' horse General Crack. Over the previous two months I had been riding winners for Paul and he asked if I was available for General Crack. But I thought a lot of Encore Un Peu and felt that if he had come out of the Stratford race well enough and we rode him differently, I would ride him.

'What do you think?' I asked Martin.

'You've been asked to ride Paul Nicholls's, you ride Paul Nicholls's.'

'But if Encore is OK, I'd rather be on him.'

'No, you ride the other one. He'll be favourite.'

And so there it was, I was on Paul's. Having his first run for three and a half months, General Crack weakened badly before the last and faded to finish fifth. Encore Un Peu, with Jonothan riding, took up the running after the second hurdle and bolted in by ten lengths. A hefty gamble had brought its price tumbling down and I knew the stable had been involved.

I went crazy after the race. I felt misled. Enraged, I went home that evening and prepared a press release saying I was leaving the Pipe yard. After sleeping on it, and consulting a few close friends, I eventually decided to stick with the job and the release was never published.

But Chester's comments a couple of days later certainly didn't help. 'What were you thinking of, going off and riding that General Crack?' He had rung to interview me about some of Ron Hodges' horses for the Pipeline. You can goad a man only so far. 'You can shove that Pipeline up . . .' From then on, these interviews dealt only with Martin's runners.

After the return from the 28-day ban, people could see how disenchanted I had become – didn't want another murderous contest for the championship, didn't want the never-ending grind of trying to ride at ten stone and didn't want the aggrava-tion that came with the Pipe job. Though we never spoke about it, it was clear to me that Adrian had no wish to repeat the 1993–94 campaign either. Such was the mental tiredness and the dread of another battle that it began to affect my riding and especially the way I fell in races. We use the expression bouncing well and through the previous campaign I had kept bouncing back up. Riding well, you fall well, you make sure you're not exposed and that mental sharpness protects you.

This season, it was different. There was weariness. If the championship came, it came; there would be no compulsive chase. By the middle of March I'd already lost days following two falls and could feel many of the falls were now awkward. The same was true for Adrian. He had lost his mother before Cheltenham and there were signs he had no stomach for another gruelling enounter. In a way, we were probably both subconsciously thinking an injury wouldn't be that disastrous. 'If I get hurt here, I won't have to go through this again. Wouldn't be the worst thing in the world.' Once you've thought that, you're already in the ambulance.

On Sunday night, 26 March, I went to the Lesters with Emma. The following day should have been three rides at Nottingham but the offer to do promotional work for the National Lottery was more appealing and for the first time in my life, a commercial opportunity came before riding. Times were changing. Thoughts of retirement came and went; a fall at Newton Abbot on the Saturday before Aintree ended with a kick in the knee that required the only cortisone injection of my career. After a couple of rides on the first day at Liverpool, the pain was pretty excruciating and I made off to the local hospital. Martin encouraged me to rest on the second day and return for the National but by then I felt as right as rain and it would have meant giving up the ride on Banjo who was fancied to win the Mumm Mildmay Novices' Chase. 'No chance,' I said, 'I'll be OK.' Banjo won well. Miinnehoma, trying to follow up last year's success in the National, made a mistake at the first, hurt himself, and I pulled him up early on the second circuit.

Adrian broke his arm in a fall off Desert Fighter at Hereford on Easter Monday and left the championship at my mercy. There was a suggestion that Norman Williamson could make it a race but that could only happen if I didn't care. Norman never got close. Brian Kilpatrick, owner of Cache Fleur, said he would like me to ride his horse in the Whitbread Gold Cup at Sandown and Martin agreed provided I could do 10st 2lb. Cache Fleur was weighted to carry 10 stone, I got down to 10st 1lb and Martin said that's OK. I was not feeling at my best, but Cache Fleur was at his. He jumped accurately and fought well when challenged by my good friend Luke and Country Member at the second last.

At Sandown, Charlie Swan mentioned that Martin had invited him over to Nicholashayne to talk about the possibility of a job for next season. Charlie and his wife Tina weren't that interested in a move to England and though Martin's approach hadn't surprised me, I was still taken aback. We don't like to think of ourselves as dispensable but of course we are. I couldn't complain. Since returning from suspension, the possibility of leaving Martin had grown in my mind. It might have happened sooner but for the fact that Martin's winners were necessary for the championship. If hanging in got me that title, then hanging in it would be.

In mid May, Ultan Guilfoyle, Robert Parsons and I met at Odette's restaurant in Camden Town. My future was on the menu. Ultan felt a change of direction would revitalise me; leave Martin, spend more time riding in Ireland and forget the jockeys' championship. That made sense. I had always enjoyed riding at Irish tracks and spending the time in Ireland would mean that the British title could be forgotten. The timing could have been better – Martin's 50th birthday was just around the corner and now he had to deal with the small matter of the stable jockey who wanted to leave. We met at his house a few days later and I spelled it out.

'Look Martin,' I said, 'I'm struggling with my weight and that's no use to you. I can't give you the commitment you expect any longer and I also want more freedom to ride abroad. I'd like to help you out where I can but this is the way it is.'

Emma came with me to Martin's birthday party and even though it was good to share a drink with Brian Kilpatrick and some of the other owners, there was coolness in the air. A couple of days later I faxed to Martin the statement drawn up for the press outlining my reasons for leaving the most success-ful yard in National Hunt racing, just as I'd explained them to him. I thanked Martin for everything he had done for me and hoped I might ride for him in the future.

I finished the season with 160 winners to Adrian's and Norman's 130 and won my third consecutive title. I'd reached important decisions about the future, my separation from Carol was easier and I had formalised my divorce from M.C. Pipe.

As horses go, James Pigg was well named. Ten months after Carol and I had split up and the day my severance from the Pipe yard became news, we were at Hereford and travelling sweetly in a handicap chase. Just past halfway I was thinking of winner 161. Then James Pigg didn't get high enough at the fence past the stands and buried me. In summertime, the fall-ing was never easy. One of the following field took my head for a football and it ached. 'Fine, just fine, not a problem,' I said when Martin asked if everything was all right. James Pigg was now my last ride for the evening and there was time to kill before setting off for home. Sitting on a bench in the weighing room, I picked up the *Sporting Life* and there it was, a front-page story that stunned me – Dunwoody To Leave Pipe. Cham-pion jockey Richard Dunwoody has decided ... Couldn't be. How could I ever leave the champion trainer? What am I doing? Then, further down in the story – Dunwoody, who is separated from his wife Carol . . . Jesus Christ, I thought, what's this, left my wife too? What's happening in my life? Left my trainer? Left my wife? I can't believe it. Carl Llewellyn, sitting further along the bench, noticed the incredulity and the tell-tale silly smile.

'It's OK, Richard,' he said, 'you're just a little concussed. It'll all make sense in the morning.'

17

GREEN SHOOTS OF RECOVERY

T here was a sense of freedom once I'd made the decision to leave Martin Pipe. There was also trepidation. Would people think of me as a has-been? It bothered me to read reports that interpreted the move as a large scaling down of my commitments when in fact it was more a reorganisation. What I wanted was more time for other things, plus as many winners as possible. For 12 years I'd raced in blinkers, unable to see anything other than the next winning post. The blinkers certainly kept my mind on the job but the narrow focus wasn't fulfilling. Glimpses of worlds beyond racing invariably left me wanting more. Every skiing trip whetted my appetite for the next one, just as an evening in London lured me to the buzz of the city.

What I didn't need was the hassle of chasing a championship that took far more than it gave. At the end of three successful campaigns, it was always the same – relief, not joy. I just thought, 'I'm glad I didn't lose that.' The game was not worth the candle. Being champion was fine but how important was it to win four rather than three titles? Martin's stable jockey was almost certainly going to win the championship but did that make him better than another top rider who rode for a trainer with a smaller string of horses?

After telling people I would like to ride more in Ireland, opportunities knocked. Dermot Weld offered me the chance to ride his select team of National Hunt horses; there were indications that Edward O'Grady would use me for his better horses and my Irish agent Ciaran O'Toole reassured me that plenty of Irish trainers would be keen to put me up. Whenever I thought about riding in Ireland and what it was I liked so much, Galway would float to the surface. Cheltenham, Ascot, Sandown and Newbury had higher quality racing but there was no meeting I enjoyed as much as the summer Galway festival. The big races, the Plate and the Hurdle, were valuable and competitive handicaps, the atmosphere was electric and Galway's groundsman kept the track in great order.

But Galway wasn't just racing. Every year I stayed with Johnny and Erna Walsh at Ely Place, not far from the city centre. Ciaran had recommended it and stayed there too with Aisling, his girlfriend. The hospitality was out of this world. It was home from home. Over the time I stayed with Johnny and Erna, they must have put up half the weighing room. There was the famous occasion when one of our colleagues stumbled out of a pub late one night and into a taxi. Before he could tell the driver where he wanted to go, he fell asleep. The taxi driver, unable to rouse him sufficiently to get instructions, delivered him to Johnny and Erna's doorstep. Of course they took him in and put him straight to bed.

Erna would cook bacon, sausages, eggs and anything else you wanted for breakfast and was it devoured! Michael Talbot's pork sausages were worth the hours we had to spend in the sauna. Michael was the butcher down the street and over the years we became good friends. 'This will be my last year. I'll be retired next time you come,' Michael used to say. For ten years it was one of the first things I checked. Michael was always there, asking for an each-way tip for the afternoon, and the pork sausages were as good as ever. Of course, retirement got me before him. Year after year, he would never let me back to England without two big bags of his pork sausages. They travelled well.

Before breakfast I would go down to Michael Farragher's newsagent's for the *Racing Post* and we'd chat about the races and the weather and life in general. Over breakfast Ronnie Ward, the postman, would drop in and seein' as we were having a cup of tea, he'd have a cup himself. What were the winners for the day? Michael Talbot's sausages. Erna would tape the races for me and that evening before going out to eat, I would disappear into the sitting room and while the others unwound, I rewound. For supper we would take Erna down to Aideen Higgins's restaurant at the back of Eyre Square and Erna would joke that she was Mother Goose chaperoning her wayward goslings. Galway is a lively spot so the poor chaperone had her hands full. A battalion of us have stayed with Erna – Peter Scudamore, Norman Williamson, Adrian Maguire, David Casey, Philip Hide, John Shortt, Francis Flood and any other rider who happened to stray through town.

Not every Irish home is as open as the Walshs', not every Irish town is as lively and welcoming as Galway, but you do see more of it in Ireland than anywhere else. After leaving Martin, I wanted less intensity in my life and that meant more time riding over there.

Before that there were other places to see. A week after the season ended, Emma and I left for two weeks in Thailand. We spent three days in Bangkok and the rest at the resort of Phuket. The Far East was a lot more appealing than a wet Wednesday at Wolverhampton. As my eyes opened to new worlds, they saw the old one more clearly. What was the point of driving off to Ludlow for two horses that couldn't win? I would learn to say no, to take a day off here and there. There was no sense in having more freedom unless I used it. Those who wondered how the champion jockey could opt out of the title race missed the point. This was abdication, not surrender.

There were other changes. No longer would I automatically agree to school horses for whoever cared to ask. Jockeys routinely say yes, wanting to improve their chances of getting rides and some are good at teaching young horses to jump. Almost every day of the week they're up at six or six thirty in the morning to do what a good few of the 30 conditional jockeys, young amateurs and lads in the trainer's yard could do equally well. During the busy periods of the season the jockeys will be tired before they get to the races and when it really matters, their performances suffer. It took me a long time to come to my senses but this season I did. 'Sorry, can't be there, won't be back from Ireland,' I'd say when asked to ride out. Generally it was

true but then there were times when the schooling was unnec-
essary and I simply avoided it and went for a run in a sweatsuit
instead. Needs must.

There was no adverse reaction, I continued to get almost as
many rides from trainers in England as before. The only fall-out
probably was that the trainer couldn't tell his owner, 'I had
Richard Dunwoody down schooling your horse this morning.' If
there was a good horse that someone particularly wanted me
to school, there wasn't a problem and as I began to spend
more time living in London, I enjoyed making the 25-minute
drive to Philip Mitchell's and Simon Dow's at Epsom to ride out
with their strings. It helped especially later on when I was
injured and they were good yards to be involved with.

Emma returned from Monaco to London in the summer of
1995 and so I began to spend more time in the capital. After a
year in the rented cottage in Great Coxwell, I bought a house in
Faringdon, Oxfordshire, but I never liked it there that much.
With Emma back in London, the city had more appeal. In the
evening we would dine out a fair bit or Annabel Vaudrey and
Nick Pegna, Emma's housemates, would put a bit of supper
together. Next morning I might go down to the gym and on the
odd day off I'd go to the FI karting track in Chelsea and drive
myself round the bend trying to beat last week's best time.

Changing the emphasis in my life never diminished the will
to win. Although not a contender for the jockeys' title, I still
wanted to ride winners and by the end of October I had
ridden 23 in Ireland and 17 in England. A further 22 winners
came in November, bringing the total to 62; not too bad for a
jockey reputed to be winding down.

My changed lifestyle attracted a certain amount of attention.
The coverage was generally fair and recognised how destruc-
tive the championship campaigns had been, even though,
ironically, the media had probably helped to create the pressure that made them so punishing. The change was also giving
me the chance to ride a lot of top-class horses. Before the
season ended, I had partnered One Man, Alderbrook, Sound
Man, Ventana Canyon, Unguided Missile, General Wolfe and
Paddy's Return among others. The big Saturday afternoons, the
big pay-days, came round more often and from that first

season, one stands out. It also brought me into fierce competition with a young gun who was to become no stranger.

It was the fourth day of Galway, 1994. With two winners at the meeting before going out on the Aidan O'Brien-trained Bally-hire Lad, there was every chance of a third. It came but only after a driving finish against a tall Irish kid whom no one seemed to know much about. Someone said he was originally from the north and that he was with Jim Bolger. For a teenager, I thought he'd given his horse an exceptional ride. So tight was the finish and so close had the horses come, it was no surprise the stewards' enquiry was announced. He was fairly grumpy. Outside the stewards' room there wasn't so much as a 'how's it goin'?' Intimidated? Not this boyo. When the stewards decided not to change the result, the kid didn't say a word, just walked sullenly away.

Afterwards I met Paddy Graffin, who was one of the top amateurs from the north.

'That conditional you just rode against, he's a real good lad. Try and get him a job over in England.'

'That miserable bugger?'

'Yeah, yeah, that's him.'

'What's his name?'

'Anthony, Anthony McCoy.'

I went back to England and told Martin about this good young conditional jockey and suggested we try to get him. Martin made some sort of contact with Anthony but, by then, Toby Balding was on the scent and the rest is now enshrined in racing's history books. What A.P. has achieved since leaving Jim Bolger's and coming to England is beyond belief – champion conditional jockey in his first season; senior champion every year since and yet always kicking on to the next target. It took me nine years to get to where he was in two and even though A.P. also spends a significant part of his day wasting, he copes remarkably well. We would talk occasionally about the difficulties and much of what I went through, he is now going through. He gets wound up, doesn't find it easy to relax and there are days when his girlfriend will find the going tough.

But tough it wasn't on Tingle Creek day at Sandown, the first

Saturday in December 1995. Hill of Tullow jumped badly in the opening race, a three-mile chase, but having survived a monumental blunder at one of the railway fences, he eventually wore down the leader, Camitrov. A.P. won the second on Redeemyourself, Sound Man won the Tingle Creek impressively and Certainly Strong was my third winner when she won the novice chase. Then came the climax. A.P. rode the mare Eskimo Nell for John Spearing and I rode Simon Dow's Chief's Song in the valuable William Hill Handicap Hurdle. Chief's Song was always close to the leaders. A.P. came from slightly off the pace and took it up going to the second last. We slugged it out from there – one moment he was getting up, the next it was Chief's Song. Racing hell for leather to the line, my horse got there by the shortest short head. I had wondered how Chief's Song would face up to a battle but that day he was like a lion. Other days, A.P. came out on top. He was very strong on Champleve when he pipped me on Hill Society in the Arkle Challenge Trophy at the 1998 Cheltenham Festival. He was always destined for the summit of the sport but it was good to stop him that afternoon at Sandown and properly introduce myself.

The four winners were a vindication of the changes I'd made in my life. There could be greater flexibility about what and when I rode, more independence, a better balanced lifestyle and at the end of the season, my earnings had improved from leaving Martin and going freelance.

After Sandown at the beginning of December, there was Unguided Missile in the Betterware Cup at Ascot two weeks later. He made a bad mistake midway through the race, hit the fourth last very hard and, with my lightest saddle on him, it slipped so far to one side that my right foot was almost touching the ground. Putting all my weight on my left iron, I managed to get the saddle back into position, we got going again and were upsides Rough Quest and Mick Fitzgerald at the last. Though he jumped the fence reasonably well, Unguided Missile stumbled badly on landing and went down on his nose. I was still there when he got back up and he gave his all to get up by a neck on the line. There was a lot of praise for that ride but my feeling was that a heavier saddle would have lessened the drama. Jockeys get paid to stay in the saddle, I had done nothing more than my job. The following season, Unguided Missile won the Perrier Jouet Handicap Chase at Aintree and even though the performance didn't earn anything like the reviews that followed the Ascot race, it pleased me more. That day at Liverpool he was giving two stones to most of his rivals and couldn't have won without jumping at his best. We set off in front, got into a good jumping rhythm and were able to dictate the pace. We won without my having to go for the stick and without making the semblance of a mistake, and that, more than anything, made me feel good. Which is the better ride? The one where you make a dramatic recovery or the one where you make sure there is no need for a dramatic recovery?

Still, the cards were falling my way as 1995 faded into 1996. One Man should have been my last big ride of '95 but the weather turned nasty and Kempton's King George meeting was cancelled. The King George itself was rescheduled for Sandown on the first Saturday of the new year and the horse was brilliant. Sandown was always one of my favourite steeplechase tracks but only if your horse could jump. One Man could, but he was also keen and as this was our first meeting, my plan was to get him switched off. By the time we got to the first fence, he was almost asleep and only woke when he hit the fence with his head. That got him going, he operated neat and accurate from then on. After a circuit, he cruised up alongside Barton Bank with Adrian on board and as we passed the stands, Adrian was slapping and kicking his horse while One Man hacked along on his outside. We hit the front entering the back straight and began to stretch clear in the last half mile.

He began to get tired after the second last but didn't fold up like he would do in future. Because he felt so fresh – the weather would have held him up in his training – he probably gave a bit more than he should have done. I always felt that the race left a mark on him. From then on when he tired, he very quickly hit a barrier and whether that was a purely physical or a mental problem or both we will never know. A couple of months later, I would ride him in the Gold Cup and going to the third last we were cantering alongside Imperial Call. I shouted across at Conor O'Dwyer, 'We've got this between us, Conor,' but before the second last the horse was legless, totally empty. It was generally felt that Cheltenham's three and a quarter miles was too far for One Man but the same alarming tendency to tie up was evident in the 1997 King George when he almost came to a stop after jumping the final fence.

The horse was a superb two and a half mile chaser with enough class to win the 1999 Queen Mother Champion Chase at Cheltenham. I could have ridden him that year but an early season agreement with the Irish trainer Arthur Moore committed me to Klairon Davis. Very Promising, Waterloo Boy, Viking Flagship, Remittance Man, Sound Man were all great two milers that I rode a lot during their careers but even though Viking and Remittance Man both won the Champion Chase, I wasn't lucky enough to be on them on the day it mattered. Given how much good fortune there was, there can be no regrets about my career but I would have traded a lot for one Champion Chase.

Luck it seemed was on my side when Graham Bradley's alarm failed to sound and he missed a schooling date with the Champion Hurdle favourite, Alderbrook. Ernie Pick, the horse's owner, ditched Brad and offered me the ride. Although Brad's punishment was greater than his crime, I couldn't turn down the offer. This was just three weeks before the race and I got to know him at Kempton in the substitute for the abandoned Kingwell Hurdle. He moved very unimpressively before the race but showed bags of class once he'd warmed up and won comfortably from Mack the Knife.

My attitude had changed from the eighties when I'd studied the videos of past performances on the evening prior to a big race. Even then I would stay out of the protracted and analytical discussions between Graham McCourt and Hywel Davies over how to ride different horses. What if you did this, what if you did that? Each race can be so different the lessons from one don't necessarily apply to another and I just preferred to keep things simple. At some stage, get your horse into a position from which he can win. Nevertheless, on the night before the Champion Hurdle, I shoved in the tape of Norman Williamson winning on Alderbrook a year earlier and watched the most confident ride imaginable. Norman dropped him in well off the pace, cruised down the hill and then just picked off those in front of him after turning in.

'That's it,' I thought, 'that's the way I'll do it. I'll ride him the same as last year.' That was the mistake, the presumption that Alderbrook was as good as he had been a year before. Norman had come down the hill swinging out of the horse and coasted up to the leaders. Starting from virtually the same point as Norman, I came down the hill squeezing and pushing for all I was worth and not getting much response. Tony Dobbin on Chief Minister carried me a little wide down to the third last and at the second last I was still four lengths down on Collier Bay. Against my principles I hadn't got him into a position I was happy with and at the line we were beaten two and a half lengths. Afterwards, you didn't have to be an expert at reading body language to see that Kim Bailey wasn't impressed. It wasn't the greatest ride I'd given a horse but, knowing the video footage well, the most significant factor was that Alderbrook was feeling his legs on the day. In a sense, justice was done with Brad falling in for the winning ride on Collier Bay after Jamie Osborne had opted for Mysilv. He and Jim Old, the trainer, deserved their success.

Alderbrook's defeat was only bearable because Ventana Canyon had been brilliant in winning the Arkle Challenge Trophy Chase 40 minutes earlier. So whatever happened, I wouldn't be leaving the Festival without a winner. Sound Man was slightly disappointing, finishing third in the Champion Chase. He was coming to the end of a long season and couldn't get home after a blunder at the third last and a mistake at the next. Edward O'Grady thought that Charlie Swan on Viking Flagship and I had got into a battle too early and in doing so set the race up for Klairon Davis. Nevertheless, I thought Sound Man wasn't quite the horse he had been earlier in the season.

That Cheltenham also proved that my enthusiasm for racing was still fragile. One of my rides had been fatally injured and Wednesday hadn't gone well but with Ventana Canyon already in the bank, it hadn't been too bad a meeting. However, as the 29 runners for the Triumph Hurdle walked round at the start on the final day, I didn't want to be there. If someone had been able to airlift me out of there, I wouldn't have looked back. Instead there was Paddy's Return to ride and in the mysterious ways of racing, he won. Despite the very negative pre-race focus, I didn't actually give him too bad a ride as we had been under pressure a long way out.

The day, though, went back downhill from there. One Man hit the wall in the Gold Cup and Martin's Lamp hit the deck in the Grand Annual Chase and had to be put down. It was a heavy fall but I could have carried on. Instead I opted not to ride Cheryl's Lad who was favourite for the County Hurdle. To feel so discouraged after such a good season was disturbing. I only stayed to the end because my two winners had made me leading rider at the meeting and I had to collect the Ritz Club trophy.

There were to be no trophies at Aintree, however. Jenny Pitman's Superior Finish tested my fitness, staying on well to be third in the Grand National but couldn't get near Rough Quest and Encore Un Peu. Afterwards Jenny said, 'I was waiting for you to give him a crack.'

The rest of the meeting was also a disappointment. The final months of the season were important because of the aim to ride 100 winners in Britain. It went to the second last day but we got there with one to spare. It turned out to be an excellent season when you added the 101 to the 42 winners in Ireland. And good too that when the race for winners was on at the end, I could still afford to take two days off and spend a weekend away at the Monaco Grand Prix. Getting to know some of Emma's friends, my interest in Formula One had intensified. And the Monaco GP? You will never beat it as a sporting occasion.

A week after the season ended, A.P. McCoy, Barry Fenton and Richard Davis came up to the city and we spent the evening together. It was a sensible night out – we had something to eat in the Sports Café, a couple of drinks and then home. Richard wasn't one of the big-name jockeys in the weighing room but he was a good rider and very easy to like. That night he stayed over with me at Emma's place. Next morning we went to the Harbour Club in Chelsea and had a work-out and after that it was off karting. Five weeks later, Richard was killed in a fall from a novice chaser at Southwell. It was a shocking tragedy for his family and a painfully sad time for all of his friends.

Richard rode a novice chaser called Mr Sox that fell at the first fence. It was a bad fall and there was a lot of anguish when it was realised he had not been taken immediately to hospital. There were only two ambulances on duty and they had to wait for a third to come to the course to pick Richard up. Vital minutes were slipping away. When they got to the hospital, the right people had not been put on alert and further time was lost. They didn't realise how serious his internal injuries were. Waiting for the ambulance, Richard had asked fellow jockey Warren Marston to look after his dog while he was in hospital. In the end he died of a heart attack; his internal injuries had been massive. Because their adrenalin is flowing at the time of a fall, jockeys are always able to say, 'I'm grand, not a bother.' But when there's ever the slightest doubt, they should be taken immediately to hospital.

Richard's parents, Ann and John, were so brave and generous in the work they did to ensure that in every future case, injured jockeys would get the best possible care. There was a huge turnout for what was an intensely sad funeral. They played the Saw Doctors because Richard was their biggest fan. It was through him and Simon McNeil that I was introduced to their music. One particular Saw Doctors' song struck a chord with every jockey present and with Richard so much on our minds, it seemed appropriate. It began 'To win just once would be enough/For those who've lost in life and love.'

Though deeply upset by Richard's death, we were back in the weighing room at Stratford the day after his funeral. From Stratford, I went to the Galway festival for the week because, if nothing else, the fun and the madness over there made us appreciate all we had.

Then it was time for a much-needed break. Emma and I went to South Africa for two weeks. Cristo, our guide in the Kruger National Park, drove us off in his jeep and we found elephants, white rhino, leopards, water buffalo and lions, as you do in the Kruger. We were also in Cape Town and stayed in a log cabin by the beach. Not far away there was a racing stable that worked its horses by the sea and Emma thought it would be nice for us to ride out together one morning. 'Any chance of riding out?' I asked, once inside the yard. 'Well, we could stick you on the hack,' said the trainer grudgingly. 'Ah, it's OK,' I said, 'maybe some other time.' There I was offering myself for riding out duty on holidays in South Africa when much of the season in England had been spent avoiding it.

Back into another season, the old horses generated new hope and old wounds began to mend. Sound Man and One Man returned fresh and well for another campaign. Martin Pipe offered me the ride on Challenger du Luc in the valuable Murphy's Gold Cup at Cheltenham and when it won, we were old buddies – well, there were less reservations in the air. My own enthusiasm for the sport was rekindling and Emma could see it in my response to her. The more tuned in I became to racing and its schedules again, the less time there was for us.

My feelings towards Emma were deep. For two and a half years she was my anchor and she helped change my outlook on life more than any other person. But I was always attracted to walking on the wild side and after the separation from Carol, I was never going to be prepared for any long-term commitment. By the middle of 1997 we were on the rocks, but it would take two years for the ship to go down. Emma saw the hungry jockey re-emerging and thought, 'No, I don't need this.' Around this time she met Carol while driving near her parents' home in Little Coxwell. They motioned to each other to stop. They chatted about this man they both knew. 'You might think,' Emma said to Carol, 'he's changed now, but he hasn't. I don't think he ever will.'

In planning for the 1996–97 season, Robert Parsons and I had opted to make sure of our 100 winners in Britain, then hopefully I could win as many races as possible in Ireland. That's how it worked out, 110 in Britain, 30 in Ireland and a total similar to the previous season's 143. Sound Man won his second Tingle Creek, despite a massive mistake at the third last, One Man won his second King George but neither did it in Cheltenham that year. Killed in a training accident at home, Sound Man never got to the Festival and One Man was again reduced to a hack canter in the last quarter-mile of the Gold Cup.

Both horses were to run in the two and a half mile Comet Chase at Ascot and forced to choose, I picked One Man. Part

With Carol after accepting the
MBE from the Queen at
Buckingham Palace in 1994.
My receiving the honour had to
be postponed on the first
occasion as it coincided with a
day's racing at Plumpton.

A blonde ambition for a good
cause – to raise money for Shane
Broderick's Appeal in September
1997. Shane had been paralysed
in a fall at Fairyhouse on Easter
Monday that year.
(George Ovington)

With Emma before a South Africa v. New
Zealand rugby match in Cape Town in 1996.

Picking our way gingerly through the mayhem at Listowel in September 1997. Owenduff and I (right) are one of the few to remain standing after this first-fence pile-up. Nine of the sixteen runners ended up on the floor. *(Pat Healy)*

Getting it wrong on Wonderman at Kempton in 1992. Fortunately, thanks to the horse's strength, we recovered to win the Bonusfilm Novice Chase. *(Gerry Cranham)*

You weren't positive! Paying the penalty for indecision on Grosvenor at the first in a staying novice chase at Ayr in April 1999. A.P. is on my inner. *(Anne Grossick)*

And may the 'horse' be with you. On the way to another winner at Tir Prince in Wales in 1996. Great fun, but as my expression shows no less competitive. *(James Griffith)*

Another tumble! This time in a Formula First car at Pembrey in 1997. *(Gary Haggaty)*

Real horse power. Driving a Porsche GT3 in the Supercup at the Silverstone Grand Prix meeting in July 1999 in front of team-mate and tennis star Henri Leconte. *(Hugh Routledge)*

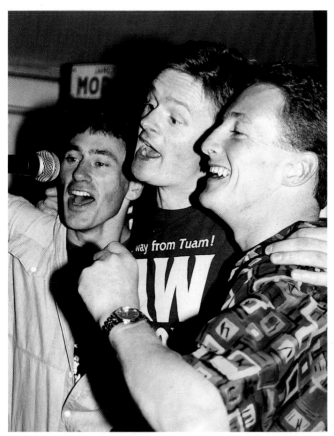

And the craic was mighty. Simon McNeil, Michael 'Corky' Caulfield and I back the Saw Doctors at our party in summer 1993.

A roster of rogues. A.P. (left), me, Mel Fordham and Carl Llewellyn on holiday in Puerto Banus four days before my last day's riding. Yet another girl is quickly vacating the area. *(Mel Fordham)*

Sound Man takes the last ditch en route to an easy success in the H & T Walker Handicap Chase at Ascot in November 1995. *(George Selwyn)*

One Man on his way to winning at Cheltenham in January 1997. Brian Harding was in the saddle for his only other victory at the course in the Queen Mother Champion Chase in 1998; I had stayed loyal to Arthur Moore's Klairon Davis. *(Les Hurley)*

Entering the winner's enclosure at the Cheltenham Festival for the final time in 1998. Florida Pearl had followed up his success in the Festival Bumper in 1997 by winning the Royal and SunAlliance Novice Chase. *(Gerry Cranham)*

At the last. Twin Falls provides me with winner 1699 on 21 August 1999. I haven't sat on a horse since. *(Anne Grossick)*

With my father, Dessie and Janice Coyle following 'This Is Your Life' in February 2000. Michael Aspel had 'caught up' with me at Ascot earlier in the day while interviewing jockey Joe Tizzard for the BBC.

Charlie with a good mate of ours, fitness trainer Barry Grinham. Barry is our running partner in the various 10km and half marathons we've contested this year.

owner of Sound Man, J.P. McManus, had agreed with Charlie Swan that if he rode the horse in the Comet, he would keep the ride for the Champion Chase. Two and a half weeks before Cheltenham, I suffered a cracked sternum. See More Business fell in the Racing Post Chase at Kempton and almost brought down Forest Sun and Brian Clifford. Forest Sun used my chest to regain his balance and I was never hit as hard in my life by a horse. Unable to move and without the breath to say much, I lay for five minutes before the ambulance came.

'You're not going to ride in the next, are you?' asked the doctor on the way back.

'No, I don't think so.'

My sister Gail and Emma came to see me in hospital that night. I was in intensive care. They brought in some Chinese food and while sitting there eating, they got a fit of the giggles. Of course that got me going – laughing that evening was one of the most painful things I have ever experienced.

There had been some controversy over the ride on Sound Man at Cheltenham. Robert Parsons, having spoken to the horse's trainer Edward O'Grady, suggested in the *Daily Express* that he couldn't see why I shouldn't be reunited with Sound Man if I was available. J.P. was not pleased because he had made his promise to Charlie. I was out of intensive care and on my way home from hospital when J.P. called. He wanted to see me in the Dorchester and even though there was a good reason for not being up and about, J.P. was a great owner to ride for, a very decent man, and I went that evening. He wanted to tell me that Robert had been out of order, publicly looking for a ride that was Charlie's. I didn't disagree. He said if Robert worked for him, he would sack him. Now that I couldn't agree with. Robert Parsons had been doing an outstanding job for me for three seasons and not in a million years would I think of ditching him.

Getting fit for Cheltenham meant a lot of running and work on the Equicizer, a wooden horse on springs that replicates the movements of the real thing. There is no better exercise for a jockey. My determination to be 100 per cent for Cheltenham was reassuring. It proved that my enthusiasm was back to what it should be. Thirteen days after cracking my sternum and spending a night in intensive care, I was back race riding. And it was well worth it. Hanakham won the Royal SunAlliance Novice Chase, the brilliant Florida Pearl flew home in the bumper and Barna Boy won the County Hurdle.

We will all remember the Grand National of 1997 for the IRA bomb scare, which caused its rescheduling from the Saturday to the Monday. As I was about to get my cap tied by Andy Townsend, the valet, who along with the Buckinghams did such a good job for me over the years, the fire alarms suddenly went off. We were told to vacate the weighing room. Not that worried, thinking we'd be back in a few minutes, I grabbed a light jacket, put it over my colours, and slowly made my way to the exit. Little did I know.

There are countless memories from the weekend. Jockeys drinking the sponsor's brandy to keep warm in the car park at the time the race was due off. Tens of people being given tea at the Buckinghams' digs in a small semi-detached across from the course. The horse-box ride with one of the intended runners, Bishops Hall, to our hotel at Runcorn on the Saturday night. And the sauna on the Monday: almost twenty jockeys piled in on top of each other, some desperate to sweat off the excess, others keen not to get too close to each other. 'Jason Titley, will you take that away from me – God knows where it's been.'

Unfortunately for my mount, the Jenny Pitman-trained Smith's Band, it would have been much better if the race had not been saved. Second time around and still in the front rank, he never took off two fences before Becher's and was killed.

Despite that cruel blow the meeting had been good to me. Four winners and that great performance by Unguided Missile. Mind you it wasn't all sweetness. The Duke's Mulligan, having already fallen at Cheltenham in the Arkle with me, launched himself at the last ditch and turned over when he probably would have won. That was disappointing. The sequel would have been even more so had I let it get to me. It seems that afterwards the Duke complained to a number of racing people that 'he's not a chase jockey. Can't ride over fences any more'. Despite my affection for the Duke, I had previously come to the conclusion that in times of disappointment or anger, he says more than his prayers.

By now the career was back on track. Dividing my time between Britain and Ireland worked a treat. Given my fondness for riding in Ireland and Ciaran O'Toole's ability to put me on winners there, the only problem was giving ourselves enough time to get the targeted 100 winners in England. At the end of the 1997–98 season we made it by three. Forty-nine winners in Ireland meant 152 between the two countries – my best all-round total for the three years since leaving Martin.

Florida Pearl, trained by Willie Mullins, was my only Cheltenham winner that year but was highly impressive in beating Escartifigue in the Royal & SunAlliance Novices' Chase. He had taken to fences brilliantly, although the first time I schooled him on a damp autumn evening at Galway racecourse I was not so sure he would. He was taking time to warm up and jumping the first fence down the back for the second time he literally stood on it. But from then he never looked back. Leopardstown at Christmas was a cakewalk.

Boss Doyle did give him a battle at the same course in February, although he wasn't fully fit and at Cheltenham the main danger was avoiding the fallers. The small field had persuaded me to drop him in behind. It was like walking through a minefield and I was very glad when, five fences from home, he pulled me to the front.

He was as fine a horse as you could sit on and, although he has won a good few races at three miles and finished placed in two Gold Cups, I will always believe his optimum trip to be two and a half to two and three quarter miles.

I was riding another Irish star at the Festival, although the circumstances in which I came to take over the ride will live with me for ever. Easter Monday 1997 at Fairyhouse, Mudahim had won the Irish National earlier in the afternoon and I had just won on Prate Box in the handicap chase. Francis Woods came back into the weighing room after a tumble in the race. 'Shane's not good.'

Huge understatement. Shane had broken his neck in a fall from Another Deadly, and due only to the outstanding work of Dr Walter Halley and his medical crew did he make it to the hospital. He was due to ride Dorans Pride in the Power Gold

Cup the next day. Tom Doran, the horse's owner, decided to run him only after much deliberation, as Shane would have expected it. I was asked to ride as I had won on him when Shane had been banned earlier in the season. It was the saddest winner I ever rode. Kay Hourigan, the trainer's daughter, led me back into the winner's enclosure with tears streaming down her cheeks, and she was not alone.

Shane had partnered Dorans in most of his runs and the memory that all of us have is of his sympathetic ride on the horse in the Stayers' Hurdle in 1995. Together with Michael Hourigan, he was largely responsible for the way the horse turned out. Dorans Pride went on to win the Kerry National at Listowel and the Hennessy Cognac Gold Cup at Leopardstown in 1997/98, and was very strongly fancied to take home the Cheltenham Gold Cup. He came within two lengths, finishing third to Cool Dawn, but I believe a race earlier in the season at Naas probably cost us. It was very heavy ground, he hated it and, well beaten going to the last, I should have pulled him up. I persevered and he nearly fell. From that day on his jumping was never quite the same and, although it was reasonable in the Gold Cup, he put in an extra stride at the downhill third last and lost us vital momentum. We could never make it up.

On the whole, life was good. It was hard but it was how I wanted it – good horses, plenty of winners and a lot of independence. Things could hardly have been better. A little incident on a summer afternoon in 1997 caught the mood of the time. Jason Titley and I were driving to Ayr races and stopped for petrol outside Carlisle. Just after arriving at the racecourse, the police turned up. They were looking for me. I froze.

'Is this yours?' one of them said, pointing to my wallet in his other hand. I had left it in the service station 40 miles back. Remembering my night in prison over four years before, I thought, 'You know, sometimes these fine upstanding men can be misunderstood.'

18

BEGINNING OF THE END

O n the bad days, I was still better off left alone. It was
something the other jockeys knew. Beaten on a horse I
thought should have won, I brooded. Maybe it was the
way I dropped the saddle on the valet's table or the way I
changed into the colours for my next ride but the lads knew
there was no point in making conversation. Some well-
intentioned person might say 'but you're only human' and I
would think, 'Sorry, it's not my job to be human.' Other jockeys
weren't that different; Peter Scudamore and A.P. especially. At
such times the real world didn't exist for me and, mindful of
my mood, the real world let me be. Saturday afternoon,
20 February 1999 was one of the dark days. Tim Reed may not
even remember our little conversation a few days later. I have
not forgotten it.

It was a little after midday and we were in the sauna at
Doncaster racecourse, Tim, a few other jockeys and me. A good
horseman, Tim is one of the older jockeys in the weighing
room. We were on the council of the Jockeys Association
together and he is a great lad.

'What happened to you on Saturday?' he asked in a good-
humoured way. Saturday was Ascot, about the worst day of my
life as a jockey and something I didn't want to discuss. 'Did you
get a bit caught up in your reins or something?' He said it with
a laugh and I suppose it did look funny to the other jockeys to
see me fumbling with the reins. Not wanting to remember, I

didn't answer. But Tim's innocent little darts hit the bull's eye.

'Christ,' I thought, 'they know there's something wrong with you. They're saying you're gone.' No disrespect to Tim but when a guy who rides about ten winners a year starts taking the mickey out of your riding, you've got problems.

Four days before, I had gone to Ascot knowing there was something wrong with my right arm. It had been sore for a month. The problem started with the Paul Eccles-trained Emerald Prince at Edinburgh five weeks earlier and a simple fall from a very tired horse. I got up, walked away but the next day there was a problem. Luckily that day's racing was lost to bad weather and, granted an unexpected afternoon off, I went for a run near my home in Fulham down to the Hammersmith Bridge. My arm felt as if it weighed a ton, the same as it had when it wasn't right previously. Why had it flared up again? Two days later on 18 January I was at Doncaster with Jenny Pitman's Princeful making his debut over fences. I could have done with a straightforward ride but unfortunately Princeful kept jumping left and landing behind other horses. If my right arm was stronger I might have been able to keep him straighter but he was not jumping well. Six fences from home it happened. Princeful jumped left, ended up behind a faller, went over the top and was brought down. To make things worse, he injured himself badly and I aggravated my arm more. In the last race at Doncaster, I tried to use the stick in my right hand going to the last but couldn't. Even though I pulled it through to my left, we were beaten a neck.

After the Princeful fall, I'd had a couple of days' physiotherapy which didn't help. The medical advice was that I shouldn't run, let alone ride. Physical exercise would be likely to stir up the nerves and slow my recovery. I stopped riding for a fortnight and to prevent myself going insane, I spent the second week in the south of France. I had to be right for Florida Pearl in the Hennessy Cognac Gold Cup at Leopardstown in Ireland on 7 February.

After returning from France, I had gone to Taunton on the Tuesday, five days before the Hennessy. Despite the break, the arm remained weak. 'Sod it,' I thought, 'from now on concentrate on using your left arm and get on with it.' If one tool in the plumber's box doesn't work, pick up another. It was a relief to win on Florida Pearl, he jumped well, didn't pull me about too much and stayed on to beat Escartifigue, his old adversary. It had been a great performance in his Gold Cup preliminary. More bad weather in Britain meant no racing for four days and more opportunity for my injury to improve. Racing resumed at Newbury on Friday, 12 February where Josh Gifford's novice chaser Kurakka fell when I flung him in on a stupidly long stride. At Haydock the following day, the Henry Daly-trained Marlborough lay down when looking a certain winner. The falls had inflamed my shoulder and arm and frustrated the hell out of me. Having had an excellent season up to the middle of January, I was now in the middle of a bad run – seconds, thirds, fallers and a worsening injury. And then, a week later, there was Ascot.

That Saturday at Ascot should have been a good day with top-quality racing, live television coverage, a good crowd, a fine racetrack and some very nice horses to ride. Marlborough, the same horse who had fallen a week earlier, was my ride in the Reynoldstown novice chase. He was mutton-headed but talented. Sadler's Realm had an obvious chance in the William Hill handicap hurdle and I was looking forward to riding Direct Route in the day's big race, the Mitsubishi Shogun Ascot Chase. I thought he could beat the favourite Teeton Mill. Once that race was over I would speed away from Ascot, catch a helicopter to Warwick racecourse and hopefully round things off by winning on Behrajan in a big race up there. It was the kind of day I lived for.

The novice chase developed into a battle between Marlborough and Lord of the River, ridden by Jamie Osborne. I tracked Jamie as we turned into the straight, going as well if not better than him. I jumped the second last OK and went to pick up my stick in my right hand. I thought, 'I'll pick it up in my right, give him one smack, put it down and pull it through into the left.' But he had been keen through the race and my arm was weak from restraining him. I picked up the stick but hadn't the strength to hit him. 'My God,' I thought, 'this is on television and I'm struggling badly.' The stick was in the forehand position. I wanted to switch it to the backhand position but couldn't do it. I tried to put my right hand back on the reins but it was completely numb. No feeling, no control and I was riding a horse that needed to be organised at his fences.

The stick was in my right hand but frozen there. I felt utterly helpless. We were going to the last, upsides Jamie and Lord of the River and there was a big race at stake. About ten strides before the fence I managed to get the stick into the backhand position and my right hand back on the rein. People who knew the game could have told what was happening. My hands were in a muddle and I was not able to give Marlborough much help. He fell. Jamie and Lord of the River went on and won very easily. I was shattered. Maybe the horse would have fallen anyway but in the middle of a depressing run this was the lowest point.

Back in the weighing room, everyone kept well away. Inside my head, the recriminations flew – 'Why the hell did you pick your stick up with your right hand?' 'Why did you have to give him a smack?' 'Why couldn't you have just gone and jumped it?' 'You looked like a prat and you've just thrown away a thirty-grand race.'

I changed for Sadler's Realm. He ran disappointingly and was never going to win but even so, it didn't pass without an incident. Around Swinley Bottom I went for a gap on the inside that was just about there, pushing Mick Fitzgerald to one side as I went through. It was more than a little cheeky but I was beyond caring. 'If Fitzy does me, he does me.' After the race, Fitzy came and said something in the weighing room. The niggle had started.

We went out for the big race. I thought I could win on Direct Route. Down the hill to Swinley Bottom I was still travelling well and went for a gap between Carl Llewellyn on Chief's Song and Fitzy on Super Coin. Carl was on the inside, Fitzy on my outside and Timmy Murphy further out on Challenger du Luc. I moved into the gap very easily but Fitzy and Timmy Murphy felt I was again creeping up on their inner, going where I had no right to go. Fitzy started to come in towards me, Timmy helped by leaning on Fitzy, squeezing everything up. I was hampered but my horse got through. On the inside, Carl and old Chief's Song were stopped in their tracks. Three fences from home I was chasing Teeton Mill and thinking I still had a chance but Direct Route emptied quickly and went backwards. I thought he had burst a blood vessel. We finished a disappointing fifth, beaten 12 or 13 lengths.

This day wasn't getting any better – disastrous on Marlborough, stupid on Sadler's Realm and Direct Route had run badly. Entering the weighing room, I heard Fitzy behind me. He was having a good run at the time and when Fitzy's having a good run, he gets a little bit louder than usual. He was riding more winners than me and even though I accept that that shouldn't have made a difference, it did. When he started saying, 'Where do you think you were fucking going out there?' I lost it. One minute we were swearing at each other, the next I grabbed hold of his goggles and ripped them from around his neck. All control had been lost. We were both on the ground, trying to fight but not doing much damage to each other. John Buckingham, the valet, and a few of the other jockeys tried to separate us. I looked up with Fitzy on top of me and saw Ashley Bealby, the stipendiary steward, standing over us.

'Would you like to come to the stewards' room. We're having an inquiry into what went on out there. Mr Fitzgerald, Mr Dunwoody, Mr Llewellyn and Mr Murphy.' We traipsed into the stewards' room but by this stage, I was beyond caring.

Carl gave his 'I've-been-murdered' line. I told them Fitzy was leaning on me and Timmy made it worse by leaning on him. Fitzy said I went where I had no right to go, a view shared by Timmy. The stewards decided Timmy was solely responsible and he got a ten-day ban. I thought Fitzy was lucky to get away scot-free. As the stewards considered the evidence, the clock ticked away and my departure for Warwick was delayed. We set off ten minutes late and discovered on the way that the helicopter company had miscalculated how long the journey would take. They reckoned on 25 minutes, it took 40. As we flew in over Warwick racecourse, I looked down to see my horse Behrajan go clear. He won easily. In a 17-year career as a jockey, there were going to be bad days. One of the worst had just ended.

Back in London I met up with Graham Bradley and we went to the Atlantic Bar. It was a night to drown sorrows but I wasn't up to drinking that much. Next morning it was not so much a hangover as feeling utterly wiped out. There was nothing left; I had a bruised body, and a spirit that felt like it had spent the previous day in a spin dryer. Emma called in at lunchtime and the recovery began. Fitzy rang to say he was sorry our little bust-up had happened but I thought it was better it had exploded and not simmered for days or even weeks. On Monday and Tuesday I went to the physio. By Wednesday, I was ready to start again. Doncaster was the venue and I won on my first two rides back, despite Tim Reed reminding me of my troubles. Winning was what I needed.

But on Friday there was another bad fall and the fear of not being all right for the ride on Dr Leunt in the Racing Post Chase at Kempton. I was still very sore but had to forget that. I had agreed to appear on Channel 4's preview programme, 'The Morning Line', but I pulled out at the last minute. I wanted to concentrate fully on being fit for Dr Leunt. Instead of television, I had physiotherapy and took a long, hot bath. Still the soreness in my neck persisted. Mentally, though, I was trying to prepare; in my head there would be no injury. But on this occasion the pain was extreme and only in the latter stages of the race did it start to subside. Dr Leunt, thankfully, made my job easier. He gave me a good ride and I steered, despite the discomfort. Ascot was history.

Throughout my career I tended to minimise the injuries. When my body spoke up, a voice inside my head told it to stop complaining. Winning horse races was the driving force and everything took second place to that. If the doctor said it would take ten days, I tried to get back in six. Then in the heat of a race the injuries usually disappeared and winning justified the risks. My body existed to serve my ambition.

Still there was no mistaking the seriousness of this injury. How could there be? As soon as I stood up in the saddle and extended my neck, I felt pain. Pins and needles were constant companions. In the middle of a race my arm would go numb, at other times the stick felt like a 20lb weight. I did undergo rigorous medical examination but when the doctors delivered their prognoses I heard what I wanted to hear. Michael Foy, an orthopaedic surgeon who works a lot with jockeys, was one of the first to say 'your neck is not in good shape' but it was his observation that he had seen rugby players 'in even worse shape' that I latched on to. Other doctors were even less encouraging but I convinced myself their fears were exaggerated. If I could still ride winners, it was ludicrous to say I shouldn't be riding. Retirement? It wasn't on the agenda.

For a three and a half month stretch in my final full season, 1998–99, I rode more winners than A.P. McCoy. Back on Sunday, 17 January 1999, two days after that fall on Emerald Prince at Edinburgh, I was at home and examining the figures. Counting from 1 October up to 15 January, I had ridden 61 winners to A.P.'s 52. OK he was still ahead in the championship because of the successes he'd had in August and September. During the period when I was riding plenty of winners, he'd had his share of suspensions. But what if he had another suspension? I could make a race of the championship. I rang Robert Parsons. 'If things continue to go right for us and A.P. has any mishap, we can give him a run for it. We have to keep it up.' Not realising the extent ot the injury I was thinking of giving him a run for the title; not beating him because with his stream of winners from Martin Pipe, that just wasn't possible. But why not make him sit up and realise that he had a rival? I felt I was riding as well as I had ridden at any time in my career and was benefiting from a higher level of physical fitness and from a calmer and more mature attitude. Being calmer did not mean being less motivated. The opposite was the case. Happier with how I was managing life, I wanted more winners.

What most pleased me was that I was actually making time for things outside racing. From being a hobby, motor racing had become a passion.

I had started driving the previous year, having visited the school at the Goodwood circuit. It was run by a relation of mine, Peter Gethin, who'd won the fastest ever Grand Prix at Monza in 1971. He had invited me down to see what I thought. After 120 laps on a freezing cold December day just before Christmas he still couldn't get me out of the car.

It was suggested I take my driver's test, buy a Formula First, a small single-seater, and enter the series. I jumped at the opportunity. But as it turned out, this business also has its share of ups and downs. In May at Goodwood, while testing, the front suspension gave. The car was demolished and I almost ended up in a neighbouring garden. In practice, two months later at Pembrey, I braked too late for the hairpin and caught the rear wheel of fellow competitor Mark McLoughlin's car. I probably went higher than I've ever been on any horse.

It was great to learn new skills, and the experience of driving Formula First enabled me to drive at two Grand Prix meetings at Silverstone in the Porsche Supercup in 1999 and 2000. I've never performed in front of bigger crowds and I only wished I could have been more competitive. Ten laps testing from one year to the next will not get you on the pace unless you are a budding Schumacher. That I am not, and I would only drive in the future if I could devote more time and energy to the sport.

In my second season driving, I was getting more to grips with the Formula First. I was driving for Mark Burdett Motorsport, the leading team in the Championship, and I felt a podium position was around the corner. Combining motor racing with horses meant an exhausting schedule but I agreed to it, and it was what I wanted.

I look back now at my diary and trace the trail after I left Punchestown on an April evening in 1998 and smile to myself. Sheer madness.

Even the journey from Punchestown to Dublin airport for my flight back to Stansted was frantic. A long line of cars inched their way towards the slip road leading to the airport motorway, time was against me and, as I have been known to do on occasions, I nipped up the inner. The policeman wasn't impressed but it seemed like he knew who I was and he certainly recognised the desperation. 'You're being let away this time but be careful,' he said. That night I stayed in a bed and breakfast near Stansted airport and flew to Edinburgh early next morning for testing with Danny Watts, my team-mate, at Knockhill, near Perth. Some people thought my involvement in motor racing created extra pressure and couldn't have been good for my riding. I found the opposite to be true. It gave me a life outside horses and the sharpness and concentration necessary for the car helped my performance in the saddle.

But it did keep me on the go. After testing at Knockhill, I drove my hired car south to Bangor for an evening meeting and rode a winner there. From Bangor, I drove up to Haydock where I was riding the next day and after Haydock I drove south for Uttoxeter's evening meeting. Two rides at Uttoxeter and I was driving back to Scotland for the Formula First races at Knockhill. Because I hadn't been able to do qualifying on the Saturday, I began from the back of the grid with a ten-second penalty and my sixth place in the second race was as good as I could have done. Then it was back to Edinburgh airport, a flight to London, a Sunday night Chinese takeaway and bed. Next morning I spent an hour in the bath trying to lose what the Chinese had put on and was then off to Fontwell races.

It was 4 May and going into that time of year when jump racing moves to the smaller tracks on summer days. With its firm ground, small prize money and its gathering of moderate horses, Fontwell on this Monday afternoon was a good example. I rode the Richard Rowe-trained Bay Lough in the second race, a novice chase. She was a good jumper but even the safest jumpers can miss a fence and she galloped straight into one that afternoon. We stumbled and collided with A.P.McCoy's mount Take My Side. I was jolted out of the saddle and fell awkwardly. I was knocked out at first, semi-conscious for a while and in no condition to continue. With concussion dulling my senses, I didn't realise the extent of my injury. All I remember is feeling annoyed that one of the rides I gave up had gone and won. That evening the lads would have known to steer clear of me in the changing room.

I left Fontwell unaware that I had seriously hurt my neck. As always, I presumed the best. A couple of days working with Mark Bender, a physiotherapist based in Fulham, would sort me out. They were easy days, light physio and plenty of time to recover. On the Thursday, three days after the fall, I went karting and did a bit of exercise on the running machine. Next day I was back riding at Stratford and was shocked when I realised my neck hadn't healed at all. Maybe the exercise had stirred up the nerves but as soon as I extended my neck on a horse, the pain was searing. My right arm was also a problem, so weak as to be almost useless. I only discovered how bad things were as

I cantered Ashwell Boy down to the start for the first race. Walking round there, I said to myself, 'I don't think I can get through this.'

Ashwell Boy is a strong horse. He sees a fence and accelerates wildly, but he is usually deadly accurate. That evening at Stratford, he took me round. I sat there, unable to do much and those who say it is 95 per cent the horse may be right. Ashwell Boy won easing down but I thought, 'That's it for this evening, can't go through that again.' By the time I got back to the weighing room, the other R. Dunwoody had reasserted himself. My second ride, Fujiyama Crest, had a good chance and as it was over hurdles, I would get away with it. The horse won but for the second time in 35 minutes, it didn't have that much to do with the jockey. I couldn't pick up my stick, could barely push but luckily Fujiyama Crest didn't need it. I had ridden my luck far enough and opted out for the rest of the evening, missing two winners. The two that got away preyed on my mind.

After seeing Jockey Club doctor Michael Turner, it was agreed that I should have a scan. It was obvious the source of the problem lay in my neck. I thought swimming would help but after two lengths, I had to stop. The scans, where you simply lie on your back in a chamber, were among the most painful things I've ever had to endure. They showed there was nerve damage and, at the time, I resented it. How could you ride horses for 15 years, take all the falls that I had taken, and suddenly be told of serious damage to your nervous system? But neither could I ignore it. I slept with painkillers beside the bed and when awoken by the pain I would take two more and drift back to sleep. At the gym, I lifted a 25lb weight with my left hand and couldn't raise 5lbs with the other. At home, if I tried to lift a jug with my right hand, I would put it down and use my left. Two visits to John Harris, an osteopath who had worked with the Wimbledon football team, brought a lot of relief but rest was what the injury needed. I didn't have a choice. Stratford had been Friday evening, 8 May. I did not ride again until 27 July, the second day of the Galway festival in Ireland. It was the longest break I'd ever had in racing and a sign of what was to come.

Even though I rode a winner on my return at Galway, the rest had not brought complete recovery. I opted not to ride over fences until confident my neck could handle it. Things that should have been easy were now extremely difficult. I couldn't use my stick in my right hand; a particular difficulty for a jockey who had been naturally strong with his right and only preferred to use his left in a finish. I felt more comfortable carrying the stick in my right hand during a race and this dependence was one I tried to combat but I never fully suc-ceeded. With the stick in that hand, I had better contact, via the reins, with the horse's mouth which meant I could restrain a strong horse more easily and could also alter his stride approaching a fence. Even though this arm was not working as it once did, I simply carried on. It had as much rest as it was going to get.

Retirement didn't enter my mind. I was 34 and felt I could go on for another five or six seasons. I had used the two-and-a-half month break to talk to people about setting up a Sports Marketing business. As joint-president of the Jockeys Association, I worked closely with Michael Caulfield, the association's executive manager, to improve working conditions for jockeys. Much of the time was spent in the area of sponsorship and marketing and I developed some understanding of what was involved. My idea was to create a business that would run alongside my riding career and when I eventually retired, it would be there for me.

That was the future. After returning from Galway I won on Master Millfield for Ron Hodges at Newton Abbot on my first ride back in England. It was Monday, 3 August, my first winner of the 1998-99 season and it was good to be up and running again. At Worcester a week later I had another two winners. At Newton Abbot on 16 August I had my first ride over fences for over three months. Village King, having his first outing over the larger obstacles, jumped great and won easily and that pleased me. I was still single-minded about racing and determined this would be the season I broke Peter Scudamore's 1,678 winner record. One hundred winners were needed to set a new mark and although it wouldn't be easy, I would do it if I stayed free of serious injury. I had ridden more than 100 winners for nine consecutive seasons. Robert Parsons and I agreed all our efforts would be channelled into setting a new record. I would not travel as much to Ireland, because winners over there would not count, and we also accepted a retainer to ride the string of horses owned by Robert Ogden. Things were beginning to sort themselves out in other ways; four weeks after my return, Gunner Sid fell in a hurdle at Worcester but I walked away unhurt. It was as good as having a winner.

August moved into September, closer to the heart of National Hunt racing. A trickle of winners became a gentle flow and towards the end of the month, things were again starting to feel good. There was already talk that I would have to decide soon between my Gold Cup horses Florida Pearl and Dorans Pride.

Towards the end of September, I went to the Listowel festival where I had 14 rides over four days. I won on the first, Enda Bolger's Risk of Thunder, but was beaten on the other 13. However, the week will be remembered for champagne, although not for the drinking of it. It began after my win on Risk of Thunder. I was due to ride Play'ntothegallery for Seamus O'Farrell in the following race and, weighted to carry 10st 6lb, I needed to be in my lightest breeches. But there was a stewards' inquiry after Risk of Thunder's win and, short on time, I didn't get to change. Not wanting to put up a pound overweight, I weighed out without a girth. I didn't see Peter Matthews, the stewards' secretary, watching like a hawk and as soon as I gave the saddle to Seamus, Peter made his move.

'You've got to weigh out with a saddle and a girth,' he said.

I had done something wrong but this horse hadn't a chance of winning and it wasn't like I was trying to cheat anybody. I weighed out again, this time with a girth, and it was 10st 7lb, one pound overweight. Play'ntothegallery finished 11th of 15, beaten 54 lengths. Before the race, I had time to change into my light breeches and when I came back after it, I weighed in at 10st 6lb, my correct weight and one pound lighter than I weighed out. But the stewards still wanted to see me.

'I wasn't trying to cheat,' I told them. 'When I changed my breeches, I was the right weight. Why the big fuss?'

I was banned for two days, a suspension that meant I would not ride at the first televised jumping meeting of the season, the Timeform day at Chepstow. I was furious. In a sport that has its share of non-triers and suspicions of doping and malpractice, jockeys get banned for not changing their breeches!

On the way to the races the next day, the hawk-eyed Peter Matthews was still on my mind, and the two-day ban for something so trivial. I stopped at a supermarket and bought a bottle of Moet & Chandon. As the jockeys weighed in after the first race, I walked up to Peter and presented him with the champagne. The other stewards were there and a good few people were milling around.

'Well done,' I said. 'That's for doing your job so well yesterday.'

'No, I don't drink,' he said, trying to hand the bottle back.

'Well, it's yours anyway. I hope you enjoy it.'

I left the champagne on his table and walked away. By now many people had seen what happened, press people were present and the stewards were not pleased. 'Mr Dunwoody, would you mind coming to the stewards' room?' So back we went and the whole sorry story was retold.

'Why did you want to ban someone who wasn't even having to cheat?' I asked.

They considered I had been sarcastic, which in a sense I had. From the atmosphere in the room, I guessed it wasn't going to help to point out that I had bought one of the finer brands in the shop. I left that second inquiry without apologising to Peter Matthews and largely because of that discourtesy I was referred on to the stewards of the Irish Turf Club. They were mature in their consideration of the case, fined me £500 and suggested the money should go to the Irish Jockeys' Accident Fund. I wrote the cheque and considered it money well spent.

One winner through the week at Listowel was disappointing but there were no falls. In the four days after the meeting I had 11 rides in England, seven of them winners. For the 11th, I travelled to Sedgefield to ride Robert Ogden's Real Tonic and I thought he was going to win. He might have too, but he dived into the first fence on the second circuit and got rid of me. Because of the unstable condition of my neck, every fall was now more dangerous and more likely to end in injury. After being unseated from Real Tonic I took a couple of days off, served my champagne ban, and was able to win on five of my first eight rides back.

We were now into October, the good National Hunt horses were returning to racing after their summer break and I couldn't wait. Philip Hobbs's horses were in great form and I was riding more and more for him. Philip is a fine trainer and a good man. On days when things didn't work, you did not mind meeting Philip in the unsaddling area. He knew losing was part of the game and understood that I didn't need to be told I had made a mistake. We got along well, I liked him a lot and one of my particular disappointments is that our partnership came to a premature end. Philip trained over 100 winners for the first time in the 1999–2000 season and I was very sad I couldn't have helped him more to achieve it.

Another regret is that I never won the Velka Pardubicka, held at Pardubice racecourse in the Czech Republic in mid October. I first rode in this four-and-a-quarter mile race on the Charlie Mann-trained Its A Snip in 1996 and had a smashing ride to finish third. With its famous Taxis fence, its steep double bank, the double hedges and its ploughed sections, the Czech Grand National is a unique race and great fun to ride. Now, two years after Its A Snip, I was heading out to Pardubice with every chance of winning their big race. Risk of Thunder had impressed in his prep race at Listowel and proven himself to be a quick and brilliant jumper over the banks at Punchestown. I travelled out there with J.P.McManus and a team of Irish enthusiasts and win, lose or fall, it was going to be fun.

What makes the Velka Pardubicka for me is that on one level it is rough and ready and yet it is also a great test of man and horse. The horses come in different shapes and sizes, some with rough coats and tails hanging down to the ground, the manes almost to their knees; neither are the jockeys the picture of neatness. Some might struggle for a licence where we earn our living. One of the Czech riders had shoulder-length hair, another wore his hair in a ponytail and a third sported a goatee beard. When I had been there previously it was the Russians who caught the eye, their long legs falling straight down into the irons; military length, I think you would call it. You didn't want to get too close to those boys in the race.

But the thing about the Velka Pardubicka is that riding short and having your hair shorter is no guarantee of success. Risk of Thunder gave me a great thrill, but only for as long as it lasted. He flew over the Taxis and was jumping well. At the sixth, Superior Finish, partnered by Ruby Walsh, tried to refuse, cannoned into another horse and suddenly there was mayhem. Nine horses came to grief but Risk of Thunder, at the head of the field, escaped. In an instant, we must have been 20 lengths clear. He was enjoying it, taking very little out of himself. Then at the tenth fence, the double hedges, he cleared the first and ducked sharply into the path between them, firing me into the second hedge. I'm sure he thought that was how it was supposed to be done.

With just a mile and a half of the journey completed, it was too early to know if Risk of Thunder would have won. Maybe the ploughed sections of the course would have sapped his strength but we were many lengths in front and it felt like he would have kept going for a long way. It was a big disappointment. In fairness to the Czech-trained winner Peruan, who was in fact ridden by the man with the goatee beard, he went on to beat Risk of Thunder fair and square in the following year's race.

Despite that disappointment, the season continued to go well. By the end of October, I had 30 winners in Britain and was well on the way to getting the 100 that I needed to beat Peter Scudamore's record. The retainer with Robert Ogden had its pluses and minuses. Financially, it was a good deal and Robert had many nice horses including Fadalko, Edelweiss du Moulin and Kingsmark. The minus was that the Ogden team did not decide in advance where they were taking their horses and Robert Parsons found it impossible to book my rides four or five days in advance. It caused no end of problems with trainers who wanted to use me on a regular basis. For example, Philip Hobbs would ring Robert on Monday morning and ask if I would be available to ride at Kempton at the weekend and Robert would say he didn't know where I was going to be tomorrow, never mind Saturday. Robert Ogden liked to have his horses blood-tested before racing and wanted to be able to react to sudden changes in the going. If a change in the ground wasn't going to suit his horse, he wanted to be able to change the plan, so it suited him to wait. It drove Robert Parsons mad. Eventually, I said to Barry Simpson, Robert's racing manager, 'Look, if this continues, Mr Ogden can forget his retainer.' I wrote to Robert Ogden explaining my dissatisfaction and things got better for a while but it remained an underlying problem. Robert Ogden was doing what was best for his horses but I wanted to ride as many winners as possible and I could only do that by planning my riding arrangements a few days in advance.

In different circumstances, I was the one who liked to delay decisions. With Dorans Pride running well and scheduled to meet Florida Pearl in the Ericsson Chase three days after Christmas, there was pressure from early in the season for me to choose one. Ideally, I wanted to leave the decision until about three days before the race as both were high-class steeplechasers and I was reluctant to get off either. Florida Pearl was unbeaten and I felt he was a better horse than Dorans. He was likely to be the choice. But Dorans Pride had been a smashing servant and what if I chose early and then something went wrong with Florida. In fairness to Dorans Pride's connections, who had to find a replacement, I did commit myself to Florida Pearl in mid December, two weeks before the race.

November was invariably a good month for me. This time, 23 winners in the month took my total for the season up to 53 and even though it was early to be talking about surpassing Scu's record, it was always in the back of my mind. December wasn't as good as November but another 12 took the total to 65 and, as the year turned, another 35 for the season wasn't going to overstretch me.

Winners are a jockey's lifeblood and the midweek meetings at the smaller tracks may be the staple diet but without the Saturdays, it wouldn't be much fun. Ascot, on the Saturday before Christmas, was one of the good days. Kurakka won the novice chase impressively and then in the big race of the afternoon, the Long Walk Hurdle, I rode Princeful for Jenny Pitman and got into a long battle with A.P. McCoy on Deano's Beeno. A.P. had kicked for home early and we were chasing him from a mile out. Under pressure, Princeful responded well in the straight, headed A.P. after the last and held on in a cracking finish. It was an exceptionally tough performance by Princeful and knowing A.P. was on the other horse didn't lessen the enjoyment.

In the days before the end of the year, there were indications that my luck might be turning. Robert Ogden sent me to Wetherby on Boxing Day. Not having a great ride in the King George at Kempton I didn't mind too much but it was still a disappointment not to be riding at one of the biggest meetings of the year. But then to cap it all, the Ogden horse didn't run at Wetherby and I ended up without a winner. Next day I had five rides at Leopardstown but no winner. Florida Pearl's rendezvous with Dorans Pride in the Ericsson Chase took place on the third day at Leopardstown and before a big crowd. The race began in earnest on the second circuit. At the ditch halfway down the back, Dorans Pride made a bad mistake and fired Paul Carberry up his neck. They recovered and Dorans was travelling well going to the third last. Florida Pearl was also going well but was a couple of lengths down and I felt we needed a good jump. He's the kind of horse who will go long at a fence if you ask him but has the intelligence to shorten his stride and pop it if he is not meeting it right. But this time he was caught in two minds, hit the fence and crashed to the ground. His jockey got a fair amount of stick.

I accept criticism. Jockeys make mistakes and the most common mistake riding over fences is indecision. Later in the season I rode Grosvenor for Robert Ogden at Ayr, dropped my hands on the approach to the first fence and hoped the horse would get it right. The horse fell and I felt largely responsible. I had not been definite. With Florida Pearl I wanted him to lengthen and jump boldly. I was definite – 'Go on, go long,' I said. I felt he could jump it on the stride we had. Maybe I asked too much of a relatively inexperienced chaser on soft ground but I believed he would handle it. You win some, you lose some. Just as it's more fun to win at the big tracks, it's pretty miserable when it goes the other way. Leaving Leopardstown that Monday evening, the anonymity of the following day's racing at Taunton had its appeal.

★　★　★

January began well. Three winners at Exeter on New Year's Day and the good run continued for the following two weeks. Then my luck changed at Edinburgh with that fall from Emerald Prince and the recurrence of my neck injury. The damage was aggravated by Princeful's fall on his chasing debut at Doncaster three days later. The rest of the season was a rollercoaster ride through the emotions – the high of Florida Pearl's victory in the Hennessy Cognac Gold Cup at Leopardstown in early February followed by the disappointment of his run behind See More Business in the Cheltenham Gold Cup. There was the immense satisfaction of passing Scu's record at Wincanton on Easter Monday. That was something I badly wanted. But through it all the frustration of not being 100 per cent fit persisted. I could shut out the injury but never banish it. Last, and probably least, there was Faye Lawrence and the *News of the World*.

Three days before Christmas, I was with James Wintle, Ez Wilson and a big group of friends at a party that began in a restaurant in Piccadilly. One of the lads noticed a couple of girls at another table and we got talking. I introduced myself to Faye, not knowing what was in store.

'Oh, you're interested in horses?' she asked.

'Ah, a bit,' I replied.

'Me too,' she said. 'I've done Lady Godiva for charity down near where I'm from in Devon.'

'Lady Godiva?'

'Who rode her horse naked and bareback.'

'Interesting.'

'Why don't you come along to the Windmill Club where I work?'

We'd had a few drinks, it wasn't that late, Christmas was in the air and even though I didn't fully realise it, a lap-dancer had invited me to watch her work. Well, it seemed a good idea at the time. I wasn't a huge lap-dancing fan and had previously come to the conclusion that you walk out of those places a little more frustrated than you walk in. But that night we went and Faye showed us all she had. Eventually we left, although I did tell her we were going on to the Café de Paris if she wanted to join us after work. We were leaving the Café as she and a friend arrived. Maybe it was all meant to happen. We invited them to join us and the rest is history.

Faye ended up staying the night. She turned up a couple of times afterwards but it was not destined to last. One night she turned up at three or four in the morning, knocking on my door. 'I can't have this,' I thought, 'can't have somebody turning up at this hour. I'm riding tomorrow.' Short and sweet was my liaison with Faye. But that wasn't the end of it.

It was the Saturday week before Cheltenham, almost two and a half months later. I had ridden three winners at Newbury – Ricardo and Queens Harbour for Jenny Pitman and Ashwell Boy for Philip Hobbs. Newbury winners put me in good form because I love the track. Then my mobile phone rang. The guy said he was from the *News of the World*, not an introduction that puts you completely at ease. He said a good friend of mine had told them all about me. Which friend? Faye Lawrence. I was silent. Was there anything I would like to say? Suspecting they already had more than enough, I declined. 'I haven't got anything to add,' I said.

My immediate concern was my parents. What would they say? I rang them and explained there would be a bit of a story about this girl and me. Although my mother was a bit upset at the time, they were OK about it. My fellow jockeys were less sympathetic. Next morning I had an early morning flight to Dublin for two rides at Leopardstown. Norman Williamson was at Dublin airport and we travelled together. Only one subject was discussed. By now I had seen and read the *News of the World*'s account of my brief fling. It was written in the newspaper's inimitable style. I wasn't sure how to react. If a newspaper makes you out to be the world's greatest Casanova, should you say it is all lies? The piece had not appeared in the Irish edition and Norman felt it was his duty to bring this piece of romance to our Irish colleagues' attention, and pretty much the entire Irish racing fraternity got to read it. He pinned the piece to the wall of the weighing room at Leopardstown. Jockeys, trainers, owners, they found it hilarious. Good that on a dull Sunday at Leopardstown I was able to brighten their lives.

Concerning the story in general, I wasn't too bothered although I felt one reference was wide of the mark. It was suggested a night spent with Faye was connected to Princeful's fall at Doncaster. That was not so. My memory is that the night before the Princeful episode was the night Faye knocked on my door at that late hour but wasn't invited in. In any event, he didn't fall, he was brought down. Robert Parsons spoke with the horse's trainer, Jenny Pitman, but she just laughed it off.

So that was Faye Lawrence, an interesting little interlude in my life. A few months later she was back in the *News of the World*, this time with Roger Taylor, the Queen drummer. And her friend, the one who turned up with her at the Café de Paris, she managed to get Jerry Springer on to the front page shortly after. The two girls were having a bit of a run.

About six months later I was riding down in Devon and there was Faye, doing her Lady Godiva performance on an inside page of the local *Herald Express*. There was also a front-page story about 'South Devon's very own Lady Godiva being stalked'. Faye told the reporter that she was being bombarded with letters and phone calls. All I can say is it wasn't me.

19

CALLING IT A DAY

We are made the way we are made. The genes that collided to produce R. Dunwoody probably argued about who hit hardest. I have always been intensely competitive, a trait that drove me and sometimes controlled me. There were times I didn't like what it led to but there wasn't much I could do about it. During the frantic seasons in the mid nineties I *had* to be champion. It was a costly journey, one that satisfied my ambition but did nothing for me in many other ways. The decision to leave Martin Pipe was based in part on my disenchantment with the life I had created for myself. What was success if it turned you into a person you barely recognised, a man you did not like?

But the more balanced human being I had now become couldn't completely banish the driven jockey. At the end of the 1997–98 season Robert Parsons and I had our customary chat about the plan for the following season. Robert knew what was possible and he understood what made me tick. Beating Peter Scudamore's all-time winners record wasn't simply an ambition, it was something I had to achieve. Years of trying to live up to my own expectations made me fearful of failing and that, as much as anything, motivated me. It would have killed me to reach the end of the season one winner short of Scu's record.

With three months of the season remaining, shortly after that fateful day at Ascot, I needed just 17 winners to overtake Scu.

The final part of the journey wasn't as smooth as it might have been. A week before the Cheltenham Festival in March, I schooled Marlborough again over a few showjumps down at Yogi Briesner's. Marlborough was just one of jump racing's slower learners, and he did win at the 2000 Festival. He was not a very clever horse and he took a long time to work out what he needed to do. Given the imminence and importance of the Festival, his rider displayed a similar lack of cop-on in agreeing to the schooling session. No one was too surprised that Marlborough spread-eagled over one of the jumps and I took another heavy fall. But nothing was broken or too bruised and I walked away, lucky to have escaped. Every jockey knows the relief, that almost euphoric feeling of having got away with it; the game kicks you in the stomach but you get up, exhale, smile and hope for better luck next time.

Cheltenham was disappointing. It is easy to remember the horses that ran well; there weren't that many of them. Tresor De Mai's low trajectory sticks in the mind in the Arkle Challenge Trophy, when he finished second to Flagship Uberalles. Celibate ran his heart out in the Queen Mother Champion Chase finishing fifth, and Edelweiss du Moulin ran keen and well to be third, but the majority of my horses ran disappointingly. The Festival, for me, hinged upon the performance of Florida Pearl in the Gold Cup because I really did think he would win. Having won at the previous two Festivals I was sure he could do it again. You do become attached to horses you win on and I suppose I was believing what I wanted to believe. Archie and Violet O'Leary were among my favourite owners, and there is a particular buzz when you ride an Irish 'good thing' in a race as big as the Gold Cup.

In past seasons I could be negative in my approach to Cheltenham. I turned up on the Tuesday and thought, 'Here we go again. Prepare yourself for hassle and disappointment.' The traffic, the crowds and the constant media demands combine to make it a pretty fraught week but my biggest problem was what I expected of myself. The top jockeys had to win at the Festival, simple as that. So I developed the habit of playing down my chances, of refusing to hype my Cheltenham horses and of anticipating the letdown. It made me negative about the sport's greatest week. This time I decided it would be different. I was going to be different. Out would go the old, pessimistic Dunwoody and in his place would be a more positive me. I convinced myself that Florida Pearl would not be beaten. He had won the Hennessy Cognac Gold Cup at Leopardstown and was still improving. I believed in the horse and banished doubt from my mind.

It doesn't matter what the jockey does if the horse is not at his best. After jumping the second fence, I sensed Florida Pearl wasn't himself. He jumped it slowly and I gave him a slap down the shoulder to see if that might sharpen him up. It didn't work and as we travelled through the race, it felt as if he was troubled by something possibly in his back. His class allowed him to get to the leaders going down to the third last but by the second last, he was gone. It was a huge disappointment but we had no excuses. Three days and 14 rides at the Festival but I had no winner. I was glad to be leaving the Cotswolds on that Thursday evening heading for London where Cheltenham mattered less and I had more space.

After the Festival, Folkestone was good the following day. My win on Montroe in the novice chase ended a run of 15 consecutive losers and in its own small way, it was important to break the sequence. On 27 March I went to Warwick for three rides, two of which won. Clifton Beat skipped round in the opening handicap chase and then in the second race, a novice chase, I got Henry Daly's Cheerful Aspect home by a short head, relying heavily on some left-hand stick use. It was a great battle with Graham Bradley on Andsuephi.

Although still having physiotherapy on my shoulder and arm, I was riding better. Cheerful Aspect's win got me to 97 and with the Easter holiday just a week away, there was every chance of getting the record. With it in my sights, the media tuned in. My three rides at Ascot on the Wednesday before Easter had winning chances and there were a lot of journalists who came thinking they might see the record broken. What better way to reach the milestone than a hat-trick of winners at one of the biggest tracks? All three were beaten. That only heightened the interest. The snowball had started to roll and the further it travelled, the bigger it would get.

Newton Abbot on Easter Saturday was the next stop. All four of my horses had chances but only Grosvenor won. Two to go and by now the interest went way beyond sport. I was on Radio 4's 'Desert Island Discs', Channel 4's 'The Big Breakfast' and gave countless other interviews. It was good the media were interested in the record but the attention created pressure that, in the end, made me want to get it over and done with. Every interviewer wondered if it mightn't be a good idea to get Scu's record and then retire. It was easy to understand the logic, a good story would have the perfect ending, except that I couldn't leave a life that totally fulfilled me.

But first things first. I hadn't expected to take the record at Ascot, nor at Newton Abbot, but I did think I would get there at Wincanton on Easter Monday. With 11 National Hunt meetings that day, I was likely to have good rides wherever I went. I went to Wincanton where I rode five Paul Nicholls-trained horses – Estate Agent, Knight Templar, Buckskin Cameo, Connaught Cracker and Yorkshire Edition. Four started as short-priced favourites, the other was a second favourite and it wasn't unreasonable to believe three or four would win. I invited my parents, so clearly I was optimistic.

Estate Agent looked likely to win the first but got turned over. Was it going to be one of those days? Knight Templar settled me when he strolled home in the second and took me to within one of the target. That close, I could sense the crowd's eagerness to see it happen. 'Come on, you can do it.' Second favourite in the fourth race, Buckskin Cameo ran listlessly and raised new doubts in my mind, fears that were not helped by Connaught Cracker's performance in the fifth race. He started a short-priced favourite and was in touch when he went down on his belly at the fourth fence and got rid of me. Never have I had such a reception for getting up on my feet, but I was running out of ammunition. Yorkshire Edition was my last chance. What had seemed likely at the beginning of the day now looked far from certain; neither did it make me feel any better that many in the big holiday crowd at Wincanton had stayed for the final race because of the record. Foremost in my mind was the fear they would go home disappointed. My parents and Gail had come to see me get the record. Emma had come along, and Peter Scudamore was there, too. This was definitely the day to do it. Thankfully Yorkshire Edition did not let us down. We jumped off in front, set a sensible pace through the first half of the race and steadily increased it through the final mile. He was well clear when walking through the last two hurdles but he still went on to win in a hack canter.

Returning to the winner's enclosure, I saw the old man. I realised what it meant to him and I think he understood what it meant to me. After Knight Templar's win earlier in the afternoon, I did my first-ever Frankie Dettori-style flying dismount. It was a pretty moderate effort but I managed a bit higher this time, although I was worried to death I'd land in an embarrassing heap on top of the horse's connections. The Wincanton crowd was appreciative. Scu was among the first to congratulate me and it is an honour for me to be ranked alongside him.

As was usual for me, there was as much relief as joy when it did finally happen. No sooner had I reached the record but I was already thinking of kicking on and riding more winners. This wasn't the end but the beginning of the final phase of my career. I wanted to leave a tally of winners that would keep A.P. McCoy busy for many years to come. In every post-record interview, I was asked about the future. In the nicest possible way, many of the journalists hinted it might be the time to go. They knew about my ongoing injury problem and with the record now safely mine, why hang around to get a really bad injury? A 35 year old jockey had just set an all-time record and was about to ride a horse named Call It A Day in the Grand National. There it was, a fairytale ending. Former champion wins National on Call It A Day and announces retirement. The difficulty was the reality.

I had no intention of retiring. Despite the injury and the never-ending battle with my weight, I was enjoying my work as much as I had ever done. How could I think of getting out with Aintree and the Punchestown festival in the immediate future? How could I give up the prospect of summer evenings at Newton Abbot, Worcester and Stratford, and trips to Killarney and Galway, with the certainty of more winners? I was already thinking of the following season. Robert Parsons and I agreed we would be better going into the new season without the retainer to ride for Robert Ogden. The constraints of the job outweighed the benefits. I would be my own boss again. Towards the end of the season, I tried to get in touch with Robert Ogden but couldn't contact him on the phone. Eventually I sent a fax saying I didn't want the retainer for the following season. He came back and said it was a bit of a shock; he thought we were to continue as in 1998–99. I went to see him. It was a friendly meeting but my mind was made up. He asked me not to say anything for a few days, which was fine. I thought it would give him a chance to line up a replacement. But a couple of days later the *Racing Post* ran the story: 'The split between the pair is seen as amicable, with Ogden deciding against taking up an option with the former champion for another year.' Fair enough . . .

In one respect, very little had changed in 17 years. The ambition to be among the best in my profession was as strong in my final season as it was ten years earlier. The desire to ride winners never really waned, the disappointment of missing a winner never lessened. On the opening day of Aintree, I was booked to ride Papo Kharisma for Philip Hobbs in the final race, a three-mile handicap hurdle. With just ten stone on his back, Papo Kharisma had a chance. It was hard for me to get down near that weight but it had to be done. First it was the bath, then the sauna and my feeling was that if I could get down to 10st 2lb, that would be OK. But the wasting drained me and after three losing rides on that first afternoon at Aintree, I felt severely dehydrated and gave up on Martin Pipe's Strong Tel and Papo Kharisma in the last two races. Strong Tel ran poorly but with Adrian Maguire deputising for me, Papo Kharisma won. You can imagine how I felt. It is a matter of pride to jockeys that they can ride at a certain weight. I accepted not being able to do 10 stone but 10st 2lb or 10st 3lb would have been OK. Philip Hobbs was always very good about it and would have had no problem with me putting up a couple of pounds overweight, but at Aintree I wasn't able to do that. I had opted out too easily and tortured myself over it. 'You could have got down to 10st 2lb but you gave it away. You're getting soft,' I thought.

Next day at Aintree, it had to go well. Village King, having had a great season, stayed on well to be second to Spendid in the novice chase and then Maitre De Musique gave me a ride you dream about over the Grand National fences, finishing third in the John Hughes. The day ended well when Edelweiss du Moulin walked away with the handicap chase. I was now looking forward to the ride on Call It A Day in the National. I'd ridden the horse at Uttoxeter on his previous run and thought he had a good each-way chance, no more than that. Struggling to go with the early pace, Call It A Day picked up on the second circuit and he was enjoying the fences, having tested one early. As we went to the last fence, I thought we were going to win. But as I waited for the old horse to go on, Bobbyjo went sprinting past. In three or four strides he went two lengths clear and Call It A Day, seeing exactly what was happening, gave up on me. He couldn't go that quick and it knocked the fight out of him. At the elbow he did get going again and was only just beaten for second. Just past the post, the Carberrys were already celebrating and Call It A Day, having seen them, pricked his ears, dropped his shoulder, threw me out of the side-door and dragged me unceremoniously towards the exit. Despite this small hiccup, it was still a thrill and, in hindsight, I am pleased my final Grand National ride was a good one. I loved riding around the course.

Cheltenham's mid-April two-day meeting brought two winners. Punchestown's four-day festival came at the end of the month and even if it wasn't the best of meetings for me, it did have its moments. Florida Pearl wasn't himself in the Heineken Chase and was beaten a long way by Imperial Call but I did manage to ride two winners – Celibate for Charlie Mann in the valuable BMW Chase and Native Fling for Philip Hobbs in a novice chase. The win on Celibate particularly pleased me because of something I heard before the race. Mick Fitzgerald had won the Game Spirit Chase at Newbury on Celibate earlier in the season but couldn't ride him at Punchestown because he was committed to ride Big Matt for Nicky Henderson. Maybe I was being wound up by Carl Llewellyn, but his story was that Fitzy reckoned that if he rode Celibate it would win. He felt he got on better with the horse than anyone and the way I heard it, there was a suggestion that I wouldn't win on him. I tried to be positive; we jumped off in front, lengthened when Direct Route attacked after the second last and the horse showed great courage to hold Space Trucker's late challenge. It was a tough, gutsy performance from Celibate, so often the bridesmaid, and his old jockey hadn't done too badly.

- By now I had learned to live with a deficient right arm. It didn't feel too bad but the strength never returned and I stopped using it. 'In time, it will improve,' I thought. If it didn't get worse, it would have to get better. I continued to have physiotherapy and Don Gatherer, the physio who treated rugby player Jason Leonard for a similar injury, put me on a specific weights programme to improve the strength in my neck and right arm. Don reckoned two or three months would bring a change for the better. Determined to stay in shape and continue the weights programme, I rode without a break through May, June and July. The flow of winners slowed down but never dried up and there were particular highs. Quinze's win in the Galway Hurdle was spectacular as he carried 11st 12lb and won by 14 lengths. To do that in a competitive £60,000 handicap hurdle was some performance and the trainer Pat Hughes had the horse ready to run the race of his life. As well as winning on Quinze I was leading rider and as was customary in Galway, we really did have a good time.

There were other good days and, occasionally, some mad nights. In that final season, the busier I was, the more I liked it. Getting up at half-five in the morning to drive to Stansted for an eight o'clock flight to Dublin never seemed a problem; neither did it bother me to drive from an afternoon meeting at Haydock to an evening meeting in Uttoxeter. I travelled on the basis that once you climbed into the saddle, you gave the horse a ride. I joked that I was too stupid to lose my nerve and it never threatened to be a problem. The prospect of long-term damage to my arm never bothered me when I was riding. I flew here and there, drove from one end of the country to the other, tried to give every horse a ride and the only thing I feared was being forced to slow down.

I was, of course, lying to myself. My neck, shoulder and right arm continued to be a problem. Sometimes a horse would throw its head back, catch me on the forehead, jolt me backwards and I would temporarily lose the power in my arm. Other times it was incredibly weak. People would ask how it was and I'd say the physio was helping. Towards the end of May, I rode Colonel In Chief for Paul Nicholls in a handicap chase at Stratford. He jumped the first fence OK but veered sharply left and ran inside a rail, out of the race. 'Oops,' I thought, 'my arm wasn't great there.' I needed to yank the horse right, with as much strength as I could muster from my right arm but it wasn't there. There was more to this problem than a lack of strength. My reflexes were slow and the co-ordination wasn't what it should be.

On 9 June, I went to Hereford to ride Premier Bay for Philip Hobbs in the novice chase. We took it up at the second last, having managed to get up A.P. McCoy's inner, went clear after jumping it and were sure to win. But as we approached the last he put on the brakes, jinked, went left-handed and I fell clean off him. It was one of the most embarrassing moments of my career. To make a bad situation worse, A.P. was left clear and went on to win. If there had been a nearby hole, I would willingly have buried myself in it. I despaired. When you spend all your life riding horses and dedicate yourself to being as good as you can, this shouldn't happen. Of course, it was at the end of a long season and tiredness had taken the edge off my riding, dulling my reaction to the horse's late change of mind. But there was more to it.

Two days later I went to Newton Abbot to ride Western Chief for Dai Williams and the anxieties increased. Western Chief had won four times in the previous month and as we went down to the start, he felt ready to win again. We didn't get a perfect view of the first fence, he launched himself at it and got rid of me. Unseated on Wednesday at Hereford, again at Newton Abbot on Friday – that was twice in the space of six rides. How could it happen? The fall off Western Chief was an awkward one and I was slightly concussed. My left shoulder was sore. Given the way things were going, I should have looked in the mirror or done the medical equivalent and had more X-rays. Such a response is not the way of the weighing room. I concentrated on hiding my slight concussion and being passed fit to ride Afon Alwen in the last race. Sore, not totally with it and very lucky to pass the racecourse doctor, I just got Afon Alwen home in a photo finish.

Stubbornness kept me going right through May and June. On 7 July I went to Worcester to ride Gee Bee Boy for Graham McCourt and although the horse was tired and well beaten when he blundered at the second last, it bothered me that I was again unseated. That was the third time in a short while. Something was clearly happening here. Exactly a week later I was at Worcester and well clear going to the last on Philip Hobbs's Nazir when lightning struck for the fourth time. Nazir slowed, almost ducked out, tried to refuse, jumped the hurdle awkwardly and got rid of me. In normal circumstances, this would have been easily explained – the horse had gone lame on his near foreleg and was reacting to the injury, but I couldn't see it in such straightforward terms. This was the fourth time in less than 40 rides. It didn't stack up. The previous season there had been a total of nearly 500 rides and two recorded cases of 'unseated rider'.

The next day, 15 July, was when I met Janet Alexander at the Harbour Club in London. She is the woman who works with the kineseologist Paul Chek and it was a good time for me to see her. I was in bits. She did the simple exercise to establish the alignment and balance of my body and, not surprisingly, found that everything was out of synch. In terms of my career, the bell sounded. I was on the last lap.

I should be grateful that on my last day as a jockey, 21 August 1999, I was able to walk out of the weighing room at Perth. It should be a source of satisfaction that over the final three days, there were six winners – six from my last nine rides. But less than a year has passed since that day and the scars have yet to heal. I'm not talking about physical injuries but the pain of no longer being a jockey. That's what hurts. Don't have sympathy for me, though. London isn't what you would call dull. Charlie has been great and, God knows, we haven't stopped enjoying life.

But, it is a lesser life. Never again will I come down the hill at Cheltenham with plenty of horse in my hands; never again will

I feel the thrill of flying those four fences down the back at Ascot, when it seems you are travelling at 100 m.p.h; and never again will I clear Becher's second time round at Aintree thinking, 'We can win this National.' In those moments your focus, your concentration, your sense of living are pitched at a level normal life cannot touch. I loved being Richard Dunwoody, jockey. I liked being publicly recognised as a top jockey and I always wanted to prove the honour was deserved.

Jockeys, they say, find retirement hard. I know that to be true. Simon McNeil, an old weighing-room colleague, didn't want to give up but when he was 40, they found him a job as a starter and he made the sensible decision. A starter's job isn't the most stressful but since making the switch, Simon suffered alopecia and lost all of his hair. I met him recently and he told me about seeing an apprentice punch the air after winning a race at Windsor one day. 'That's what we'll never experience again,' he said. I do miss that but so much more. I miss the life – the winners and the losers, the saunas and the motorways, wasting our bodies and wasting our time, the impossible schedules, the early mornings and the late nights.

Yes, it was good to be champion jockey three times, to ride more than 100 winners for ten consecutive seasons and to leave the sport having ridden more winners than any jump jockey in history. But that wasn't what it was about. It was about my place in that world. I loved riding, I loved winning, I loved competing. I felt I rode a racehorse as well as anyone else. I needed to believe that every time I walked into the weighing room. That was the obsession.

EPILOGUE

The after-life was never going to be easy. I knew that from the December afternoon in 1999 when Jack Phillips, the neurosurgeon, told me it was over. A couple of months later a friend asked if I saw myself as a jockey or an ex-jockey? I wasn't sure. It is one thing to say you are retired, another to accept it. But life moves on and me too. Over the last ten months I've had good days, fun days, hard days and depressing days, but I've been going forward. The future doesn't frighten me as much as it did at the beginning.

Dunwoody Sports Marketing and writing this book have consumed much of the time. I enjoy being busy and wouldn't have it any other way. The business is now getting there. This time last year it wasn't going well and, totally unprepared, I found myself taking charge of a company that had to be turned round. Changes have been made and thanks to Nick Jackson's hard work and excellent advice from Mike Diamandis, there is now a future for us. Craig Hutchinson joined at the beginning of the year and has done well on the football side of our business.

Although I enjoy the marketing of sports, especially those outside of racing, there is a yearning for a greater challenge. I cannot live in my past and don't want racing to be the crutch that carries me into the future. Punditry is not for me. I did it at Aintree for the 2000 Grand National and cannot think of anything worse than commenting on A.P.'s or Norman's performance. Actually, maybe I can. Talking racing in a corporate box and then spending the afternoon praying that not all of your tips run as if their legs are tied together: that's worse. If I can't ride the race, I don't want to watch it from the sidelines.

Maybe it is simply a case of needing some time away from the sport. After two or three years, it might be different. I'm not so sure. Training never interested me. As for the administrative side? No chance. The problem for me is that the jockey experiences the best of the racing life. Anything else is just a poor substitute.

Two months ago the Victoria Racing Club in Australia asked me to ride in a five-furlong sprint against Lester Piggott and other former stars. The race was to be held at Flemington in Melbourne and for the few days that it was a possibility, it excited me. Lining up in a stall alongside the incomparable Lester would have been one of the great thrills of my life. He has long been a hero of mine. But the Jockey Club doctor, Michael Turner, thought it would be foolish to return for such a race. My career ended through injury and the insurance companies would be entitled to ask questions if I started competing again. Lester and I spoke about it a couple of times but for me it was destined not to happen.

There has had to be a lot of adjustment. Gail, my sister, manages my day-to-day life and does a difficult job well. Over the last year Charlotte 'Charlie' Hutchings has helped keep me sane. She has been a terrific companion – our life together is good. Socially, London's been good for me. Tom Maher, James Wintle, Don Shanks and the lads are not interested in who I once was.

I would love Ireland to be some part of the future. Competing over there, I was conscious of the public's enormous support and a challenge that involved Ireland would make me sit up and listen. Physical challenges also appeal and now that I am running half-marathons, I can see myself going the full distance. If serious money could be raised for worthwhile causes in the process, then so much the better.

I realise full well how special the jockey's life was and how hard it is to find anything that comes near it. That won't stop me trying, nor will it tempt me to settle for soft options that pay the mortgage but don't fulfil me. Along the way I will have to adapt but that's okay.

A part of me will always be with the lads in the weighing room. I see very little of them now and don't spend much time following their careers. Occasionally I ring one of them or one of them calls me and it is good to talk. But they have all-consuming lives and, more than most, I understand. They know whose side I'm on.

The thing is you can ever be an ex-jockey. I am just an old jock who is now doing something else.

CAREER RECORD

1

CAREER TOTALS

Key to abbreviations
unpl. unplaced
unstd. unseated rider
b.d. brought down
sl. slipped up
p.u. pulled up
other refused, ran out, refused to race, etc.

GREAT BRITAIN

ON THE FLAT

year	rides	results
1982	1 ride	1 second
1983	4 rides	4 unplaced

POINT-TO-POINT

year	rides	won	2nd	3rd	unpl.	fell	unstd.	b.d.	sl.	p.u.	other
1983	13	2	2	1	3		1		1	2	1
1984	1	1									
total	14	3	2	1	3		1		1	2	1

NATIONAL HUNT RULES

season	rides	won	2nd	3rd	unpl.	fell	unstd.	b.d.	sl.	p.u.	other
1982-3§	23	4	3	2	8	4	2				
1983-4§	213	24	34	29	92	20	4	1		9	
1984-5	383	46	41	41	194	23	8	5	1	23	1
1985-6	504	55	51	60	238	31	10	2		57	
1986-7	560	70	71	75	254	41	7	4	3	34	1
1987-8	582	79	60	87	276	29	5	4	2	39	1
1988-9	671	91	114	90	275	34	7	3	1	52	4
1989-90	604	102	102	84	212	32	5	2	1	62	2
1990-1	646	127	122	78	233	33	8	2	1	40	2
1991-2	715	137	128	108	252	32	6	2		50	
1992-3	740	173*	121	89	268	28	9	3		47	2
1993-4	890	197*	145	117	322	39	8			60	2
1994-5	745	160*	117	102	262	32	8	3	1	56	4
1995-6	492	101	76	77	183	21	6	1	1	26	
1996-7	558	110	101	70	212	26	3	1		29	1
1997-8	517	103	76	64	210	24	4	1		34	1
1998-9	491	108	80	63	182	24	2	2		29	1
1999-00	65	12	8	11	23	3	4			4	
total	9399	1699	1450	1247	3701	476	106	36	11	651	22

§ = RD riding as amateur
* = champion jockey

IRELAND

season	rides	won	2nd	3rd	unpl.	fell	unstd.	b.d.	sl.	p.u.	other
1984-5	4	1			2						1
1985-6	4		1	1	1	1					
1986-7	4	2	1	1							
1987-8	4			1	2	1					
1988-9	7	1		2	3	1					
1989-90	15	2	2	1	8		1			1	
1990-1	11	1	1	3	6						
1991-2	27	4	1	2	17					3	
1992-3	67	14	11	8	26	3				5	
1993-4	48	4	6	6	30					2	
1994-5	30	7	1	3	17	1	1				
1995-6	248	42	35	35	116	13			3	4	
1996-7	162	30	27	17	74	5	3			6	
1997-8	199	49	23	26	81	10	1			9	
1998-9	95	14	14	9	51	3				4	
1999-00	14	4	1	1	6		1			1	
total	939	175	124	116	440	38	7	3	3	35	1

CAREER TOTALS OVERSEAS

97 overseas rides: 10 winners

USA: 18 rides, 4 winners, 7 placed
Jersey: 24 rides, 3 winners, 12 placed
Belgium: 15 rides, 2 winners, 2 placed
Australia: 4 rides, 1 winner
Germany: 10 rides, 5 placed
France: 12 rides, 2 placed
Norway: 3 rides, 1 placed
Czech Republic: 2 rides, 1 placed
Italy: 1 ride, 1 placed
New Zealand: 4 rides
Sweden: 2 rides
Switzerland: 2 rides

2

THE BIG RACES

(a) THE CHELTENHAM RECORD

NATIONAL HUNT FESTIVAL WINNERS

1985 Coral Golden Handicap Hurdle Final: VON TRAPPE (trained by Michael Oliver)

Ritz Club National Hunt Handicap Chase: WEST TIP (Michael Oliver)

1986 Grand Annual Challenge Cup: FRENCH UNION (David Nicholson)

1988 Daily Express Triumph Hurdle: KRIBENSIS (Michael Stoute)

Tote Cheltenham Gold Cup: CHARTER PARTY (David Nicholson)

1989 Arkle Challenge Trophy: WATERLOO BOY (David Nicholson)

1990 Waterford Crystal Champion Hurdle: KRIBENSIS (Michael Stoute)

Ritz Club National Hunt Handicap Chase: BIGSUN (David Nicholson)

1991 Waterford Castle Arkle Challenge Trophy: REMITTANCE MAN (Nicky Henderson)

1992 Sun Alliance Novices' Hurdle: THETFORD FOREST (David Nicholson)

Tote Festival Bumper: MONTELADO (Pat Flynn)

1993 Tote County Handicap Hurdle: THUMBS UP (Nicky Henderson)

1996 Guinness Arkle Challenge Trophy: VENTANA CANYON (Edward O'Grady)

Daily Express Triumph Hurdle: PADDY'S RETURN (Ferdy Murphy)

1997 Royal & SunAlliance Novices' Chase: HANAKHAM (Ron Hodges)

Weatherbys Champion Bumper: FLORIDA PEARL (Willie Mullins)

Vincent O'Brien County Handicap Hurdle: BARNA BOY (Nicky Henderson)

1998 Royal & SunAlliance Novices' Chase: FLORIDA PEARL (Willie Mullins)

RIDES IN THE BIG THREE FESTIVAL RACES

CHAMPION HURDLE

1985	Northern Trial (fell last behind See You Then)
1986	Ra Nova (twelfth behind See You Then)
1987	Stepaside Lord (fifth behind See You Then)
1988	Celtic Chief (third to Celtic Shot)
1989	Kribensis (seventh behind Beech Road)
1990	KRIBENSIS (won)
1991	Nomadic Way (second to Morley Street)
1992	Kribensis (fourteenth behind Royal Gait)
1993	Flown (eighth behind Granville Again)
1995	Jazilah (tenth behind Alderbrook)
1996	Alderbrook (second to Collier Bay)
1997	Sanmartino (sixth behind Make A Stand)
1998	I'm Supposin (third to Istabraq)
1999	Blowing Wind (brought down behind Istabraq)

QUEEN MOTHER CHAMPION CHASE

1987	Very Promising (second to Pearlyman)
1988	Very Promising (third to Pearlyman)
1990	Waterloo Boy (second to Barnbrook Again)
1991	Waterloo Boy (second to Katabatic)
1992	Waterloo Boy (third to Remittance Man)
1993	Waterloo Boy (sixth behind Deep Sensation)
1995	Travado (eighth behind Viking Flagship)
1996	Sound Man (third to Klairon Davis)
1997	Viking Flagship (third to Martha's Son)
1998	Klairon Davis (fourth to One Man)
1999	Celibate (fifth behind Call Equiname)

CHELTENHAM GOLD CUP

1986	Von Trappe (fell 19th behind Dawn Run)
1987	Charter Party (fell 5th behind The Thinker)

1988 CHARTER PARTY (won)
1989 Charter Party (third to Desert Orchid)
1990 Desert Orchid (third to Norton's Coin)
1991 Desert Orchid (third to Garrison Savannah)
1993 Rushing Wild (second to Jodami)
1995 Miinnehoma (third to Master Oats)
1996 One Man (sixth behind Imperial Call)
1997 One Man (sixth behind Mr Mulligan)
1998 Dorans Pride (third to Cool Dawn)
1999 Florida Pearl (third to See More Business)

(b) THE AINTREE RECORD

RIDES IN THE GRAND NATIONAL

1985 West Tip (fell second Becher's behind Last Suspect)
1986 WEST TIP (won)
1987 West Tip (fourth to Maori Venture)
1988 West Tip (fourth to Rhyme 'N' Reason)
1989 West Tip (second to Little Polveir)
1990 Bigsun (unplaced behind Mr Frisk)
1991 Bigsun (pulled up before second Canal Turn behind Seagram)
1992 Brown Windsor (fell first Becher's behind Party Politics)
1993 Wont Be Gone Long (did not start: void race)
1994 MIINNEHOMA (won)
1995 Miinnehoma (pulled up before 21st behind Royal Athlete)
1996 Superior Finish (third to Rough Quest)
1997 Smith's Band (fell 20th behind Lord Gyllene)
1998 Samlee (third to Earth Summit)
1999 Call It A Day (third to Bobbyjo)

COMPLETE RECORD OVER THE GRAND NATIONAL FENCES

1985 Whitbread Trophy: Run To Me (brought down)
     Seagram Grand National: West Tip (fell)
1986 Whitbread Trophy: GLENRUE (won)

Seagram Grand National: WEST TIP (won)
1987 Whitbread Trophy: Rouspeter (unplaced)
Seagram Grand National: West Tip (fourth)
1988 Glenlivet Trophy: Woodside Road (unplaced)
Seagram Grand National: West Tip (fourth)
1989 Seagram Grand National: West Tip (second)
1990 John Hughes Memorial Trophy: WONT BE GONE LONG (won)
Seagram Grand National: Bigsun (unplaced)
1991 Seagram Grand National: Bigsun (pulled up)
1992 John Hughes Memorial Trophy: THE ANTARTEX (won)
Seagram Grand National: Brown Windsor (fell)
Crowther Homes Becher Chase: The Antartex (third)
1993 Martell Grand National: Wont Be Gone Long (did not start: void race)
Crowther Homes Becher Chase: Hey Cottage (unplaced)
1994 John Hughes Memorial Trophy: Tri Folene (unplaced)
Martell Grand National: MIINNEHOMA (won)
1995 Martell Grand National: Miinnehoma (pulled up)
1996 John Hughes Memorial Trophy: Pims Gunner (brought down)
Martell Grand National: Superior Finish (third)
1997 John Hughes Trophy: Coonawara (pulled up)
Martell Grand National: Smith's Band (fell)
1998 John Hughes Trophy: Kibreet (unplaced)
Martell Grand National: Samlee (third)
1999 John Hughes Trophy: Maitre de Musique (third)
Martell Grand National: Call It A Day (third)

(c) OTHER BIG RACE WINS

In addition to the Grand National twice, the Champion Hurdle and Cheltenham Gold Cup once each and the other Cheltenham National Hunt Festival and Aintree winners listed above, Richard Dunwoody won most of the other major races of the jumping season:

Mackeson Gold Cup (Cheltenham)
1986 VERY PROMISING (trained by David Nicholson)

1991 ANOTHER CORAL (David Nicholson)
1996 CHALLENGER DU LUC [run as Murphy's Gold Cup] (Martin Pipe)

Tingle Creek Chase (Sandown Park)
1985 LEFRAK CITY (Capt. Tim Forster)
1987 LONG ENGAGEMENT (David Nicholson)
1991 WATERLOO BOY (David Nicholson)
1992 WATERLOO BOY (David Nicholson)
1995 SOUND MAN (Edward O'Grady)
1996 SOUND MAN (Edward O'Grady)

William Hill Handicap Hurdle (Sandown Park)
1984 PRIDEAUX BOY [run as Mecca Bookmakers Handicap Hurdle] (Graham Roach)
1995 CHIEF'S SONG (Simon Dow)

Tripleprint Gold Cup (Cheltenham)
1992 ANOTHER CORAL (David Nicholson)

King George VI Chase (Kempton Park)
1989 DESERT ORCHID (David Elsworth)
1990 DESERT ORCHID (David Elsworth)
1995 ONE MAN [run at Sandown Park in January 1996] (Gordon Richards)
1996 ONE MAN (Gordon Richards)

Christmas Hurdle (Kempton Park)
1988 KRIBENSIS (Michael Stoute)
1989 KRIBENSIS (Michael Stoute)
1992 MIGHTY MOGUL (David Nicholson)

Castleford Chase (Wetherby)
1990 WATERLOO BOY (David Nicholson)
1991 WATERLOO BOY (David Nicholson)

Welsh National (Chepstow)
1993 RIVERSIDE BOY (Martin Pipe)

Anthony Mildmay, Peter Cazalet Chase (Sandown Park)
1985 WEST TIP (Michael Oliver)
1989 MR FRISK (Kim Bailey)

Victor Chandler Chase (Ascot)
1992 WATERLOO BOY (David Nicholson)
1994 VIKING FLAGSHIP [run at Warwick] (David Nicholson)

Agfa Diamond Chase (Sandown Park)
1988 CHARTER PARTY (David Nicholson)
1991 DESERT ORCHID (David Elsworth)
1994 SECOND SCHEDUAL (David Nicholson)

Tote Gold Trophy (Newbury)
1989 GREY SALUTE (John Jenkins)

Kingwell Hurdle (Wincanton)
1989 FLOYD (David Elsworth)
1990 KRIBENSIS (Michael Stoute)
1994 VALFINET (Martin Pipe)
1997 DREAMS END (Peter Bowen)
1998 I'M SUPPOSIN (Richard Rowe)

Racing Post Chase (Kempton Park)
1990 DESERT ORCHID (David Elsworth)
1996 ROUGH QUEST (Terry Casey)
1999 DR LEUNT (Philip Hobbs)

Martell Cup (Aintree)
1991 AQUILIFER (Martin Pipe)
1994 DOCKLANDS EXPRESS (Kim Bailey)

Mumm Melling Chase (Aintree)
1992 REMITTANCE MAN (Nicky Henderson)

Aintree Hurdle (Aintree)
1988 CELTIC CHIEF (Mrs Mercy Rimell)
1992 MORLEY STREET (Toby Balding)

Scottish Champion Hurdle (Ayr)
1996 ALDERBROOK (Kim Bailey)
1998 BLOWING WIND (Martin Pipe)
1999 FADALKO (Paul Nicholls)

Whitbread Gold Cup (Sandown Park)
1993 TOPSHAM BAY (David Barons)
1995 CACHE FLEUR (Martin Pipe)

IRELAND

Galway Hurdle (Galway)
1999 QUINZE (Pat Hughes)

Kerry National (Listowel)
1997 DORANS PRIDE (Michael Hourigan)

Hennessy Cognac Gold Cup Chase (Leopardstown)
1998 DORANS PRIDE (Michael Hourigan)
1999 FLORIDA PEARL (Willie Mullins)

Power Gold Cup (Fairyhouse)
1997 DORANS PRIDE (Michael Hourigan)

Irish Grand National (Fairyhouse)
1990 DESERT ORCHID (David Elsworth)

Heineken Novices' Chase (Punchestown)
1992 SECOND SCHEDUAL [run as the Woodchester Bank Gold Cup]
(Arthur Moore)

USA

Breeders' Cup Chase
1989 HIGHLAND BUD [run at Far Hills, New Jersey] (Jonathan Sheppard)

> **1992** HIGHLAND BUD [run at Belmont Park, New York] (Jonathan Sheppard)
>
> **Colonial Cup** (Camden, South Carolina)
> **1989** HIGHLAND BUD (Jonathan Sheppard)

3

JUST FOR THE RECORD ...

- With 1,699 winners from 9,399 rides, Richard Dunwoody is the winningmost jump jockey in the history of National Hunt racing in Great Britain. The three most recent holders of that record were Peter Scudamore (1,678 winners), John Francome (1,138) and Stan Mellor (1,035). This exclusive quartet of jump jockeys who have ridden more than 1,000 winners in Britain was joined in December 1999 by Tony McCoy.
- Richard's strike rate of winners to rides is 18 per cent.
- As well as being champion jockey in terms of winners ridden in 1992-3, 1993-4 and 1994-5, Richard was leading jump jockey in terms of prize money earned by his mounts five times: 1989-90, 1990-1, 1991-2, 1992-3 and 1995-6.
- Richard rode over 100 winners in ten consecutive seasons. The previous record for centuries was Peter Scudamore with eight.
- At the time of his retirement, Richard was the only jockey then riding to have won the 'Big Three' races of the jumping season: Champion Hurdle (on Kribensis in 1990), Cheltenham Gold Cup (Charter Party in 1988) and Grand National (West Tip in 1986 and Miinnehoma in 1994). The only other jockeys to have achieved this feat since the Second World War are Fred Winter, Willie Robinson and Bobby Beasley
- Richard's fellow jockeys voted him National Hunt Jockey of the Year at 'The Lesters', the annual awards ceremony

of the Jockeys' Association, on five occasions: 1990, 1992, 1993, 1994 and 1995. He was also voted National Hunt Jockey of the Year by the Horserace Writers' Association at the Derby Awards in 1993.

- Richard won the Ritz Club Trophy for leading rider at the Cheltenham Festival in 1990 and 1996, and for leading rider at the Aintree Grand National Festival in 1986, 1988, 1992 and 1997.

- Two of Richard's performances in the saddle were voted 'Ride of the Year' by readers of the *Racing Post*: on Unguided Missile in the Betterware Cup at Ascot in 1995, and on Challenger du Luc in the Murphy's Gold Cup at Cheltenham in 1996.

- The horse on which Richard won most races is Waterloo Boy: the partnership registered fifteen victories.

- Richard had rides in fifteen consecutive Grand Nationals between 1985 and 1999, finishing in the frame eight times from fourteen valid rides (taking into account the void race of 1993): two winners, one second, three thirds, two fourths. Only once did he complete the course but fail to reach the frame, and even then his horse got into the money: Bigsun's sixth in 1990 earned his owner £1,336.05. Richard's first five rides in the National were all on West Tip, and the pair finished in the frame on four of those five occasions.

- With eighteen winners, Richard is the most successful rider at the Cheltenham Festival in the modern age. (Most successful of all is Arkle's rider Pat Taaffe, with twenty-five wins.)

- Catterick is the only jumps track in Great Britain on which Richard did not ride a winner. Of jumps courses in Ireland, only Bellewstown and Wexford failed to register on his score sheet.

INDEX